EARLY CHINESE LITERATURE

PREPARED AS ONE OF THE COMPANIONS TO ASIAN STUDIES

WM. THEODORE DE BARY, EDITOR

LITERATURE: A VITAL FORCE

IN THE ORDERING OF THE STATE,

A GLORIOUS ACHIEVEMENT

THAT NEVER GROWS OLD.

EMPEROR WEN OF THE WEI

EARLY

CHINESE

LITERATURE

by BURTON WATSON

COLUMBIA UNIVERSITY PRESS

NEW YORK

The preparation of *Early Chinese Literature* in the series "Companions to Asian Studies" was made possible by a grant from the Carnegie Corporation of New York. That Corporation is not, however, the author, owner, publisher, or proprietor of this publication, and is not to be understood as approving by virtue of its grant any of the statements made or views expressed therein.

ISBN 0-231-02579-3 *Cloth*

ISBN 0-231-08671-7 *Paperback*

LIBRARY OF CONGRESS CATALOG CARD NUMBER: 62-17552
PRINTED IN THE UNITED STATES OF AMERICA
10 9 8 7 6 5 4 3

FOREWORD

THIS INTRODUCTION to early Chinese literature is the first of a series of guides to the study of Oriental thought and literature being prepared by the Columbia University Committee on Oriental Studies. It is a companion to the series, Translations from the Oriental Classics, by which the Committee makes available to the general reader major works of the Oriental traditions. These are the peaks that dominate the Asian landscape, that may be admired even at the great distance which separates us from the time and place of their creation—in one sense admired the more because at such a distance their full contours stand out.

But there is another mode of appreciation which comes from intimate acquaintance and involves for us a journey thence. Mt. Fuji is awesome in its solitary grandeur; Hiroshige, viewing it along the Eastern Sea Road, makes it a friend of ours in wayside villages and fields. In this book we approach the great heights of ancient Chinese literature; with Mr. Watson as our guide, their surroundings are now made familiar to us, and the peaks themselves, no less impressive, are found after all approachable.

WM. THEODORE DE BARY

CONTENTS

FOREWORD, *by Wm. Theodore de Bary*   vii

INTRODUCTION   1

HISTORY   17

PHILOSOPHY   121

POETRY   199

CHRONOLOGY   295

INDEX   299

INTRODUCTION

THIS BOOK is intended to answer some of the questions a general reader might be expected to have concerning early Chinese literature, its major forms, its themes, its particular characteristics, and its works of distinction. The period covered is that from the earliest literary writings down to about the year A.D. 100, a span of almost a thousand years. Actually the oldest examples of written Chinese we possess are the inscriptions found on oracle bones and bronze vessels dating from the latter part of the Shang or Yin dynasty (traditional dates 1766–1123 B.C.). But these are very brief and are of interest to archeologists alone, and I have accordingly begun my discussion with the literary works of the following Chou dynasty, which officially came to an end in 249 B.C.

My choice of the terminal date A.D. 100, which falls in the middle of the Latter Han dynasty (25–220), may at first seem arbitrary. The closing years of the Latter Han, however, did not produce any prose works of outstanding importance, while the poetry of the period, much of it in the new five-word meter which began to gain popularity at this time, belongs rather to the following age of Chinese poetry. The old unified empire of early Han times was beginning to crumble in the second century A.D., and China was entering upon an age of social turmoil, disunity, and intellectual doubt and reevaluation which continued until the unification of the empire under the Sui in the early years of the seventh century. Moreover it was around A.D. 100 that Buddhism became established in China, and though its influence was not immediately felt, the ideas, institutions, and art forms which it brought with it were in time to have a far-reaching effect upon the culture of the nation. The year A.D. 100 has therefore seemed a fitting date with which to close a discussion of the earliest literature of the Chinese people.

I should explain that I use the word literature here not in the restricted sense of "pure literature" or belles lettres, but to mean all types of writing—historical, philosophical, or poetic—whose aim is to express ideas or emotions with clarity and artistic finesse. The distinction between belles lettres and writing which is primarily didactic or informative was, to the best of my knowledge, never made in early China, and moreover seems to me to be quite false to the thought of the time.

Though I do not recall ever having seen it stated in so many words in any ancient work, the men of early China, if questioned, would, I believe, have distinguished not between pure and utilitarian literature, but only between literature that is reasonable or refined, and literature that is vulgar. By refined they would have meant any type of writing, in any form and directed toward any purpose, that was morally sound in content, clear in thought, and expressed in suitably gracious and dignified language. Vulgar, stupid, or rustic, on the other hand, were their terms for any kind of writing that seemed to them absurd or shallow in content or uncouth in expression. The former writings they took care to preserve and hand down, adding what exegetical material they deemed necessary, and it is these in most cases which constitute the body of works I shall be discussing here. The vulgar type of writings they ignored or preserved only for curiosity's sake. Thus most of this literature has been lost, or even deliberately destroyed, as in the case of the voluminous prophetic and apocryphal literature of the less respectable of the Han Confucian scholars, which was destroyed by imperial command.[1]

I mention this because it helps to account for the somewhat lopsided character of the early literature which has come down to us. We have, for example, no collections of popular folk tales or works on sexual regimen, and almost no popular ballads or works on divination from later than the sixth century B.C., though many such works existed and are listed in the catalogue of the imperial archives compiled at the beginning of the first century B.C. and preserved in the "Treatise on Literature" of the *Han shu* or *History of the Former Han Dynasty*. Likewise, although the *Han shu* and other early histories often contain memorials, letters, poems, or other incidental writings which have been copied in by the historians to illustrate some point in their narrative, we have no diaries or collections of letters or other private papers attributed to the men of these early times. We must hence view them, and their age, almost entirely through their formal, published writings and through the equally formal and selective accounts of the historians.

This lopsided character is in part due merely to neglect, the cumbersome nature of the writing materials of the time, and the ravages of time. But, as I have suggested above, it is also in part purposive, a reflection of the interests of the men who were the producers and custodians of so much of this early literature. Nearly all the authors whose works we shall be discussing, whether poets, historians, or philosophers, were at the same time government officials or members of philosophical schools which sought official sanction and support. They were, in other words,

---

[1] It is important to note that, while much of the literature of the Classical West has been recovered from actual ancient manuscripts, that of ancient China, with the exception of some government documents of little literary interest, is known only through later texts. The oldest extant texts of the works are in most cases printed editions dated a thousand years or more after the composition of the works themselves.

either members of the ruling class or aspirants to such member-
ship, and their principal intellectual concern was, as Stephen
Spender puts it, "that human experience so neglected in modern
art—the art of ruling, the art of being a prince and being responsible for the use of power." [2] As the quotation suggests, it
is a subject which is foreign to much of our modern literature,
and the western reader may therefore be unprepared for the extent to which, explicitly or implicitly, it dominates the literature
of ancient China. That literature contains works in many forms
and on many subjects, but again and again, as we examine it and
sift its ideas, we realize that its real intent is to illumine or
comment upon some aspect of political science.

Interest in this question of the proper ordering of the state,
though by no means confined to followers of Confucianism, was
particularly associated with that doctrine, and in time, especially
after Confucianism received recognition as the official creed of
the state in the second century B.C., came to color all Chinese
literary theory and practice. It led scholars, for example, to impose allegorical interpretations on older literary works such as
the folk songs of the *Book of Odes,* in order to extract a political
meaning from them, and to ignore other types of literature, which
seemed of no political significance, until in time they were lost.
The allegorical interpretations we can attempt to strip away; the
losses we can only deplore. But if we are to understand early
Chinese literature at all, we must at least understand, if we do
not wholly sympathize with, this overriding concern with
questions of politics and the ordering of the state. I have therefore
devoted considerable space in what follows to Confucian doctrines
and their influence upon literary theory and practice, though I
am aware that such doctrines, with their occasional air of sancti-
moniousness and their refusal to venture beyond the realm of

[2] *The Making of a Poem* (London, 1955), p. 133.

common sense, may not strike a very responsive note in many modern readers.

I would like to emphasize one more point here. Lionel Trilling, in his essay "The Sense of the Past," points out that "the literary work is ineluctably a historical fact, and what is more important, . . . its historicity is a fact in our aesthetic experience." [3] I have no intention of apologizing for early Chinese literature; its intrinsic excellence is such that it certainly needs no apology. But I want to stress a fact that seems almost too obvious to mention: namely, that these are the earliest works in a great literary tradition that continues unbroken to the present day. As the oldest works in the language, they command a very special respect and affection in the eyes of native critics. No English-speaking person is insensible to the peculiar appeal of the early English ballads, Chaucer, or the archaic language of the King James Bible, particularly since, as in the case of the Bible, such language may so often be associated with beautiful music and solemn surroundings. In the same way we must imagine that the quaint and archaic language of these early Chinese works, the ancient songs of the *Book of Odes,* the resounding phrases of the *Analects* or the *Book of Rites,* have for Chinese readers a particular beauty which is inseparably bound up with their antiquity and the exalted role they have played in the formation of the literary tradition of China. We should keep this in mind when we read these works and the appraisals of them by native critics, although we ourselves, bred in another culture, may be able to catch only the faintest echoes of the music that reaches Chinese ears.

I have dealt with early Chinese literature under three headings: history, philosophy, and poetry. The distinction between the first two is not always easy to make, since many works of history are colored by philosophical bias, and many philosophical works

[3] *The Liberal Imagination* (Anchor A13), p. 181.

abound in historical anecdotes and allusions. On the whole, however, I believe the two groups of writings can be satisfactorily separated. I have divided the philosophical writings by schools—Confucianism, Taoism, Legalism, etc.—though in the case of some of the eclectic works I have followed traditional Chinese practice by treating them as a separate category. Unlike some other writers, I have not attempted to treat the Five Classics as a unity, since they embrace a variety of texts and were only lumped together in late Chou times because of their antiquity and their supposed connection with Confucius and his school. Hence the *Book of Documents* and the *Spring and Autumn Annals* are discussed under historical writings, the ritual texts and the *Book of Changes* under philosophical writings, and the *Book of Odes* under poetry.

I have endeavored to treat all important works of early Chinese literature still extant, and frequently to illustrate their nature by translated excerpts, particularly in cases where the work as a whole has not yet been translated into English. I have not, however, attempted to describe every text that has been handed down from antiquity, nor to deal exhaustively with all the works mentioned. My criterion for deciding what to discuss, and at what length, has been my own interest in the work and, by extension, what I hope will be the interest of the reader. Needless to say, I am not without my own prejudices and favoritisms, which are inevitably reflected in my approach to the subject. But if the reader finds himself prompted by them to challenge my views by turning to the works themselves, they will have served a purpose.

Unfortunately, I realize that this is not always possible without a knowledge of the language of the original. I have at the end of each section listed English translations of the works discussed which are easily available and which seem to me to do justice to the works. Much fuller listings, including those of translations into other European languages, will be found in James Robert Hightower's *Topics in Chinese Literature* (revised edition, Harvard University Press, 1953), a work which contains in its limited pages an enormous amount of sound information and opinion, and to which I am greatly indebted.

CLASSICAL CHINESE

It may be well at this point to give for the benefit of readers who are not familiar with its general nature and characteristics a brief description of the language in which these early works are written.

The earliest examples of Chinese writing we possess are, as I have said, diviners' notations and inscriptions on vessels, and of course are of a special nature. From the early centuries of the Chou dynasty we possess examples of poetry, political speeches and exhortations, and a manual of divination. These are followed by a number of philosophical and historical works dating mostly from the fourth and third centuries B.C., in which the written language shows remarkable progress in richness and clarity of expression. How close the language of these works was to the actual speech of the period we do not know, though some of them apparently attempt to reproduce a deliberately conversational tone. By the first century B.C., with the unification of China under the Ch'in dynasty and its successor, the Han, the written language achieved considerable uniformity of style and diction. This more or less "standard" written language, though undergoing numerous stylistic changes and fluctuations, continued to be used as the vehicle for most serious writing until the present century. If it ever represented the actual speech of the time, it probably ceased to do so in the early centuries of the Christian era. As the spoken language underwent its own process of development, it diverged farther and farther from the formal written language, until the two became almost separate languages. It is this written language, formed in the centuries before the Christian era and thereafter employed, with only minor stylistic variations, until the present century, that is known as classical Chinese.

As everyone knows, Chinese is written not with an alphabet or syllabary but with characters, which to Dickens looked "like bird-cages and fly-traps" and, to later Westerners who began to delve enthusiastically into their meaning, seemed to be nothing but little pictures, wonderfully graphic and expressive. It is now generally realized in the West that the Chinese characters are in fact the highly conventionalized and sophisticated products of a long, complicated process of development. Though many of them were originally pictographs, or contained pictographic elements, these elements were in many cases confused or obscured in the centuries before the characters reached their present form, and hence play only a minor part in the system of writing as it is used today. True, certain of these pictographic elements, the so-called radicals, still serve to give important (though sometimes misleading) clues to the meanings of the characters. Thus, for example, though one may be unfamiliar with a certain character, he can often surmise from its radical that it is the name of a kind of fish, bird, plant, or stone. In most cases, however, the average educated Chinese is scarcely conscious of the pictographic elements underlying or embedded in the characters he uses.

Once the form of the characters had been conventionalized and standardized around the second century B.C., the system of writing underwent little change. Thus, while the pronunciation of the characters differed widely in different periods and different localities, the characters remained the same, providing a strong bond between the literature of past and present, of province and province, or, when the characters were adopted in Korea and

Japan, between China and the foreign countries within its sphere of cultural influence. Allowing for minor differences of style and diction, it is as easy to read a page from a Chinese author of the second century B.C. as to read one from an author of the present century who uses the classical language.

The same would not be true, however, of a page from an author of the centuries before 300 B.C., when the language was still in its formative stage. In *The Way and Its Power* (p. 101), Arthur Waley writes: "The earliest use of connected writing . . . was as an aid to memory. That is to say, its purpose was to help people not to forget what they knew already, whereas in more advanced communities the chief use of writing is to tell people things they have not heard before."

This is an important point to keep in mind when considering the oldest writings in the Chinese language. The men who transcribed the speeches of the *Book of Documents,* the poems of the *Book of Odes,* or the oracles of the *Book of Changes* were undoubtedly concerned to get the meaning noted down as accurately and elegantly as possible; but probably the last thing they would have asked themselves was whether what they had written would be intelligible to someone who did not already know what the piece was about. They would assume that anyone to whom the text was transmitted would receive instruction in its meaning when he received the text. Writing was still a sacred thing and it was hardly thinkable that written works would ever come into uninitiated or unauthorized hands.

As a result, the earliest writings in Chinese are couched in an extremely brief, laconic style, a sort of shorthand designed "to help people not to forget," which today presents difficulties of interpretation at every turn. Commentaries purporting to represent the traditional interpretations handed down over the centuries do exist, but they are often separated by almost a thousand years from the texts they essay to elucidate, and their interpretations are in many cases patently no more than plausible guesses. In recent years scholars, using the methods of modern textual criticism, have gone far in establishing the original meanings of the texts, but there are still countless doubtful passages. This is of course true of the ancient literature of other countries; but the reader should perhaps be reminded that when he reads these early Chinese works in translation, he is at many points reading not an incontrovertible rendering of the meaning of the original, but only one of a variety of tentative interpretations.

As literacy spread more widely through Chinese society and books became more plentiful in the fourth and third centuries B.C., written Chinese shed some of its early arcane, laconic quality and became more easily comprehensible to the uninitiated. But the old fondness for brevity remained one of the outstanding characteristics of classical Chinese. Words that could presumably be supplied by a thoughtful reader on the basis of context were often left unexpressed, so that the student of classical Chinese is sometimes led to conclude despairingly that even in the later centuries of the language he is still dealing not with a medium for the communication of new ideas but a mnemonic device for calling to mind old ones. Is it too much to ask that the writer indicate at least the subject of the sentence? he may ask. In the case of classical Chinese the answer is usually, yes.

Another characteristic of classical Chinese, which does much to assist this penchant for brevity, is the fine versatility of its words. Chinese grammarians have traditionally distinguished only two classes of words, "full words" and "empty words." The latter are particles used as connectives or expletives and may often be omitted without any great loss in meaning; the former include what we would call nouns, verbs, adjectives, and adverbs. The reason the Chinese have not attempted to break down the "full word" group into such narrow categories as our noun, verb, etc., is that full words may, depending upon context, function in any one of these capacities.

English words possess some of the same versatility. In conversation, for instance, we may "fox" a rival or "dog" someone we admire, and Shakespeare could picture Cleopatra disdaining to be taken captive to Rome where some actor might "*boy* my greatness i' the posture of a whore." But we are often inhibited by grammatical convention, especially in writing, from converting our nouns into verbs too freely, even when the meaning would be perfectly evident.

Classical Chinese, however, knows no such inhibitions, and there is apparently no limit to the number of nouns, or what we would call nouns, that may be used verbally, thus allowing the language to achieve a vigor and brevity of expression that is only partially realized in English. In classical Chinese, for example, one finds such usages as the following: "O King, I would *jewel* you"—i.e., make you as perfect as a jewel (*Odes* # 253); "I will *corpse* you here"—i.e., look for your corpse here (*Tso chuan,* Hsüan 12); "Are you trying to *King of Wu* me?"—i.e., assassinate me as the King of Wu was assassinated (*Tso chuan,* Ting 10); "Do you *door* Confucius?"—i.e., consider his teachings as the entry into the Way (*Fa yen,* sec. 2). And centuries later the T'ang Confucian scholar Han Yü, in a fiery denunciation of Buddhism and Taoism (*Yüan tao*), called upon the authorities to take steps to suppress the two religions and "*men* their men!" —that is, force the members of their clergy to become ordinary citizens again, implying by his powerful use of "men" as a verb that, in retiring from active productive life to become priests, they have ceased to deserve the name of men.

There are indications that ancient Chinese was once inflected to a limited degree, but such inflections certainly ceased to be of any importance by the second century B.C. From that time on the language depends almost entirely upon word order to make clear the relationships between words. Classical Chinese word order is strikingly like that of English, so that an English-speaking reader generally knows just where he is in a Chinese sentence; he need not wait until the end of the sentence, as in Japanese, for example, to find out whether all that has gone before is to be affirmed or negated. Since the language is uninflected, substantives contain no indication of number and verbs no indication of tense. If a writer feels he is in serious danger of being misunderstood he may indicate number and tense by the use of additional words. Most writers of classical Chinese, however, appear to entertain a highly optimistic view of the reader's ability to divine the sense without such aids.

Classical Chinese is essentially monosyllabic, one character being used to represent one monosyllable. Thus a single sentence of subject, verb, and object may be expressed in three characters, though there has been a tendency since early times to combine words of related meaning to form two-character substantives, verbs, etc. Classical Chinese tends to use short, simple thought units, often arranged in neat patterns of three, four, five, or six characters each, the same grammatical construction being repeated in a series of parallel units. Such fixed-length, parallel phrases assist the reader's comprehension (since originally no punctuation was used), and give the passage a rhythmical swing, though they may at times produce an air of irritating monotony. The general effect of this brevity, monosyllabism, and tendency to group thoughts in parallel units may perhaps be suggested in English by a passage like this:

Sky spans high   earth bears up   beast herds teem there   winged flocks fly by   four seas close round   ten streams race on   so too kings reign lords aid men plow wives spin good sires rear sons good heirs serve sires, *etc., etc.*

More will be said later on concerning the characteristics of particular prose and poetic styles. But the foregoing paragraphs will serve, I hope, as a description of the general nature of classical Chinese, a language remarkably brisk and pithy in expression, dispensing magnificently with the inflections and connectives that are required in European languages, moving now in swinging parallel clauses, now in short, staccato utterances. At its best it is capable of both clarity and vigor but, if one element must take precedence over the other, it usually prefers, like English, to slight the demands of clarity. It moves with a speed and economy that defy reproduction in any other language and sometimes tax the ingenuity of the reader in divining the sense. But it is undoubtedly one of the great languages and has served for over two thousand years as the vehicle for some of the world's finest poetry and prose. What follows will introduce the reader to the principal works written in this language when it was in its youthful and perhaps most vigorous period.

HISTORY

POETRY AND HISTORY, it is generally agreed, are the two glories of Chinese literature. While drama and pure fiction developed comparatively late in China, and philosophical writing sporadically waxed and waned, poetry and history (in the broadest sense) appear among the earliest extant writings in Chinese and continue almost without break to occupy a major position in Chinese letters up to our own day. The volume and continuity of historical literature is particularly impressive. From 721 B.C. to the present there is scarcely a single year to which the Chinese chronicles do not ascribe some fact or event.

This is not to say that such a mass of historical writing is uniformly valuable. Much of the early literature is of questionable reliability and contains patently fictional elements; much of the later is dry and uninspired. As the centuries advance, the broader developments of Chinese history become all but obliterated by the wealth of political detail; the mass of recorded information swells to such proportions that only the most indefatigable reader can hope to control it.

And yet Chinese scholars have never ceased to study the histories of the past, even as the chroniclers continued year by year their interminable scribble, scribble, scribble; for the Chinese never wavered in their conviction that somewhere, buried among all the detail and trivia, were vital lessons to be learned.

The heroine of Robert Henryson's *Testament of Cresseid*,

after relating the sad history of her downfall, warns the women of Greece and Troy: "And in your mynd ane mirrour mak of me." This same mirror image has been used by the Chinese from earliest times to express their belief in the didactic value of history. We find it at the beginning of the Chou dynasty in the speeches which the Chou leaders made to the men of the newly conquered Yin state. "We should not fail to mirror ourselves in the lords of Hsia," admonishes the duke of Chou. "We likewise should not fail to mirror ourselves in the lords of Yin" (*Book of Documents, Shao Kao*). The successes and failures of the preceding Hsia and Yin dynasties must be a mirror to guide the inexperienced Chou leaders and to reconcile the Yin people to subjection by showing them the reasons for its necessity. The *Book of Odes* repeats the image: "Yin, your mirror is not far;/It is in the generations of the lords of Hsia!" (*Ta-ya*, T'ang). And in late Chou times a minister of the state of Chin, commenting sadly upon the errors and extravagances which brought about the downfall of the rulers of antiquity, concludes, "And so they came to destruction and could not grasp in their hands the mirror of past remembrance" (*Kuo yü*, Chin yü 1).

A mirror which sheds such light, a study which purports to hold the key to an understanding of the central problem of early Chinese thought—the ordering and preservation of the state—could not help but command the serious attention of scholars and statesmen. It is for this reason that examples and lessons from history or allusions to the events of the past occupy so much space in Chinese philosophical writing and that works of history, whether bare chronicles like the *Spring and Autumn Annals* or elaborate, semifictional re-creations of the past such as the *Tso Commentary,* have been accorded such a high position in the Chinese canon. Poetry, ritual, the metaphysical structure of the universe—all these have a place in the education of the scholar, for all bear, in one way or another, upon the problems of state-craft. But it is history alone that shows what political problems have actually arisen in the past, how and with what measure of success they have been dealt with. Its place must therefore be primary.

The *Shu ching* or *Book of Documents*

The first Chinese work of history—taking the word in its broadest sense to mean a record of past events—is the *Shu ching,* the *Classic of History* or *Book of Documents,* also known as the *Shang shu,* or *Documents of Antiquity*.

According to tradition, the documents which make up the work were assembled and arranged by Confucius, who wrote brief introductions to each one explaining the circumstances of its composition. There may well be a core of truth in this account, since it is known that Confucius and his disciples often cited passages from some of the documents in their teaching. Whatever Confucius' collection of documents may have been, however, it was certainly added to in the centuries after his death, and the introductions to the documents which we now possess appear to be from a later hand.

When the First Emperor of the Ch'in dynasty attempted to silence the criticisms of his totalitarian policies and to suppress the scholars of the Confucian school, he ordered the confiscation and burning of the texts that were the basis of Confucian teaching, among them the *Book of Documents*. A few copies escaped de-struction and were recovered by the scholars of the following Han dynasty, but these copies do not seem to have contained all the sections that existed in the pre-Ch'in version of the work. The Han version therefore consisted of 28 sections (or, since several of the longer documents are divided up in some editions, 32 sections). Later, in the third century A.D., a number of clever forgeries, purporting to be the lost sections of the work, appeared. These consisted of genuine fragments of the lost sections preserved in quotation in other texts, pieced together and filled out with a shrewd antiquarianism that fooled Chinese scholars for a thousand years. It was not until the Ch'ing dynasty that the spurious nature of these chapters was finally proved beyond doubt. These forged sections, 26 in all, because they were for so long accepted as genuine, have had a certain influence upon later thought and literature. But here we shall confine our discussion to those sections which are generally accepted as dating from pre-Ch'in times.

The first point to be noted about the documents is that each is a separate unity. Though many of them deal with the same period and the same rulers and ministers, they contain no cross references or connecting narratives relating one to another. What we have in the *Book of Documents,* therefore, is no more than an assortment of early pronouncements or papers, arranged in chronological order by the compiler. It is easy to believe, for this reason, that earlier versions of the text contained many more sections, since, under the circumstances, there would presumably be no evidence to indicate where a section had dropped out in the course of transmission. The earliest documents purport to deal with the reign of the legendary Emperor Yao, the latest with the return of the defeated army of the state of Ch'in in 626 B.C. This terminal date has no particular historical significance and the work might just as well contain documents pertaining to a later period. In other words, though the individual documents relate, or claim to relate, segments of the history of the past, there has been no attempt (fortunately for us) to weave these segments together into a connected narrative. The text as it stands is a collection of source materials.

The second point to note is that, with one exception, all the documents contain large portions of direct speech, and many of them consist almost entirely of the texts of pronouncements or declarations made by early rulers or their ministers. What little narrative there is serves in most cases simply to identify, in the briefest terms, the speaker and the occasion for the speech.

This fondness for direct speech is a salient characteristic of later Chinese historical writing and it is significant that it should have its model in the earliest extant work in the historical genre. Partly it may be explained as a reflection of the idiom of the language. Early Chinese has ways to express indirect discourse; but they are sparingly used, customarily to summarize some statement that has previously been expressed in direct discourse, or to convey a single word or two of discourse. There are no extended passages of indirect discourse in early Chinese literature. The use of direct discourse, therefore, would seem to have been the most natural mode of expression, and we may suppose that neither writers nor readers of history in early China attached to such a mode of expression the momentous significance which we attach today to anything appearing within quotation marks.

Toynbee has remarked, "The semi-fictitious speech is clearly a dangerous instrument in a historian's hands," and if one is inclined to condemn it in a historian such as Thucydides, who informs us beforehand that he has made use of the device, one will perhaps be even more inclined to condemn it in the Chinese historian, who does not bother with a warning. Nevertheless, we may assume, I think, that the conscientious Chinese historian, like his Greek or Roman counterpart, when he knew in general what a particular person had said on a particular occasion, did his best to convey the gist of the pronouncement faithfully, though he might not be able to reproduce the exact wording. As for unconscientious historians, East or West, none of the conventional devices invented by scholarship for the purpose of assuring accuracy has ever been known to hamper their inclination to distort and falsify, and the discourses in their narratives, whether direct or indirect, must always be equally suspect.

Whatever the dangers to strict historical accuracy involved in the use of the fictitious or semifictitious speech, we must in fairness note the distinct literary advantages of the device. It allows the writer to cast his narrative in a highly dramatic form and, like the dramatist, to illuminate the character of the speakers through their manner of speech. The set speech on a particular topic, moreover, may serve as a convenient and effective way to enumerate the points of a problem and list the steps for its solution, or to convey in the most persuasive form a particular viewpoint. A great deal of early Chinese philosophical thought is expounded in just such dialogues and speeches, sometimes in works associated with the name of a particular philosopher, sometimes in semihistorical works such as the *Tso Commentary* or the *Intrigues of the Warring States*. It is precisely in these passages of direct discourse, particularly the set speeches, that the line between history and philosophy becomes most tenuous, since we know that it is a device of Chinese philosophers to give the expositions of their ideas a concrete historical or pseudohistorical setting and a device of Chinese historians to elaborate their narratives with lengthy moral pronouncements put, with what justice it is often difficult to determine, into the mouths of historical figures. For this reason many so-called historical works of early Chinese literature could just as well be labeled works of philosophy. In the case of the *Book of Documents,* Chinese scholars, aware of this difficulty of distinguishing between history and philosophy, circumvent it by calling the book a *ching* or "classic." By the word *ching* they mean a work which, though the product of a particular time and place, conveys truths that are timeless, a combination of history and philosophy whose value transcends both categories.

The language of the *Documents,* in both its narrative and its speech passages, is extremely difficult. Bernhard Karlgren terms it lapidary, which seems a particularly apt way of conveying the terse, archaic impression which it gives: something stiff, stone-carved, difficult to make out, and blurred in places beyond intelligibility. It stands with the *Book of Odes* and the older portions of the *Book of Changes* at the dawn of Chinese literature, preceded by the bone inscriptions discovered in the last century and paralleled by inscriptions on bronze, but set apart in style and vocabulary from everything that follows. No one, not even a scholar, picks up the *Documents* and reads it right off; the meaning of many passages remains today the subject of endless dispute among specialists. Nevertheless, in spite of individual words or phrases whose meaning is doubtful or lost, the general sense of the text can still be made out. As in later Chinese style, there is a tendency to use balanced, parallel phrases, and to treat ideas in the form of numerical categories—the five felicities, the three virtues, etc. The basic ideas expressed in the *Documents* have influenced later Chinese thought to an incalculable degree. But the style, because of its difficult and archaic quality, cannot be said to have had a similar influence. Although we find in later literature occasional passages, usually imperial edicts, which seem to be conscious imitations of the *Documents* style, they are no more than isolated pieces of pedantry. While the thought of the *Documents,* rephrased and reinterpreted, lived on, the style happily died with antiquity.

The sections of the *Book of Documents* may be said to fall into two main groups: (1) those speeches and pronouncements which are pegged to specific persons, problems, and times, principally the early years of the Chou dynasty; (2) those pieces which, though presented in the form of speeches or dialogues, are in fact treatises on abstract principles of government or idealized descriptions of the deeds of the sage rulers of high antiquity. (A case apart is the *Yü kung* or "Tribute of Yü," which contains no discourse at all but is an idealized geography of the empire as it was supposed to have existed in very ancient times.)

The pieces in the first group are most likely to be genuine, that is, to reflect the actual ideas, perhaps even the words, of the men and times to which they are attributed. The most important among these are the pronouncements and advisory pieces attributed to Chou Kung or the duke of Chou, the younger brother of King Wu, the founder of the Chou dynasty. Most of these are addressed to the people of Yin, the subjects of the Yin or Shang dynasty that had been conquered by the Chou leaders; others are addressed to King Wu's successor, King Ch'eng, to whom the duke of Chou acted as regent. These may be called the heart of the *Documents;* they contain the most important ideas and probably represent the work as it was compiled by, or known to, Confucius. Of less importance are several sections dealing with events in the history of the feudal states of the early Chou period, and some pieces which are said to deal with certain events during the preceding Yin dynasty, such as the moving of the Yin capital.

The pieces in the second group, as I have said, though presented in a pseudohistorical form—usually that of a dialogue between a ruler and his minister, or ministers—are actually not accounts of historical fact or pronouncements on specific problems, but philosophical expositions of the general principles of government. Among these the most important is the *Hung fan* or "Great Plan," dealing with the political, economic, moral, and religious principles to be observed by the ruler; the *Lü hsing* or "Code of the Marquis of Lü," on the proper way to

administer punishments (but not on specific criminal laws); and
the opening section of the *Documents,* the *Yao tien* (divided in
some editions into *Yao tien* and *Shun tien*), and the *Kao Yao
mo* (divided in some editions into *Kao Yao mo* and *I Chi*).

All of the sections in this latter group, most scholars agree,
date from middle or late Chou times. In other words, the date of
their composition or compilation is far removed from the time
of the persons purportedly described therein—in the case of the
account of the sage rulers Yao and Shun, almost two thousand
years removed by traditional dating. These pieces have no historical value, therefore, except as reflections of the ideas, and
idealizations of the past, current at the time of their compilation,
and as embodiments of earlier legends. They belong rather to
the philosophical literature of the late Chou, though they have
customarily been accepted by later Chinese scholars as reliable
accounts of ancient history.

The sentiments expressed in the *Documents,* as befits a work
which has been accorded such high honor in Chinese society,
are uniformly pious and lofty. The ruler is to be the moral leader
and norm for his people, serving the spirits with reverence, carrying out his duties with diligence and alacrity, selecting wise
counselors and heeding their advice, examining into the grievances of the people and alleviating their hardships. One could
ask for little more, except perhaps a bit of concrete instruction
on how this happy state of affairs is to be achieved and maintained. Among the profusion of vague and noble sentiments, we
may distinguish two important ideas that play a significant role
in later Chinese political thought. The first is propounded in the
first group of documents mentioned above, particularly in the
speeches of the duke of Chou to the conquered people of Yin.
This is the famed concept of *t'ien ming,* the mandate of Heaven.

Like all farsighted conquerors, the Chou leaders, after having defeated the armies of the Yin state and deposed its ruler, Emperor Chou (or Shou, as he is called in the *Documents*), sought for some philosophical principle or concept to justify their action and assist them in persuading the Yin people to cooperate with the new regime. They found such a justification in the concept of the mandate of Heaven, which teaches that the would-be founders of a new dynasty, by their just and virtuous actions, receive from Heaven—a vague, half-personalized spiritual power which rules the universe—a command to set up a new rule. So long as the successive leaders of the new dynasty continue to follow the virtuous course which first entitled their predecessors to the mandate, Heaven will continue to sanction their power. But if subsequent rulers turn their backs upon virtue and sink into negligence and evil, Heaven will withdraw its blessing and bestow it instead upon another family or group of leaders, who will then rise up, depose the erring dynasty, and establish a new reign of virtue in its place. The fact that they succeed in doing this is in itself the necessary proof that Heaven has withdrawn its mandate from the old dynasty and conferred it upon the new. In other words, it is virtue alone that entitles a ruler to rule, and when he sets aside virtue he sets aside the right to call himself a sovereign. The throne is never conferred by Heaven upon a dynasty for the period of a generation or a century or a millennium, but only for as long as the dynasty proves worthy of it.

Whether this idea was already current in Chinese thought at the time of the Chou conquest or whether it was an invention of the Chou leaders, we cannot say. The urgency with which the duke of Chou declaims it rather suggests that, if it was already known, it was by no means universally accepted. It seems to have taken the Chou leaders considerable time and effort to stamp out all resistance to their conquest and to win the sincere allegiance of their new subjects. The duke of Chou resorts to all manner of threats and cajolery to convince the Yin people that they must forget their former king and accept the new one. But the core of his exhortations is always the concept of the Heavenly mandate. The last ruler of the Yin dynasty by his wickedness forfeited the right to rule. The Chou leaders, King Wen, who began the conquest, and King Wu, who brought it to completion, have, by their virtuous ways, won it. Their very success is proof of this.

To bolster this assertion, the duke of Chou resorts to a favorite argument of Chinese thinkers; the proof of history. Look back at the history of your own defunct dynasty, he urges the people of Yin. There you will find evidence of exactly the same process in the past, when Ch'eng T'ang (King T'ang the Completer), the founder of the Yin dynasty, deposed Emperor Chieh, the last and notoriously evil ruler of the preceding Hsia dynasty.

We have no archeological evidence to show whether or not the Hsia dynasty ever existed. But the Yin people obviously believed that it had, and also believed, or allowed themselves to be convinced, that its rulers, though virtuous at first, had eventually sunk into evil and been toppled by the virtuous founder of the Yin. If this analogy from the past was originally only a piece of propaganda invented by the Chou leaders to persuade their new subjects that it was useless and wanton to resist the conquerors any longer, it ended by being accepted as historical fact.

According to this argument, therefore, a dynasty, to borrow Arthur Wright's expressive terminology, always begins with a "good first ruler" and ends with a "bad last." In the *Li cheng,* the last of the pronouncements attributed to the duke of Chou, the series works out as follows:

Dynasty	*"Good First"*	*"Bad Last"*
Hsia	—	Chieh
Shang or **Yin**	Ch'eng T'ang	Shou (Chou)
Chou	Wen/Wu	—

Elsewhere in the *Documents* the sage Yü is added to the series
as the "good first" of the Hsia dynasty.

The clearest expression of this concept of the mandate of
Heaven is found in the speech of the duke of Chou in the *Shao
kao* or "Announcement to the Duke of Shao," from which I
shall quote. The passage will also serve to illustrate the balanced,
symmetrical style characteristic of the set speeches in the *Documents*.

We should not fail to mirror ourselves in the lords of Hsia; we likewise should not fail to mirror ourselves in the lords of Yin. We do
not presume to know and say that the lords of Hsia undertook
Heaven's mandate so as to have it for so-and-so many years; we do
not presume to know and say that it could not have been prolonged.
It was that they did not reverently attend to their virtue, and so they
prematurely renounced their mandate. We do not presume to know
and say that the lords of Yin received Heaven's mandate for so-and-
so many years; we do not know and say that it could not have been
prolonged. It was that they did not reverently attend to their virtue
and so they prematurely threw away their mandate. Now the [Chou]
king has succeeded to and received their mandate. We should then
also remember the mandates of these two states and, in succeeding to
them, equal their merits. . . . Being king, his position will be that of
a leader in virtue; the small people will then imitate him in all the
world. . . . May those above and below labor and be anxiously careful; may they say: we have received Heaven's mandate; may it
grandly equal the span of years of the lords of Hsia and not miss the
span of years of the lords of Yin.

This, then, is the concept of kingship and the explanation of
the process of dynastic rise and fall expounded in the *Book of
Documents*. It is profoundly moral and rational, characteristic
of the best in Confucian thought. By making the virtue of the
ruler prior to, and the cause of, spiritual sanction, rather than
the other way around, as in other concepts of kingship in the
ancient world, it places a heavy moral responsibility upon his

shoulders. Hence the endless and impassioned injunctions to the rulers, in the *Book of Documents* and later Confucian texts, to eschew idleness and indulgence, to be diligent in the practice of virtue, and to promote good counselors and follow their advice. At the same time, by citing the decay of virtue which marked the latter years of the Hsia and Yin dynasties—in the *Wu i,* the duke of Chou speaks of the later Yin rulers who were "born to ease" and hence did not understand or care about the hardships of the people—the concept implies that it is habitual, indeed inevitable, for a dynasty to abandon its righteous ways in the course of time and to fall into evil and decay. Thus the periodic change of dynasties becomes a normal phenomenon; no such thing as an eternal dynasty is to be expected. Though the theory was originally expounded as a justification for the establishment of a new dynasty, it could easily, one can see, be interpreted as an excuse for revolt and regicide. For this reason it has sometimes been regarded with misgivings by later Chinese thinkers, and with horror by the Japanese, who are committed to the opposite concept, that of one never-ending dynasty. As recently as the period of ultranationalism in Japan before and during the Second World War, the passage in *Mencius* (IB, 8), in which Mencius defends the deposition of the last rulers of the Hsia and Yin by saying that they had, by their evil actions, forfeited the right to be regarded by their subjects as sovereigns, was expunged from copies of the texts used in the schools.

The other important idea expressed in the *Documents* is the "ceding of the throne" theme, clearly stated in the first section, the *Yao tien* or "Canon of Yao," and implied in the second, the *Kao Yao mo* or "Pronouncement of Kao Yao." According to the former, the sage ruler Yao, said to have reigned sometime before the Hsia dynasty, passed over his own son and selected a commoner, Shun, to be his successor to the throne. After employing

Shun for a three-year trial period and finding his conduct satisfactory, he abdicated, turning over the business of government
to Shun. According to very early legend (though it is not stated
explicitly in the *Documents*), Shun in a similar manner passed
over his own son and bequeathed the throne to one of his ministers, Yü, the founder of the Hsia dynasty. Again according to
other texts rather than to the *Documents,* Yü attempted to be-
queath the throne to a minister named I, but after his death
the other ministers deserted I and gave their allegiance to Yü's
son Ch'i, so that from then on the throne remained in the family
until the fall of the dynasty.

It is agreed by scholars today that Yao, Shun, and Yü were
originally not historical figures at all, but local deities or culture
heroes. They are mentioned frequently in Chou texts, along with
various other legendary figures, such as Fu Hsi, Shen Nung, or
the Yellow Emperor, as heroically wise and virtuous rulers of
antiquity. In the version of the legend found in the *Documents,*
however, none of these other figures is mentioned.

As stated above, the section of the *Documents* dealing with
Yao and Shun is now believed to date from late Chou times.
The theme of the emperor who cedes, or attempts to cede, his
throne to a worthy man who is not his son, is found frequently
in later Chou literature, being attributed in one text or another
to almost all the famous rulers of antiquity.[1] It was a particular
favorite of the Taoist thinkers who, because they regarded power
and authority as basically evil and corrupting, always picture
the person to whom the offer of succession is made as rejecting
it violently and often going into seclusion afterward to purify
himself from the stain of such a vile suggestion. Confucius speaks
admiringly of Yao, Shun, and Yü in a number of passages in

---

[1] For a detailed study of these legends, see Bernhard Karlgren, "Legends and
Cults in Ancient China," *Bulletin of the Museum of Far Eastern Antiquities,* XVIII
(1946), 291 and *passim.*

the *Analects,* and this may be one reason why the compilers of
the *Yao tien* chose to pay exclusive honor to these figures. But
it is only in the last chapter of the *Analects* that any mention
is made of the ceding of the throne by Yao to Shun, and by
Shun to Yü, and this chapter is generally agreed to be considerably later in date than the early portions of the text. Mencius,
however, in Book V, Part 1, discusses the *Yao tien* and the ceding theme at some length, and so we may assume that the legend
and the text of the *Yao tien* was well known by his time.

The appearance of such a legend, in which a ruler passes over
his son and selects a successor from among his subjects or ministers, is so curious in a society that placed such emphasis upon
the ties of familial duty and affection and in which, so far as we
know, rulership always passed from father to son or, in some
cases, from brother to brother, that one is immediately impelled
to ask how and why it could have originated.

There is no easy answer, though various attempts have been
made by scholars in recent years to suggest an explanation. Some
see the legend as a distorted and misunderstood remnant of a
matriarchal society—that is, Shun was actually an adopted son-
in-law; or of a tribal society in which the principle of hereditary
succession to leadership had not yet been established. Others explain it as an attempt to link up in some significant manner two
quite different sets of legendary figures, those of the Chou people
(the lineage of Yao), and those of the older Yin people (the
lineage of Shun). Still another suggestion, and one which has
many plausible arguments to support it, is that the legend is a
creation of the philosophers of late Chou times (probably mainly
those of the Mohist school), men of plebeian origin who were
seeking employment in the governments of the time and who
attempted in this way to "prove" that in antiquity rulers were so
concerned about promoting men of talent and worth, regardless

of birth, that they even at times turned over their thrones to virtuous commoners.

Whatever its genesis, the legend and the concept which it embodies, like the concept of the mandate of Heaven, often proved an embarrassment to later thinkers, particularly since it was enshrined in the *Book of Documents,* the oldest and most sacred of historical texts, and attributed to the greatest sages of antiquity. Later rulers sometimes wondered, or professed to wonder, if they themselves should not attempt to imitate the example of the wise and virtuous Yao by ceding their thrones to worthy aides; ministers no doubt sometimes secretly hoped that they would. But everyone who could see that an attempt to put such an ideal into practice would lead to political chaos was at pains to explain why, in this case alone, the deeds of the ancient sages did not necessarily constitute an inflexible guide for rulers of later ages. Like the concept of the mandate of Heaven, with its implied right of revolution, the theme of the cession of the throne to a commoner required careful handling and interpretation if it was not to undermine the principle of hereditary succession. It is interesting that China, noted for the length and durability of its imperial institutions, should honor as a classic a work enshrining two such "dangerous" ideas.

The direct discourse style which figures so prominently in the *Documents* has already been amply illustrated. It may be well to close with an example of one of the rare narrative sections of the work.

The only passages of extended narrative in the *Documents* (aside from the descriptive geography of the "Tribute of Yü"), are to be found in the "Canon of Yao," the *Chin t'eng* or "Metal-bound Casket," and the *Ku ming* or "Deathbed Commands." The first, as we have seen, is probably of late date; the last, though perhaps early, is merely a description of the rituals accompanying the death of King Ch'eng. The date of the "Metal-bound Casket," the most interesting of the three, is likewise uncertain; the narrative portions, in particular, may well be of quite late date. The typically primitive and naïve belief, expressed in the prayer of the duke of Chou, that one can hoodwink the spirits, and the miraculous reversal of the wind, however, suggest that the legend, if not the wording of the piece, date from rather early Chou times. If the piece is in fact earlier in composition than the *Tso Commentary*, it represents the oldest example we have of historical narrative style in Chinese literature, with its typical dramatic form and large admixture of direct speech. The translation, like the one above, is based on that of Karlgren.

After he had completed the conquest of the Shang people, in the second year, King Wu fell ill and was despondent. The two lords, the duke of Shao and T'ai-kung Wang, said, "For the king's sake let us solemnly consult the tortoise oracle." But the duke of Chou [King Wu's younger brother, named Tan] said, "We must not distress the ancestors, the former kings!"

The duke of Chou then offered himself to the ancestors, constructing three altars within a single compound. Fashioning one altar on the southern side facing north, he took his place there, holding a jade disc and grasping a baton of jade. Then he made this announcement to the Great King, to King Chi, and to King Wen, his great-grandfather, grandfather, and father, and the scribe copied down the words of his prayer on tablets:

"Your chief descendant So-and-so [King Wu's personal name is tabooed] has met with a fearful disease and is violently ill. If you three kings are obliged to render to Heaven the life of an illustrious son, then substitute me, Tan, for So-and-so's person. I am good and compliant, clever and capable. I have much talent and much skill and can serve the spirits. Your chief descendant has not as much talent and skill as I and cannot serve the spirits! . . ."

Then he divined with three tortoises, and all were auspicious. He opened the bamboo receptacles and consulted the documents, and they too indicated an auspicious answer. The duke of Chou said to the king, "According to the indications of the oracle, you will suffer no harm."

[The king said,] "I, the little child, have obtained a new life from the three kings. I shall plan for a distant end. I hope that they will think of me, the solitary man."

After the duke of Chou returned, he placed the tablets containing the prayer in a metal-bound casket. The next day the king began to recover.

[Later, King Wu died and was succeeded by his infant son, King Ch'eng. The duke of Chou acted as regent and was slandered by King Wu's younger brothers, whom he was eventually forced to punish.]

In the autumn, when a plentiful crop had ripened but had not yet been harvested, Heaven sent great thunder and lightning accompanied by wind. The grain was completely flattened and even large trees were uprooted. The people of the land were in great fear. The king and his high ministers donned their ceremonial caps and opened the documents of the metal-bound casket and thus discovered the record of how the duke of Chou had offered himself as a substitute for King Wu. The two lords and the king then questioned the scribe and the various other functionaries, and they replied, "Yes, it is true. But his lordship forbade us to speak about it."

The king grasped the document and wept. "There is no need for us to make solemn divination about what has happened," he said. "In former times the duke of Chou toiled diligently for the royal house, but I, the youthful one, had no way of knowing it. Now Heaven has displayed its terror in order to make clear the virtue of the duke of Chou. I, the little child, will go in person to greet him, for the rites of our royal house approve such action."

When the king came out to the suburbs to meet the duke of Chou, Heaven sent down rain and reversed the wind, so that the grain all stood up once more. The two lords ordered the people of the land to right all the large trees that had been blown over and to earth them up. Then the year was plentiful. (*Chin t'eng.*)

The *Ch'un ch'iu* or *Spring and Autumn Annals*

The next work of history, the *Ch'un ch'iu* or *Spring and Autumn Annals*, like the *Book of Documents*, is included among the Five Classics. It is a chronicle of events in the feudal states during the period from 722 to 481 B.C., known consequently as the Spring and Autumn period. The term "spring and autumn" is an abbreviation of "spring, summer, autumn, winter" and was used in the state of Lu, where the chronicle was compiled, to designate such a season-by-season record of events. We know that similar chronicles were customarily kept by official scribes or historians at the courts of the various feudal leaders of the later Chou period, though they were known by different names in different states. The First Emperor of the Ch'in, when he unified the empire, ordered these chronicles to be burned because they contained derogatory references to the state of Ch'in, and consequently most of them were lost long ago. The only ones that survive are the *Spring and Autumn Annals;* a chronicle of the state of Ch'in preserved in Chapter 6 of the *Shih chi;* and the *Chu-shu chi-nien* or *Bamboo Annals,* a chronicle of the state of Wei, which was recovered from a grave in the third century A.D. and subsequently lost, but partially reconstructed from quotations preserved in other works.

Though they vary in time span, all these chronicles are written in the same concise, laconic style; in contrast to the *Documents* and later historical works, they contain no direct discourse. They are in fact not narratives at all, but collections of brief notices of events—accessions, deaths, battles, unusual natural phenomena, etc. Because of the complete lack of background explanation or detail for the events noted, the historical value of the chronicles is limited, and their literary interest is nil.

In spite of this, the Chinese have since early times held one of these chronicles, the *Spring and Autumn Annals,* in extravagantly high esteem. This is because, according to tradition, it was compiled by Confucius himself on the basis of records preserved in his native state of Lu. This tradition, moreover, as it is recorded in *Mencius,* asserts that the *Annals* deals with "matters proper to the emperor," and quotes Confucius as saying, "Yes! It is the *Spring and Autumn* which will make men know me, and it is the *Spring and Autumn* which will make men condemn me" (*Mencius* IIIB, 9). As a result, the time span of the *Annals,* the order of its wording, and the exact terminology employed, have been studied and pondered by generations of scholars in an effort to discover some hidden message which Confucius was attempting to relay to posterity. An elaborate system of interpretations, highly forced and often contradictory, was worked out which purported to reveal how certain inclusions, omissions, or slight variations of terminology express Confucius' "praise" or "blame" of the persons or events mentioned. Later scholars pointed out the fatuousness of such interpretations. But because of the tradition associated with the *Annals,* few were ever able to free themselves from the conviction that the work must somehow be more than it appears to be—a fairly accurate but wearisomely dull and colorless chronicle.

One may avoid the dilemma easily enough by denying that there is any basis to the tradition. But this does not explain how and why it arose. Perhaps it was for no other reason than the fact that both Confucius and the *Annals* came from Lu, though I am inclined to think there is more to it than that. We know the fondness of Chinese thinkers of all ages for illustrating political principles by means of concrete historical examples. We also know from the *Analects* that Confucius himself often commented upon the actions of the statesmen of his own day or of the past, indicating what he approved or disapproved of in their conduct. It seems quite possible, therefore, that Confucius or his immediate disciples might have had a copy of the Lu chronicle, perhaps one which Confucius had compiled from the court records for his own convenience, which was used as a framework for discussions of political theory and practice, certain principles or "lessons" customarily being pegged to certain entries in the chronicle. It would then be this body of teachings and judgments, orally transmitted, and not the actual text of the *Annals,* which Mencius would be referring to as containing matters—i.e., principles of government—proper to an emperor, and which would cause men to honor or condemn Confucius in the future.[2]

Whether such a body of orally transmitted lessons and exegeses ever existed in the early days of the Confucian school, we cannot say. By late Chou and Ch'in times we find scholars writing commentaries in an attempt to explain the background and significance of the events recorded in the *Annals,* and these may to some extent have drawn upon such an early body of exegesis. But all of the commentaries which have been preserved attempt to discover some deep meaning in the text of the *Annals* itself. By the time these commentaries were composed, men were apparently convinced that Confucius had somehow altered the text of the old chronicles of Lu in such a way as to imbue it with profound moral significance.

Of these various commentaries, three exist today and are included in the Confucian canon. Two of them, the *Kung yang* and *Ku liang* commentaries, are in the form of a catechism: the commentary poses a question on the significance of some nota-

---

[2] The Han historian Pan Ku seems to have held such a view. In his "Treatise on Literature," *Han shu* 30, the section on the *Spring and Autumn Annals,* he asserts that, with regard to the *Annals,* Confucius "had certain things which he praised or blamed, respected or condemned. He could not put these in writing, but transmitted them orally to his disciples. After his disciples had dispersed, however, their explanations began to differ."

tion in the *Annals* and then answers itself, explaining what Confucius intended by the inclusion of the notation and the way in which he worded it. Occasional historical narrative is added to elucidate the text or support the interpretation. Though the ideas expressed are of some importance in the history of Chinese thought, the commentaries themselves contain too little narrative to be of significance as historical works and are of slight literary interest.

The third commentary, the *Tso chuan* or *Tso Commentary,* contains similar passages which seek to interpret the moral import of the form and wording of the *Annals.* Far more significant, however, is the fact that the work contains lengthy sections of narrative on the history of the period, which constitute the longest and most important historical text of the Chou period. At the same time, because of its vivid, powerful style and wealth of detail, it ranks with the *Chuang Tzu* as one of the greatest prose works of ancient China. It deserves, therefore, to be treated not as an appendage to the brief and dreary *Annals,* but as an independent work of literature.

The *Tso chuan*

The *Tso chuan* takes its name from its putative author, Tso Ch'iu-ming or Tso-ch'iu Ming, who has sometimes been identified with a man of the same name praised by Confucius in *Analects* V, 24. In fact, however, nothing is known of who he was, when he lived, or what connection he had with the work that bears his name.

Most scholars today agree that the *Tso chuan* is a genuine work of Chou times, compiled probably in the third century B.C., though it appears to contain additions made toward the end of the Former Han. Attempts have been made in recent years, partly with the purpose of giving more glory to the *Kung yang*

Commentary, to demonstrate that the *Tso* was forged by Liu Hsin, a supporter of the usurper Wang Mang at the beginning of the Christian era. Liu Hsin was an enthusiastic advocate of the *Tso chuan* and may in fact have made some additions to the text. But Karlgren has demonstrated by linguistic analysis that the historical sections of the *Tso* observe certain grammatical rules and distinctions which would have been unknown to a man of Liu Hsin's time. Moreover, even without such proof, it should strike anyone familiar with the peculiar style of the *Tso chuan* as highly unlikely that even the most skilled Han antiquarian could have concocted out of whole cloth a narrative so far removed from the style of his own time.

We do not know what the original form of the *Tso chuan* was. At present its accounts of events in the various feudal states are broken up and arranged chronologically to fit with entries in the *Spring and Autumn Annals.* Some entries in the *Annals* have no corresponding passages of explanation in the *Tso chuan,* however; some passages in the *Tso* have no corresponding entry in the *Annals;* and sometimes the accounts in the two texts are in conflict. It would seem, therefore, that the two works were originally quite separate, though it may have been an interest in the events mentioned in the *Annals* itself which inspired the compilation of the *Tso chuan.* In addition, as stated above, the *Tso* contains passages similar to those in the *Kung yang* and *Ku liang* commentaries which comment upon the wording and significance of the *Spring and Autumn Annals.* These passages, explicitly relating the *Tso chuan* to the *Annals,* may well be of later date.

The *Tso chuan* begins in 722 b.c., the first year of the *Annals,* but carries its narrative down to 468 b.c., thirteen years after the *Annals* stops. Undoubtedly the narrative contains a large admixture of legend and romance. The lengthy, formal speeches of its numerous rulers and statesmen, in particular, are in most cases probably no more than literary fictions. Yet it undoubtedly includes a great deal of sound fact and information of real value on the life and history of the period. If we had only the *Annals* to go by, we could construct no more than the barest outline of the history of the age. With the *Tso,* however, we have a portrait which, while perhaps somewhat idealized and confined almost wholly to the life of the aristocracy, is remarkably vivid and detailed. Regardless of what light it can be made to shed as a commentary on the *Spring and Autumn Annals,* therefore, it is a work of primary importance for the study of Chou history and society.

The world glimpsed in most of the sections of the *Documents* is a remote realm of heroes and sages, of primitive mythico-religious themes and pious ideals, shrouded in antiquity. By contrast, the world of the *Tso chuan* is starkly real. The religious rites and themes are still here, the lofty sentiments still pronounced. The Son of Heaven, the Chou king, though pitifully weak and the pawn of one after another of his powerful barons, still radiates an aura of ritual sanctity. The high ideals and noble standards of conduct which were said to have characterized the society of early Chou continue to command not only lip service, but at times true fidelity. We read of statesmen who sincerely seek peace from the incessant feudal wars and work to alleviate the sufferings of the common people, of rulers who attempt to fulfill not merely the letter but the spirit of the old rites and religious ceremonies; of a general who refuses to condone the betrayal of an enemy, or a minister who defies the wrath of his lord by weeping over and cradling the head of a murdered comrade. But such isolated acts of altruism—the deeds which, in the eyes of the compilers of the *Tso,* made the history of the age worth telling—are set against a background of violence, greed, and sordid political strife.

Perhaps the contrast between this period and the previous one seems greater because the picture of the society drawn by the *Tso* is so much more detailed than that of earlier days found in the *Documents*. The *Tso* shows us the rulers of China not only making high-flown pronouncements, but plotting the ruin of an enemy, riotously drinking and dining, setting their mastiffs on an offending courtier, or wearing on their arms the badges of adultery: bits of the undergarment of an aristocratic slut. Perhaps the whole image of the peaceful and enlightened days of early Chou is no more than a dream born in the minds of the men who had to live in the strife-ridden society of the Spring and Autumn period, and the even fiercer, more chaotic period that followed it. But though the writers of the *Tso* may have fabricated from their dreams a golden age of antiquity, they were fearless in recording the harsh and feculent realities of their own day.

It would be naïve, of course, to suppose that the narratives in the *Tso chuan* were originally compiled and handed down merely with the purpose of giving an objective account of the history of the period. The *Tso* betrays no indication of who its author or authors were; its beginning and ending dates have no particular historical significance; and there is no formal structure to the work, at least in its present form, other than chronological order. Nevertheless, it is dominated throughout by a single philosophy, a single outlook on the nature and significance of its material. The raw stuff of the narrative may be historical fact, or legend and romance in pseudohistorical guise. But its purpose from beginning to end is didactic. In a passage under Duke Ch'eng 14th year, the *Tso* states that the *Spring and Autumn Annals* was designed "to encourage good and censure evil." Whatever its applicability to the *Annals,* the phrase is a fitting description of the *Tso chuan* itself.

The *Tso chuan* is essentially a work of the Confucian school of thought, and this outlook has no doubt strongly colored its picture of the Spring and Autumn period. It is true that many of the figures who appear in its pages voice sentiments that are repugnant to Confucian teaching. There are militarists who eulogize the glories of warfare, cynics who deny the value of benevolence and a sense of duty in politics, advocates of strict totalitarian government, fatalists who would shift all responsibility for human failure to the gods. In addition there is frequent mention of baleful spirits, prophetic dreams, and consultations with shamanistic mediums—elements of ancient superstition which have often distressed Confucian admirers of the *Tso* in later, more rationalistic ages.

In spite of these elements, however, the *Tso* narratives, and particularly the frequent moralizing speeches and comments strewn through them, are on the whole firmly dedicated to the proposition, basic in Confucian thought at least from the time of Mencius on, that man is the author of his own fate, that good deeds insure success and evil deeds failure. On the basis of this axiom the *Tso* orders its material, an endless series of variations on the theme of virtue triumphant; or, more aptly, since these are dark and disordered times, of evil and delusion as the cause of failure.

In the numerous speeches of the wise statesmen and scholars of the *Tso,* we find frequent evocations of the traditional Confucian concepts of *te* (virtue), *jen* (benevolence), and *i* (righteousness or a sense of duty). But the key term of the *Tso*'s doctrine is *li* (rites, ceremonies, a sense of propriety). In many passages in the *Tso* this word *li* refers to the specific rules of conduct which govern religious and social ceremonies, the points of etiquette to be observed in public and private life. But in other passages, as so often happens in early Chinese philosophical writing, the word is expanded in meaning and scope until it has ceased to refer to details of ceremony alone but has become, as in the teachings of the Confucian philosopher, Hsün Tzu (fl. 298–238 B.C.), a comprehensive moral standard which embraces all phases of human behavior and even extends to the natural and supernatural worlds. Thus under Duke Chao 25th year we read: "Ritual (li) is the constant principle of Heaven, the righteousness of Earth, and the proper action of mankind. . . . Ritual determines the relations of high and low; it is the warp and woof of Heaven and Earth and that by which the people live." A correct understanding of ritual, both in its detailed manifestations and in its essence, therefore, is the basis of all correct action and the key to success. In the *Tso,* to describe a man as *wu-li* (without a sense of ritual or propriety) is to say that he is ignorant, evil in action, and doomed to certain failure.

A whole section of the Confucian canon, the books on ritual, is designed to impart this understanding of the rules of proper conduct. The *Tso,* by means of historical anecdotes, imparts the same type of knowledge by showing men in the act of conforming to or violating these rules of behavior and by noting the consequences of their behavior. The figures in the narrative are repeatedly pictured as concerned about the correctness of their actions. Rulers question their ministers and advisers on the propriety of some action; statesmen gather to exchange opinions on the behavior of some important personage. These are the occasions for numerous formal speeches on the principles of ritual and on what particular attitude, approach, or course of action is correct in particular circumstances. And scattered throughout these exchanges, in case the reader should miss the point of the historical sequence of the narrative, are the endless prophecies for which the *Tso* is famous.

Some of these prophecies are based upon the ancient arts of divination by tortoise shell or milfoil stalks. A ruler consults a diviner on some question of policy; the latter reports the results of the divination in appropriately arcane language and then explains its significance, prophesying the future and suggesting what course of action is appropriate.

But the large majority of the prophecies in the *Tso* are not based upon such formal processes of divination or consultation with the spirits or ancestors. They are based rather upon what we may best describe as common sense and an acute sensitivity to the implications and consequences of particular types of behavior. To put it more simply, in this second type of prophecy one looks at a person, decides to what degree his actions conform to the principles of *li,* and on this basis predicts his success or failure.

If a man commits outrageously cruel or immoral acts, it is not difficult even for him to foresee that, in the rapidly fluctuating society of the Spring and Autumn period, he may well meet with disaster. Thus the evil King Ling of Ch'u, when informed of the murder of his sons, replies, "I have killed many sons of other men—how could I help but come to this?" (Chao 13).

But not all the sequences of cause and effect, of evil and downfall, recorded in the *Tso* are so easy to foresee. Under Duke Ting 15th year, we read of a visit of Viscount Yin of Chu to the court of Lu. When Viscount Yin presents his jade symbol to Duke Ting of Lu (who is nominally his sovereign), he holds the symbol high, with his face upturned, while the duke receives it in a low-bent position with his face turned downward. Tzu-kung, one of Confucius' disciples, observing the proceedings, immediately predicts that "these two rulers will soon die or be forced into exile!" Justifying his prediction, he explains, "The high position and upturned face are indicative of arrogance; the bent position and downturned face are indicative of apathy. Arrogance is not far removed from rebelliousness and apathy is not far removed from sickness."

Tzu-kung, a diligent and talented disciple of Confucius, presumably developed through his association with the Master an unusually acute moral sensitivity which allowed him to make such predictions on the basis of subtle and seemingly insignificant details of posture and behavior. Few other figures in the *Tso* could be expected to possess such acuity, and therefore, in a period marked by constant warfare between states, rebellions, depositions, murders, and incessant court intrigues, it is natural that many of the men portrayed in the *Tso* should feel uneasy about the correctness of their actions and should be constantly questioning each other and offering each other advice. The advice of a friend or minister which opens one's eyes to fatal error and restores one to the path of rectitude is a priceless gift. One incautious statesman, gratefully acknowledging the value of such a piece of lifesaving advice from a fellow courtier, says, "This is what it means to give life to the dying and to flesh again the bare bones!" (Hsiang 22).

By heeding such advice, by wise judgment and moral acuity, some of the men in the *Tso* are able to escape the disasters which overtake their less prudent contemporaries. And the stories of their lives, as well as those of the lives of the imprudent, the speeches of advice and warning, and the frequent prophecies, provide the reader with a comprehensive set of examples and case studies from which he may deduce the principles necessary to guide him in his own conduct. The *Tso* is thus a handbook of moral cause and effect, a system of divination based not upon numbers or omens, but upon the more complex, but infinitely more trustworthy, moral patterns discernible in actual human history. A proverb of the time says, "He who is in doubt about the present should examine ancient times; he who does not understand the future should look to the past" (*Kuan Tzu,* Sec. 2). Works on philosophy or ritual may teach one the principles of virtue or the rules of correct behavior. But it is works of "history" like the *Tso chuan* which, in the opinion of the early Chinese, were best able, by demonstrating to the reader the actual effects of the application or neglect of such principles, to "give life to the dying and to flesh again the bare bones."

In the *Documents* we find an explanation of dynastic change in the concept of the mandate of Heaven, according to which a family qualifies itself to rule the empire by practicing virtue, and disqualifies itself by neglecting it. In the *Tso chuan* this principle is extended to apply to all successes and failures in political life.

The later dukes of Lu described in the *Tso* were on the whole a weak and incompetent lot, and the actual power of government came to be concentrated more and more in the hands of the Chi family, a collateral branch of the ducal family, who for generations had served as high ministers to the dukes of Lu. Duke Chao finally blundered into an open contest for power with the leader of the Chi family and was obliged to flee from the state. He spent eight years in exile and died there in 510 B.C. After recording his death, the *Tso* describes a conversation in which one court official asks another why the people of Lu allowed their ruler to be exiled and why neither they nor any of the other feudal lords attempted to punish the Chi family. The official's explanation runs in part as follows:

The rulers of Lu have for generations pursued a course of error, while the Chi family have for generations practiced diligence. Thus the people of Lu have forgotten who their ruler is. Though he has died abroad, who is there to pity him? The altars of the state are not always tended by the same family; ruler and subject do not remain in their respective positions forever. From ancient times this has been so. Thus the *Odes* says:

> The high banks become valleys;
> The deep valleys become hills.

The descendants of the rulers of the three dynasties of antiquity are mere commoners today—as you well know! (Chao. 32.)

Once again the lesson is driven home: it is goodness and ability, not birth alone, that entitle a man to rule.

Such, then, is the philosophy of history revealed in the earliest important historical work to be compiled under the influence of Confucian thought. It is a philosophy which, like that of the early Confucian thinkers Mencius and Hsün Tzu, is strikingly and, in view of the dark age which produced it, almost miraculously optimistic. History, for all practical purposes, is motivated solely by the human will. Its course is governed by no inexorable laws other than those of human morality; supernatural forces play little or no part in its unfolding except as responses to, and reinforcements of, the good or evil deeds of man himself. All men are free moral agents; all, in theory at least, are morally perfectible through education and effort. And history is one of the most important tools in this educational process, making it possible for the men of later ages to imitate the excellencies and avoid the errors of their predecessors. Accordingly there is nothing to prevent the men of any time or place from reaching, by their own wisdom and striving alone, the millennium. Early Confucian thought is marked by a humanism so sanguine and thoroughgoing it would startle even the Greeks.

Let us turn now to a consideration of the style of this remarkable work. It is probable that the narrative portions of the *Tso* were compiled from a variety of earlier accounts and legends belonging to various periods and geographical areas. In the process of compilation, however, they have been reduced to a uniform style and, as Karlgren has shown, a uniform grammar. It is possible, therefore, to discuss the style of the *Tso* as a single entity.

Like the *Book of Documents,* the *Tso* contains a large amount of direct speech. True, the narrative portions are far more complex and important than the brief, scattered narratives in the *Documents.* But it is still the speech portions which carry the burden of the story. The narrative in most cases still serves merely to set the stage for a dialogue or a discussion.

The dialogue passages may be divided into two groups. First are the brief remarks or conversational exchanges between two or more persons. These are phrased in a succinct and forceful style and presumably conform rather closely to the actual speech of the period of the compiler, though not necessarily to that of the period and locality of the speaker to whom they are attributed. In this respect they are much like the conversational exchanges recorded in the *Analects* and *Mencius.*

The second group is made up of longer and more formal speeches, pronouncements, or replies to questions. These have all the characteristics of set literary pieces. Like the speeches in the *Documents,* they are cast in a balanced, rhythmical style employing series of phrases made up of the same number of words—four-character phrases, five-character phrases, etc.—and having a parallel grammatical construction. In addition, to increase their effectiveness they use the standard Chinese rhetorical devices—similes, historical examples, quotations from the *Odes* and the *Documents,* homey analogies, proverbs, and numerical categories. In other words, unlike the shorter passages of dialogue, these make no attempt to convey a conversational or spontaneous impression, but are consciously formal and literary. The degree to which this is so may be conveniently illustrated by a passage under Duke Chao 28th year. Two retainers are invited to dine with their lord, and in the course of the meal they sigh three times. Their lord asks them why they sigh and, the narrative tells us, "the two replied in the same words, saying . . . ," after which follows an elaborate explanation of the three sighs. Obviously we have here not an attempt to reproduce realistic speech —it is impossible to imagine two men giving an identical reply of such length and complexity—but a literary convention like the chorus in a Greek play. The purpose of the device, of course, is to allow the writer to express his ideas and assertions in the most effective and memorable fashion by putting them into the mouths of historical or supposedly historical personages. It is in these set pieces, with their literary embellishments, that we find the principles of proper ritual behavior, of political theory and practice, of benevolence, wisdom, loyalty, and the other traditional virtues expounded. These are the main vehicle for the didactic element of the work.

On the whole these speech passages are fairly easy to read, particularly the longer and more florid ones, and are not very far removed from similar passages in works of the succeeding Ch'in and Han periods, in spite of occasional oddities of vocabulary and construction. The same, however, cannot be said for the narrative passages.

The narratives may likewise be divided into two groups. Sometimes, though not often, the *Tso* will contain a passage of straight narrative uninterrupted by dialogue, such as the description of the government policies of Tzu-ch'an in Hsiang 30 or of the walling of the Chou capital in Chao 32. These correspond to the second group of speech passages described above, the formal orations. They are set literary pieces of description and, like the formal speeches, fall generally into a rhythmical, parallelistic style.

But by far the larger part of the *Tso*'s narrative passages employ no such formal style. As already stated, they are mostly in the nature of framework or connectives for the dialogue passages, and the writer therefore strove apparently to phrase them in an appropriately rapid and succinct style. Unfortunately for the reader, the result is often so succinct as to be nearly incomprehensible.

The *Documents,* as we have seen, contains almost no narrative passages, the "Metal-bound Casket" being the only important exception, and it is of uncertain date. Aside from this the only examples of historical narrative we possess which antidate the *Tso chuan* are those in the *Spring and Autumn* and the other chronicles, which are extremely limited in subject and vocabulary. The *Tso,* then, represents the earliest extant piece of extended and detailed historical narrative. This fact may help to account for its peculiar, archaic, and sometimes rather crude quality. In style it is close to the inscriptions found on early and middle Chou bronzes, and yet it essays a length and complexity of expression which is undreamed of in the curt inscriptions.

One of the things which makes the narrative passages of the *Tso* so difficult to read today is the vocabulary. The writer of the narrative can certainly not be blamed for using terms and names of things which were common in the life of the period. But since almost our only literary source for the life of the period is the *Tso* itself, scholars today naturally find it difficult in many cases to discover the exact meaning of such names and terms.

A second difficulty, and one which the writer might have avoided with a little forethought, is the erratic use of proper names. The identity of persons appearing in the narrative is seldom explained, so that we must gather from the context itself who the person is, or rely upon later commentaries (though how the commentators acquired their information is another question.) Moreover, the same person will at one time be identified by his familiar or personal name, at another time by his polite name, at another time by his official title, and perhaps at another time even by his posthumous title, all without any indication that he is the same individual. Presumably a reader of the period would not find this too troublesome, since he would be familiar with these various names of the famous persons of the time. But the practice is surely out of place in a work of history which is designed to convey a knowledge of the past to distant generations in the future. This is merely one of many indications that the *Tso chuan* is basically less a history in our sense of the word than a treatise on ethics set in historical form.

A third difficulty is caused by the extreme succinctness and compression of the narrative, due in part, no doubt, to the fact that the compilers were incorporating materials written in an earlier and more archaic style. Actually, this is one of the qualities of the *Tso* most lavishly praised by later critics. Liu Chih-chi (661–721), who wrote the first important work on Chinese historiography, the *Shih t'ung* or *Generalities on History,* states flatly that brevity is the most important quality in historical narrative, praises the *Tso* for possessing this quality to such an exemplary degree, and berates later historians for falling into verbosity (*Shih t'ung* 22, "Narrative"). The reader may wonder why brevity alone, even at the expense of clarity, should be so extravagantly admired. He should recall, however, that educated Chinese like Liu Chih-chi (as Liu himself states in his "Autobiography," *Shih t'ung* 36) studied the *Tso chuan* and other classics as children under a tutor and were customarily made to memorize the texts. They therefore mastered the gist of the narrative at a very early age. In their later years, therefore, when they came to write their critical comments, since they already knew what the text said, they were free to admire the wonderful economy with which it said it. Hence their case is rather different from that of the foreign scholar who comes to the text without such a background and tries to discern the meaning simply by reading it off.

In order to convey something of the effect of this brevity, I shall give a painfully literal translation of one of the most famous, and most bizarre, narrative passages in the *Tso,* the description of the assassination of Duke Hsiang of Ch'i by Kung-sun Wu-chih and his band of rebels in 686 B.C. I am aware that such a style of translation is grossly unfair to the original; even the most beautiful and lucid classical Chinese prose can be made to sound like pidgin if one omits all the words which must be expressed in English but may be left unexpressed in Chinese. I hope, however, that it will serve to illustrate some of the difficulties I have enumerated.

Winter, twelfth month. Lord of Ch'i [Duke Hsiang] traveled to Ku-fen, then hunted at Shell Hill. Saw big pig. Attendant said, "Sir P'eng Sheng!" [who had been killed by men of Ch'i some years before because he had caused the death of Duke Huan of Lu when the latter was visiting Ch'i]. Duke angrily said, "P'eng Sheng dares show himself?" Shot it. Pig stood up manlike and wailed. Duke frightened, fell in carriage, injured foot, lost shoe. Returned, demanded shoe from attendant Pi. Failed to get it, beat him till blood showed. Ran out, met rebels at gate. Seized and tied him. Pi said, "Would I dare stop you?" Doffed robe and showed back. Believed him. Pi asked to go in first. Hid duke and came out, fought, died in middle of gate. Shih-chih Fen-ju died at foot of stairs. Eventually entered, killed Meng Yang in bed. Said, "Not the ruler! No resemblance!" Saw duke's feet under door. Proceeded to assassinate him and set up Wu-chih. (Duke Chuang 8th year [685 B.C.].)

One of the reasons this narrative is so mysterious on first reading is that, though the subject often changes from sentence to sentence, the new subject is seldom expressed. Thus unless one reads very carefully and ponders the scene, he will not realize that, though the duke beat his attendant Pi, it was *Pi,* not the duke, who ran out and into the arms of the rebels who were at the gate; and though it was Pi who ran out, it was the rebels who seized and tied him. It would also be helpful to the reader to realize that Meng Yang had gotten into the duke's bed and was impersonating the duke in an effort to fool the rebels, which explains their remarks when they discovered their error. The sudden appearance of Shih-chih Fen-ju, an otherwise unknown minor official of Ch'i who remained loyal to the duke, is typical of the way in which the *Tso* introduces names without any explanation of the individual's identity.

Professor Yoshikawa Kōjirō, writing on the style of the *Tso,* says: "As the reader pauses at the end of each phrase, he must consider carefully what it means before he can grasp its logical connection with the next phrase and so move on. The writer seems to have written with the expectation that the reader would perform such a mental exercise at the end of each phrase, and would thereby obtain a sensation of intellectual pleasure" ("Kŏ-chaku no bungaku," in *Raihōtō* [Tokyo, 1956], p. 29).

It is true, as Professor Yoshikawa says, that in this style one must usually grasp the meaning of the first phrase before he can move on to the second. But in other cases one finds he must move on to the second phrase before he can understand the first. And when, as sometimes happens, these two phenomena coincide, it is difficult to see where the pleasurable sensation comes in.

However, I do not wish to labor the point. Once one has perceived the meaning, the style of the *Tso* is indeed magnificent, as the Chinese say. I only wish to warn the reader that when he reads the *Tso* in translation he may be sure that, for better or worse, he is certainly missing a good deal of the flavor of the original.

Because of the economy of its narrative style, the *Tso* is able to achieve a power and a rapidity which are unparalleled in later Chinese literature. Consider, for example, the following scene which takes place just before the famous battle of Yen-ling, 575 B.C., in which the Chin armies defeated King Kung of Ch'u. Here the writer, instead of describing in his own words the preparations of the Chin forces for battle, conveys the description through the words of an anxious onlooker, the king of Ch'u. In the dialogue passage, beyond the first phrase, "asked the king," there is no indication whatsoever of who is speaking. As in a modern novel, one must judge from the content who the speaker is.

The king of Ch'u climbed up into a towered carriage and gazed afar at the armies of Chin. Tzu-chung ordered the minister Po Chou-li [a man of Chin who had deserted to the Ch'u side] to attend the king and stand behind him.

"Why are those people rushing about to left and right?" asked the king.

"They are calling together the army officers."

"They're all gathering in the center of the camp!"

"They are plotting their strategy."

"They're putting up a tent!"

"So they may respectfully consult the former rulers by divination."

"They're taking down the tent!"

"They are going to issue the orders."

"Such a commotion, and all that dust rising!"

"They are filling in their wells and smashing their cooking pots in preparation for the advance."

"They're all mounting their carriages! Now those on the left and right are holding their weapons and dismounting!"

"They will take the oath of battle."

"Will they fight now?"

"I cannot tell yet."

"They've mounted, but now those on the left and right are all getting down again!"

"The prayer of battle." (Duke Ch'eng 16th year [575 B.C.].)

The Spring and Autumn period was an age of incessant feudal warfare, and the battle descriptions of the *Tso* are justly famous. They are, however, far less elaborate than those found in the histories of the Classical West, where the battle scene was a set literary piece, an opportunity for the historian to draw a vivid picture of massive columns of moving men, onslaughts, breakthroughs, and endless gore. By contrast the *Tso* battle scenes are relatively restrained. A good part of the description is concerned with the preparations for battle, including speeches for and against its advisability, and notes on the disposition of prisoners and booty after the battle. The description of the actual battle is often jerky and lean. We are told that large forces of soldiers participated in these battles, their number and disposition being recorded at the outset of the action. But once the action starts, we generally lose sight of the masses of fighting men while the narrative focuses upon the individual deeds of a few famous leaders or heroes. Presumably the common soldiers were there, milling around in the background. In the description of the battle of Pi, for example, at which Ch'u inflicted a crushing defeat on Chin, we are given, in a particularly grisly vignette, evidence of their presence and numbers: as the Chin forces, completely routed, attempted to flee across a river, those who arrived late clung to the boats of their comrades who had already embarked and threatened to overturn them; the men in the boats began chopping off the fingers that clutched at the gunwales until there were so many severed fingers in the bottom of the boat that, the narrative tells us, "one could scoop them up by the handful" (Hsüan 12).

But the *Tso* is the product of a feudal and aristocratic age, and the writer appears not to have known or cared what these common soldiers were doing in the field of battle; he concentrated instead upon the exploits of their leaders. As a result we seldom see the over-all sweep of a battle, but only a series of disconnected scenes of encounters between individual heroes, rather like the battle scenes in an Elizabethan play: "alarums, excursions, enter two warriors fighting"—then a shift to "another part of the battle field."

The following excerpt, though hardly a battle description, since the actual battle is disposed of in a single sentence, will illustrate some of the characteristics of the *Tso*. Note, for example, how the locale of the narrative skips back and forth from Ch'in to Cheng to Chin and back again, without even so much as a conventional "Meanwhile, back in ———." Note also the prophecy of the young prince of Chou based upon his observation of the behavior of the Ch'in troops. In the translation only one name has been used to refer to each person, though the original employs a variety of names.

In the winter [628 B.C.] Duke Wen of Chin died. On the day *keng-ch'en* preparations were made to inter the body at Ch'ü-wo, but as it was being carried out of the capital at Chiang, a sound issued from the coffin like the lowing of an ox. The diviner Yen urged the high officials to bow down, saying, "Our lord is speaking to us of a grave affair. He says that an army will come from the west to invade our land and that if we attack, we will win a great victory!"

Ch'i Tzu [the commander of a garrison of Ch'in troops stationed in the state of Cheng] sent a report from Cheng back to his sovereign in Ch'in saying, "The men of Cheng have given me custody of the keys to their north gate. If you send an army in secret, you can capture the city!"

Duke Mu of Ch'in questioned his minister Chien Shu about this, and he replied, "I have never heard of wearing out the army attempting to make a surprise attack on a distant state! If our army is worn out and its strength exhausted, while the ruler of the distant state has meanwhile been preparing for our attack, will not the outcome be disaster? If our army knows what it is doing, then Cheng will certainly find out as well, and if in spite of all our precautions we fail to win success, we will surely be faced with discontent. Anyway, if we have to march a thousand *li,* who could fail to guess what we were up to?"

But the duke declined to listen to his advice and, summoning Po-li Meng-ming, Hsi Ch'i, and Po I, he ordered them to lead the army out of the eastern gate.

Chien Shu wept and said, "Lord Meng-ming, I see the army going forth, but I shall not see it return!"

The duke sent someone to reproach him, saying, "What do you know about this, old man? If you had died at a decent age, the trees on your grave mound would be a span around by now!"

Chien Shu's son was with the army. Chien Shu wept and, taking leave of him, said, "If the men of Chin move to block your advance, it will surely be at Yao. There are two ridges at Yao. That on the south bears the grave of Emperor Kao of the Hsia dynasty. That on the north is where King Wen of the Chou dynasty retired to escape the wind and rain. You will die between these two and I will go to gather up your bones there!"

The Ch'in army then proceeded east.

Thirty-third year [627 B.C.], spring. The Ch'in army passed by the northern gate of the king's capital at Chou. The archers on the left and the lancers on the right of the carriage drivers doffed their armor and dismounted out of respect for the king, but when they came to mount again, the men of some three hundred carriages leaped up into their vehicles without waiting for them to stop. The royal prince Man, though still a young lad, watched them and then said to the king, "The army of Ch'in is overconfident and has no sense of propriety. It will surely be defeated. He who is overconfident lays few plans and he who has no sense of propriety easily slips up. If one enters a dangerous situation and slips up, and if on top of that he does not know how to plan, can he escape defeat?"

The army had reached the city of Hua [on the Cheng border] when Hsien Kao, a merchant of Cheng who was on his way to market in Chou, chanced to meet it. Quickly grasping the situation, he presented four tanned hides, followed by twelve oxen, as a gift to the army, saying, "My sovereign, the ruler of Cheng, hearing that you were about to lead your army through his humble territory, takes the liberty of presenting these gifts to your followers. Poor as are the resources of his humble territory, he has made preparations to provide your troops, who have been so long away from home, with a full day's supply of grain and fodder if you should decide to make camp, and an escort throughout the night if you should decide to march straight through without halting."

He then sent a fast rider to report the advance of the Ch'in army to the ruler of Cheng.

Having received the news, Duke Mu of Cheng sent men to keep a watch on the guest lodge where the Ch'in envoys Ch'i Tzu, P'eng Sun, and Yang Sun were staying. They found the envoys busy getting their baggage together, sharpening their weapons and feeding their horses. The duke then sent Huang Wu-tzu to say to the envoys, "Gentlemen, you have resided for a long time in my humble territory, and I fear that the supplies of dried meat, grain, fresh meat, and animals which were provided you are all used up. That is the reason, I suppose, that you are preparing to leave. However, Cheng has its Yüan Gardens, much like the Chü Park of your native state of Ch'in. How would it be if you gentlemen were to help yourselves to the deer from the Yüan Gardens and remain at leisure here a while longer?"

Their plot discovered, Ch'i Tzu fled to the state of Ch'i and P'eng Sun and Yang Sun fled to Sung.

Po-li Meng-ming said to the other commanders of the Ch'in army, "Cheng has already made preparations for our attack. We can hope for nothing! Now, even though we attack we cannot win, and though we surround the city we cannot maintain a siege. We had better go home!" With this they destroyed the city of Hua and began the march back. . . .

At the Chin court, Hsien Chen said, "Ch'in ignored Chien Shu's advice and has worn out its people on a mission of greed. Heaven presents us with this opportunity, and an opportunity thus presented must not be lost! One must not allow an enemy to escape, for to do so means trouble in the future, while to reject the offer of Heaven is unlucky. We must attack the Ch'in army!"

Luan Chih objected, saying, "We have not yet repaid the kindness which our late sovereign, Duke Wen, received from Ch'in in the past. Now if we were to attack its army, this would be to treat him as dead indeed!"

But Hsien Chen replied, "Ch'in, without showing any pity for the fact that we are in mourning for our sovereign, has attacked Hua, a city·of our own clansmen. It is obvious that Ch'in has no sense of propriety. Why worry about obligations to such a state? I have always heard that he who acts leniently towards his enemy for a single day brings on himself generations of trouble. If we plan now for the future safety of the sons and grandsons of the ruling family, how can we be said to be treating our late sovereign as dead?"

So the order was finally issued to attack the Ch'in army and a fast rider was dispatched to enlist aid from the Chiang barbarians. The late duke's heir dyed his mourning garments black and put on a white hemp sash. Liang Hung drove his chariot for him and Lai Chü stood by his right side in the chariot. In the summer, the fourth month, the day *hsin-ssu,* he defeated the Ch'in army at Yao and took Po-li Meng-ming, Hsi Ch'i, and Po I prisoner. Then he returned to Chin and, still wearing his black garments, buried his father, Duke Wen. This was the beginning of the Chin custom of wearing black mourning garments.

Wen-ying [a princess of Ch'in who became the wife of Duke Wen but was not the mother of Duke Wen's heir] asked her stepson, the new ruler of Chin, about the fate of the three Ch'in commanders. "It was they who actually brought about the trouble between the rulers of the two states!" she declared. "If my former lord, the ruler of Ch'in, could only lay his hands on them, his wrath would scarcely be appeased even by eating their flesh! Therefore, my lord, why demean yourself by executing them here? Send them back to Ch'in to be punished and you will make it possible for the ruler of Ch'in to accomplish his desire for vengeance!"

The new duke consented to this proposal.

When Hsien Chen appeared at court, he asked what had happened to the Ch'in captives.

"At the urging of my father's widow, I set them free," replied the duke.

Hsien Chen was furious. "Prizes won by the warriors at great labor on the field of battle—and at a word from a woman they are allowed to leave the state! He who deliberately discards the fruits of battle and nourishes the strength of his enemy need not wait long for the day of his destruction!" he exclaimed and, without turning his head, he spat.

The duke dispatched Yang Ch'u-fu to pursue the Ch'in commanders, but when he reached the banks of the Yellow River he found that they had already embarked in a boat. He immediately unharnessed the left horse from his team of four and shouted to Po-li Meng-ming that the duke wished to present the horse to him. But Po-li Meng-ming was not taken in and only bowed his head from the boat and replied, "Through the kindness of your lord I have been spared the usual fate of prisoners—having my blood smeared on the war drums. Instead I have been sent back to be punished by Ch'in. Even though I should be executed by my sovereign in Ch'in, I shall never forget the gratitude I owe your lord. And if my sovereign out of pity should pardon my offense, I will assuredly be back within the next three years to accept your lord's gift!" [3]

The ruler of Ch'in, wearing white mourning garments, camped in the suburbs of his capital to await the return of the army. He greeted the commanders with tears, saying, "I failed to heed the advice of Chien Shu and brought this shame upon you. The fault is mine!"

He did not deprive Po-li Meng-ming of his command, but said, "I was in error. What fault have you committed? How could I, because of one failure, forget the great deeds you have done?" (Duke Hsi 32–33 [628–627 B.C.].

The excerpts quoted so far have all been in the form of historical narratives relating to specific times and events, and this is the usual form of the *Tso* material, however much the history involved may be expanded and embroidered by the use of legend and literary imagination. There are other sections of the *Tso*

---

[3] I.e., to attack Chin again and wipe out the disgrace of his defeat.

which are more in the nature of out-and-out didactic fables. The following excerpt, for example, which centers about the wise statesman Tzu-ch'an of Cheng, is no different in form from similar anecdotes about Kuan Chung of Ch'i found in the *Kuan Tzu* or about Yen Ying of Ch'i found in the *Yen Tzu ch'un-ch'iu,* both philosophical works. The time and place of the incident could as easily be shifted and Kuan Chung, Yen Ying, or some other wise statesman substituted for Tzu-ch'an without affecting the moral of the piece. As a matter of fact, this has actually happened, for in the next work to be considered, the *Conversations from the States* (Chou yü 1), we find an almost identical anecdote concerning the tyrannical King Li of Chou and his wise counselor, Shao Kung.

The people of Cheng were in the habit of discussing the administration of the state when they gathered at leisure in the village schools. Jan Ming said to Tzu-ch'an, the head of the government, "How would it do to abolish the village schools?"

"Why do that?" said Tzu-ch'an. "In the morning and evening when the people have finished their work and are at leisure, they gather to discuss the good and bad points of my administration. The points they approve of I encourage, and those they criticize I correct. They are my teachers. Why should I do away with them? I have heard of wiping out resentment through goodness and loyal service, but I have never heard of stopping it by force. True, one can cut it off for a time. But it is like damming a river. When there is a major break in the dikes many men are bound to suffer. If the people's resentment were to break out in the same way, I would never be able to save the situation. It is better to leave a little break in the dikes for the water to drain off. It is better that I hear the people's complaints and make them my medicine!" . . . When Confucius later heard of this incident, he remarked, "People say that Tzu-ch'an was not a good man, but judging from this I find it impossible to believe." (Duke Hsiang 31 [542 B.C.].)

Another characteristic of the *Tso* which I have already mentioned is the large part that spirits, prophetic dreams, and other
manifestations of the supernatural play in its narrative. This has
always been counted as one of the faults of the *Tso* by later,
more rational-minded scholars. Thus Fan Ning (339–401), in his
preface to the *Ku liang Commentary,* says of the *Tso chuan,*
"It is colorful and rich, but it errs by its attention to sorcery." The
reader today, however, who does not have to approach the *Tso*
with the reverence expected of a traditional Chinese scholar, can
only be thankful for such elements, which provide invaluable information on the beliefs and superstitions of the period. The
following account of the death of Duke Ching of Chin is a good
example of the macabre side of the *Tso chuan.*

Duke Ching dreamt that he saw a huge ogre with disheveled hair
that hung to the ground, beating his chest and leaping about, saying,
"You killed my grandsons [Chao Tung and Chao K'uo], an evil deed!
God has promised me revenge!" The ogre broke down the main gate
of the palace, and then the door to the inner apartments, and came
in. The duke fled in terror to his chamber, but the ogre broke down
that door as well. At that moment the duke awoke and sent for the
sorcerer of Mulberry Field. The sorcerer, without asking what had
happened, described the duke's dream just as it had been.
    "What will become of me?" asked the duke.
    "You will not live to eat the new grain!" replied the sorcerer.
    The duke fell gravely ill and sent for a doctor from the state of
Ch'in. The ruler of Ch'in dispatched a physician named Huan to
treat the duke. Before the physician arrived, the duke dreamt that his
illness appeared to him in the form of two little boys. One boy said,
"He is a skilled physician and I am afraid he will do us injury. Where
can we flee?" The other replied, "If we go to the region above the
diaphragm and below the heart, what can he do to us?"
    When the physician arrived, he told the duke, "I can do nothing
for your illness. It is situated above the diaphragm and below the
heart, where treatment cannot affect it, acupuncture will not pene-
trate, and medicine will not reach. There is nothing I can do."

"You are a good doctor," said the duke and, entertaining him with all courtesy, he sent him back home.

On the day *ping-wu* of the sixth month the duke decided he wanted to taste the new grain and ordered the steward of his private domain to present some. When his butler had prepared it, he summoned the sorcerer of Mulberry Field and, pointing out the error of his prophecy, had him executed. Then he started to eat the grain, but his stomach swelled up and, hurrying to the privy, he fell down the hole and died.

One of the duke's servants had dreamt in the early morning hours that he was carrying the duke on his back up to Heaven, and consequently he was delegated that day to bear the duke's body on his back out of the privy, after which he was executed so that his spirit might accompany the duke in death. (Duke Ch'eng 10 [581 b.c.].)

As already stated, a great deal of the *Tso* is concerned with moral cause and effect, with frequent prophecies of what kind of fate will overtake what kind of person and when. For this reason the time and manner in which death comes to men is always, to the writer of the *Tso*, an important consideration. One statesman, speaking of a king who derived such pleasure from mourning ceremonies that they threatened to be his undoing, remarked, "A man will meet his end doing what he enjoys" (Chao 15). If one enjoys doing good, he will meet a good death, if evil, an evil one. In the *Tso*, the manner of death is thus a key to the personality and moral worth of the dead man. I shall close this description of the *Tso*, therefore, with a brief excerpt on the death of a minor feudal ruler which illustrates this point, and at the same time is typical of the swift, stark quality of the *Tso* narrative.

The duke of Chu was on the terrace at the top of the palace gate, looking down into his courtyard. The gatekeeper at the time was dousing the courtyard with water from a pitcher. The duke, spying him from afar, was greatly annoyed. When he questioned the gatekeeper, the latter explained, "Lord I Yeh-ku pissed in the court there!"

The duke ordered I Yeh-ku arrested. When I Yeh-ku could not be found, the duke, more furious than ever, flung himself down on his bed with such violence that he fell off into the ashes of the brazier and burned to death. . . . Duke Chuang was a very impetuous and fastidious man, and therefore he came to such an end. (Duke Ting 3 [507 B.C.].)

The *Kuo yü* or *Conversations from the States*

As stated earlier, the author of the *Tso chuan* is traditionally supposed to have been Tso Ch'iu-ming. In some early accounts he is also mentioned as the author of another work, the *Kuo yü* or *Conversations from the States*. The *Kuo yü* covers roughly the same period as the *Tso chuan,* deals with many of the same persons and events, and even contains passages that are almost identical with the *Tso* narrative, though more often the accounts in the two works differ slightly. Tradition asserts that, after Tso Ch'iu-ming had finished compiling the *Tso chuan,* he took the material he had left over and variant versions of the same events which he had rejected in writing the *Tso,* and put them together to form the *Kuo yü.* More likely, however, the differences and similarities between the two works can be accounted for by assuming that both of them drew upon the same early body of legend and narrative.

The narratives in the *Conversations* are arranged not according to the chronology of the dukes of Lu, as the *Tso*'s are, but according to the states to which they pertain, namely the central court of Chou and the feudal states of Lu, Ch'i, Chin, Cheng, Ch'u, Wu, and Yüeh. Within the sections devoted to each state, the narratives are arranged chronologically, but there is no attempt to give a year by year account of the history of each state. Particularly in the chapters dealing with the earlier history of the states, the narrative is no more than a collection of disconnected anecdotes.

As in the *Tso chuan*, dialogue and direct speech play a very important part. Indeed, in the Chou, Lu, and Ch'i sections the anecdotes are hardly more than an excuse to present a lofty speech, or series of speeches, on some problem of statecraft. This is no doubt the reason the work has been entitled *yü* (conversations, or discussions).

With the section on Chin, the longest in the work, we enter upon a lengthy and elaborate account of the reign of the fatuous Duke Hsien of Chin, the tragic downfall of his son, the crown prince Shen-sheng, and the exile, wanderings, and eventual accession to the throne of Chin of another of Duke Hsien's sons, the famous Ch'ung-erh, posthumously known as Duke Wen of Chin. Parts of this legend, or cycle of legends, are to be found in the *Tso*, but the account given in the *Conversations*, particularly that portion dealing with the crown prince Shen-sheng, is much more elaborate and detailed, and suggests that the author or authors of the *Conversations* might have had some special connection with the state of Chin. The last two sections of the work deal with another famous legend, also found in the *Tso*, the tale of the struggle between King Fu-ch'a of Wu and King Kou-chien of Yüeh and the eventual conquest of Wu by Yüeh.

Because each of these anecdotes or legends is presented without interruption, rather than being broken up and scattered under the years of the Lu chronology, as in the *Tso*, the narrative is usually easier to follow than in the *Tso chuan* versions. (The Tso anecdotes, of course, may have been arranged in this same fashion originally, and broken up and scattered only later when the work was made into a commentary on the *Spring and Autumn*.) The style of the *Conversations*, though closely resembling that of the *Tso*, also gives the impression of being somewhat more relaxed and verbose, suggesting that many of the anecdotes may have been written down at a rather later date than those in the *Tso*. Though the *Conversations* is for these reasons sometimes easier to read, it lacks the rapidity and tightness of the *Tso*. Particularly in the formal speeches there is a tendency to repeat the same parallel constructions and even the same words and phrases *ad nauseam,* resulting in a monotony of which the *Tso* is never guilty.

The didactic purpose of the narratives, just below the surface in the *Tso* but usually cleverly disguised, becomes in the *Conversations* obtrusively obvious. The vivid, realistic impression so often conveyed by the *Tso* accounts gives way in most cases in the *Conversations* to a highly stylized and artificial construction in which characters and viewpoints are carefully paired and balanced. Thus, for example, in the section in Chin yü 2 in which, after murdering the heir of Duke Hsien, the ministers of Chin send messages to Ch'ung-erh and his brother I-wu, who are both in exile, offering them the throne of Chin, each prince is attended by a minister who makes a speech explaining why the prince should or should not accept the offer. Not only are the two princes and their respective ministers neatly paired, but even the two speeches of advice and their wording are made to match and balance each other in a wholly artificial manner.

We find this excessive formalism throughout the *Conversations,* as though the historical incidents and legends upon which it is based had been reworked and polished over the centuries until they acquired these trimly symmetrical shapes. Because of this symmetry, the narrative often moves with a kind of measured dignity. But we can no longer even pretend that in it we are reading an account of actual historical events as they happened. The narrative has passed over, rather, into the realm of allegory and fable.

Whatever its value as history, however, the *Conversations* contains passages of considerable beauty and effectiveness. Perhaps the most impressive is the story of the downfall of the crown prince Shen-sheng, sections of which I shall present below. Shen-sheng was the eldest son of Duke Hsien of Chin and had accordingly been designated as crown prince to succeed his father. But his mother, a woman of Ch'i, had died some years earlier and his position at court was consequently weaker than that of the other sons of the duke by the later consort or concubines who were still living. The course of his downfall begins with his father's ill-advised attack on a branch of the Jung barbarians, a non-Chinese people, living in the vicinity of Mount Li to the west of the state of Chin.

Duke Hsien divined to see whether he should attack the Jung barbarians of Li. The historian Su conducted the divination and replied, "The attack will be victorious but unlucky!" . . .

The duke, ignoring his prediction, proceeded to attack and defeat the Jung barbarians of Li. He brought back as a captive Lady Li, the daughter of the barbarian chief, and treated her with great favor, making her his new consort.

The duke dispensed wine to his ministers, ordering the master of ceremonies to fill a goblet and give it to the historian Su. "I give you wine, but no meat to go with it," he said. "When I was planning the campaign against the Jung barbarians of Li, you said that the attack would be victorious but unlucky. Therefore I reward you with this cup for your prediction of victory, but punish your prediction of ill luck by withholding the meat. What greater luck could there be than to conquer a state and win a consort?"

The historian Su drained the cup, bowed his head twice, and replied, "That was what the oracle said. I dared not hide the prophecy. If I were to hide the meaning of the prognostication and fail to carry out the duties of my office, I would be guilty of a double fault. How then could I serve my lord? I would call down upon myself a punishment far greater than being deprived of meat with my wine!

"Yet, my lord, while you delight in this good luck, I would have you also prepare for misfortune. If misfortune never occurs, what harm will there have been in the preparations? And if it should occur, the preparations will mend it. If my prediction proves to have been wrong, it will be a blessing to the state. How could I object to being punished for such a happy error?"

Having drunk the wine, he departed. (Chin yü 1.)

The duke, completely under the spell of the evil Lady Li, who had borne him a son, is persuaded to consider removing Shen-sheng from the position of heir and designating Lady Li's son Hsi-ch'i in his place. In the following highly stylized scene, three ministers of Chin appear, as though upon a stage, state their respective opinions on the move, and then exit.

Lady Li gave birth to Hsi-ch'i, and her younger sister gave birth to Cho-tzu. The duke wished to remove his son Shen-sheng from the position of crown prince and set up Hsi-ch'i in his place. Li K'o, P'i Cheng, and Hsün Hsi met one day. "The misfortune which the historian Su predicted would come to the state is about to fall upon us," said Li K'o. "What shall we do?"

"I have heard that when you serve your lord, you carry out your duties with all your might," said Hsün Hsi. "I have never heard that you go about disobeying orders. Whomever the ruler sets up we should proceed to follow. What right have we to question the move?"

"I have heard," said P'i Cheng, "that when you serve your ruler, you follow what is right, but you do not flatter the ruler's delusions. If the ruler is deluded, then the people will be misled, and if the people are misled, they will abandon virtue. This is nothing less than to cast the people aside. The reason the people have a ruler is so that he may guide them in doing right. Right brings profit, and profit enriches the people. How can a ruler live with his people and still cast them aside? Shen-sheng must be retained as crown prince!"

Li K'o said, "I am no good at making speeches but, though I may not know what is right, neither will I flatter delusion. I had best remain silent."

With this the three ministers parted. (Chin yü 1.)

Misfortune draws nearer as Lady Li, conspiring with one of the duke's palace actors named Shih, with whom she is carrying on an affair, plots the downfall of her son's rival, Shen-sheng. By means of deceit and hypocritical tears, she succeeds in arousing the duke's suspicion against Shen-sheng. On one pretext or another she manages to have the crown prince sent on various expeditions of conquest, from each of which he returns victorious. His success, however, only makes the duke more anxious about his son's increasing fame and favor with the people. Finally Lady Li begins to slander Shen-sheng openly, playing upon the duke's fear that the prince may be plotting a revolt. In the following scene, as her plot nears the moment of consummation, she attempts to discover which side the minister Li K'o will support in the event of an open break.

Lady Li said to the actor Shih, "The duke has already promised me that he will kill the crown prince and set up my son Hsi-ch'i as heir. But I am worried about what Li K'o will do."

"I can bring Li K'o over to our side in a day's time!" said the actor. "Prepare a feast of the meat of a ram for me and I will take wine and go wait on him. I am an actor. I know how to avoid saying anything indiscreet."

Lady Li agreed to do as he said. When everything was prepared, she sent him to drink with Li K'o, and when the drinking had reached its height, the actor Shih rose from his place and prepared to dance. "Lady Meng," he said to Li K'o's wife, "if you will give me a bite to eat, I will teach this contented gentleman how to serve his lord." Then he began to sing:

> "Contented gentleman, aloof and solitary,
>   No match for the flocks of birds.
>   While others gather in the flourishing grove,
>   You perch alone on a withered branch."

Li K'o laughed and said, "What is the grove? What is the withered branch?"

"The mother a royal consort, the son a lord—is this not a flourishing grove? The mother long since dead, the son ill spoken of—is this not a withered branch? What is withered will be cut off!"

With this the actor took his departure.

Li K'o ordered the gifts of food to be taken away and, without eating any supper, retired to bed. In the middle of the night he sent for the actor Shih and said, "Were you only joking earlier? Or have you really heard something?"

"I have," replied Shih. "Our lord has already promised Lady Li that he will kill the crown prince and set up her son Hsi-ch'i as his heir. The plans are all settled."

"I could not bear to assist my lord in killing the crown prince," said Li K'o. "And yet, now that I know of the plot, I would not dare to associate with the crown prince as I have in the past. If I were to remain neutral, do you think I could escape harm?"

"You will escape," said Shih. (Chin yü 2.)

Lady Li is ready now to deliver the final blow. Shen-sheng, though fully aware of her machinations and of the way she has managed to delude his father, remains throughout apprehensive but unwilling or incapable of taking any steps to combat the forces opposing him. He is the model of passive suffering, refusing to do anything that will discomfit his father, a figure tragically paralyzed by the ideal of filial piety. According to the *Tso chuan,* his death took place in Duke Hsi 4th year, or 656 B.C. Shen-sheng's speech is an example of the excessively formalized and mannered style described above, which achieves verbal symmetry at the expense of meaning.

Lady Li came to Shen-sheng with an order from the duke, saying, "Last night our lord dreamt of your mother, the princess of Ch'i. You must sacrifice to her spirit at once and bring him a portion of the sacrifice!"

Shen-sheng consented and, having performed the sacrifice at his fief in Ch'ü-wo, returned to the capital with the sacrificial meat and wine. The duke was out hunting and Lady Li received the offerings.

Then she mixed poison with the sacrificial wine and soaked the meat in deadly aconite.

When the duke returned, he summoned Shen-sheng to present his offerings. The duke poured a libation of the wine on the ground, but the ground boiled up. Shen-sheng was frightened and left the palace. Lady Li threw some of the meat to one of the dogs and the dog died. She gave the wine to a servant to drink and the servant died too. The duke ordered the execution of Shen-sheng's tutor Tu Yüan-k'uan. Shen-sheng fled to the New City, his fief in Ch'ü-wo. . . .

Someone said to Shen-sheng, "You have committed no fault. Why do you not leave the realm?"

"I cannot," he replied. "If I were to evade the blame by departing, then it would fall upon my lord. This would be to defame my lord. If I were to expose the faults of my father and make him a laughing stock among the other feudal lords, what land could I look to for refuge? He who incites the disfavor of parents at home and of the feudal lords abroad only doubles his disfavor. He who abandons his lord and runs away from blame is an evader of death. I have heard that the good man does not defame his lord, the wise man does not double disfavor, and the brave man does not evade death. If my guilt cannot be pardoned, then I would only double it by departing, and this would be to show my lack of wisdom. To evade death and defame my lord would show my lack of goodness, while to be guilty and yet decline death would show my lack of bravery. Fleeing would only compound the evil. Evil cannot be doubled, death cannot be evaded. I shall bow down and wait my lord's command."

Lady Li appeared before Shen-sheng and wept. "If you could bear to do this to your own father, what would you not do to your countrymen? You would sacrifice your father in order to curry favor with others, but who would favor such as you? You would kill your father in order to seek gain from others, but who would grant *you* gain? Deeds such as these all men despise. You will not live long!"

After Lady Li had left, Shen-sheng hanged himself in the ancestral temple in the New City. (Chin yü 2.)

These excerpts from the *Tso chuan* and the *Kuo yü* should give a general idea of the type of historical or pseudohistorical narratives to be found in these works and the highly dramatic form in which they are cast. Thanks to these two works, we are able to form a vivid and fairly detailed picture of the life of the period, which without them would be an almost total blank. How true the picture may be to historical reality we shall probably never know, but it is a picture which has had a powerful influence upon the Chinese imagination. In keeping with the essentially didactic intent of the works, the figures who appear in them have become eponyms of wisdom, benevolence, delusion, greed, or craftiness; its battles have passed into the language as metaphors for victory or crushing defeat, its plots and campaigns as bywords for recklessness or caution. Chinese historiography inherited in these two works an unparalleled example of vivid, dramatic style, a model of narrative art which later historians could draw upon for instruction and inspiration.

The *Chan-kuo ts'e* or *Intrigues of the Warring States*

The next work to be considered is the *Chan-kuo ts'e* or *Intrigues of the Warring States*. The *Spring and Autumn Annals,* and the period to which it lends its name, ended in 481 B.C. It has been estimated that at the beginning of the Spring and Autumn period, China was divided into over a hundred feudal states and principalities. By the end of the period, the number had been reduced to about forty, the smaller and weaker states having been conquered and absorbed by their more powerful neighbors. This process continued until in 403 B.C., when the old state of Chin officially split into three parts, there were only seven important states left. The period from 403 until the unification of the empire under Ch'in Shih-huang-ti, the first emperor of the Ch'in dynasty, a process which was completed in 221 B.C., is known as the Warring States period and gives its name to this work.

Actually some of the material in the *Intrigues* deals with events as early as 475 B.C., and it thus covers, though in a sketchy way, the entire period from the end of the *Tso chuan* to the unification of the empire. It is, however, by no means a year by year account of the period, but rather, like the *Conversations from the States,* a collection of anecdotes arranged in more or less chronological order in sections devoted to twelve states: the Chou court, the seven "Warring States"—Ch'in, Ch'i, Ch'u, Chao, Wei, Han, and Yen—and a few smaller ones that perished early.

The *Intrigues* contains a certain amount of valuable historical information, and it was used as early as the Han dynasty as a source for the history of the period, there being no other comparable work on the history of the period extant. For this reason Chinese scholars have often classified it as a work of history. But at other times they have treated it as a philosophical work, and this is the more realistic view.

We have seen that the *Tso chuan* and the *Kuo yü,* while dealing with historical or semihistorical persons and events, are, so far as we can judge, less interested in presenting an objective account of the past than in displaying the lessons which the past has to teach. They are works on ritual and ethics cast in historical form. In the case of the *Intrigues,* the connection with anything that we today could call history becomes even more tenuous. If the *Tso chuan* and *Kuo yü* are handbooks on morality illustrated by historical cause and effect, the *Intrigues,* while making use of the same "examples from history" form, is a handbook on rhetoric and persuasive speaking.

As in the case of the two earlier works, we do not know when, where, or by whom the *Intrigues* was written or compiled, though it probably dates from the early part of the second century B.C. The anecdotes which it records are arranged according to the various states to which they pertain, but since one anecdote may deal with persons or events belonging to several different states, there seems to have been some doubt as to which state it should be assigned to, and the arrangement of the anecdotes therefore varies somewhat with different editions. The text has suffered considerable damage in transmission and parts of it are garbled beyond repair.

During the Spring and Autumn period, the Chou court, with its king who was theoretically the supreme ruler of the empire, still commanded a certain ritual and religious respect, though it possessed almost no actual power. From time to time there arose in one or another of the powerful feudal states a leader who attempted to exercise *de facto* control over the rest of the empire while pretending to be acting in the name of the Chou ruler and restoring authority to him. Such leaders were called *pa*. Various translations—dictators, overlords, hegemons—have been suggested in an attempt to convey the exact meaning of the term. The most famous of these overlords were Duke Huan of Ch'i (of whom we shall have more to say in the section on the *Kuan Tzu*) and Duke Wen of Chin.

By the time of the Warring States period, however, the feudal rulers scarcely bothered even to pretend to acknowledge the sovereignty of the Chou court. It was obvious to men of the time that the Chou rulers had sunk to a level of such insignificance that the idea of a revival of Chou authority was unthinkable; the only question was which of the contending states would become strong enough to force its will upon the rest of China and establish a new dynasty. Han, Chao, and Wei, the three small states created out of the former state of Chin, were never strong enough to become serious contestants in this struggle for supremacy, nor was the state of Yen, far on the northeastern border. The real contest was between Ch'in in the far west, Ch'i on the northeastern seaboard, and Ch'u in the south.

Since there was no central authority that could insure peace and order in China as a whole, the smaller states, in an attempt to protect themselves from invasion, and the larger ones, in order to advance their dreams of supremacy, entered into a complex series of pacts and military alliances with one another. These alliances are customarily referred to as the Horizontal and Vertical Alliances because they followed two geographical patterns—an east-west alignment of states under the leadership of Ch'in in the west and calculated to further Ch'in's interests, or a north-south alignment under Ch'i or Ch'u in the east designed to block the spread of Ch'in's power.

Many of the ancedotes in the *Intrigues* center about the exponents of these two alliances, Chang I, the spokesman for the Horizontal, or pro-Ch'in, alliance, and Su Ch'in, the spokesman for the Vertical, or anti-Ch'in, alliance. These men are pictured traveling tirelessly from state to state, persuading the various rulers to join one or the other of the alliances. In addition there are anecdotes dealing with numerous other famous statesmen, political theorists, military leaders, court favorites, etc. Much of the material is of dubious historical value or is obviously apocryphal. The fact, for example, that the same speech or argument is found in different places in the text attributed to quite different persons and periods suggests that there was an original story which, in the process of transmission, became attached in various versions to the names of several different men, just as today we hear a witty remark attributed at one time to a famous actress, at another to a woman novelist.

In the *Shih chi* or *Records of the Historian,* a diviner of the early Han, in argument with two court scholars, describes the art of persuasive speaking in these words:

Surely, gentlemen, you have observed the rhetoricians and orators. All their plans and schemes are simply the products of their own minds. But if they merely blurted out their own ideas they could never capture the imagination of the ruler. Therefore they always begin their speeches by discussing the kings of antiquity and open their orations with a description of ancient times. In setting forth their schemes and plans they make up elaborate tales about the successes of the former kings or tell about their failures in order to move the ruler to admiration or fear and thereby achieve their objective. When it comes to talking exaggerated and imposing nonsense, as you put it, no one can match them. Yet if one wishes to strengthen the state, insure the success of the ruler, and fulfill his duty as a loyal minister, he must resort to such means or his words will never be heeded. (*Shih chi* 127.)

This passage should be borne in mind when we read the *Intrigues,* for it is speeches such as those the diviner describes which fill its pages, and the "history" which they cite to prove their points in most cases no doubt has about as much real value as the diviner suggests. Not only this, but the anecdotes themselves, which serve as a setting for the speeches, become in time the source of more "historical examples" for later rhetoricians, so that the mass of legend and pseudo history grows by feeding upon itself. Fact, legend, and rhetorical embellishment become inextricably jumbled.

Most of the anecdotes in the *Intrigues* follow a set pattern. They begin with some problem: a ruler is about to enter into an alliance or launch an attack or to be attacked himself. Someone then comes forward with advice. Sometimes the speaker is identified as a well-known statesman or one of the political theorists who at that time wandered from state to state offering advice and seeking employment; sometimes the speaker is unidentified, and we are told only that "Someone advised the king, saying, . . ." Then follows the speech, the heart of the anecdote, often a long and extremely complicated proposal couched in what we may suppose was the most persuasive style of the period.

The anecdote ends with a short notation on whether or not the ruler followed the advice and what the results were. If the ruler followed the advice, as he is usually said to have done—completely won over, apparently, by the trenchant arguments and powerful rhetoric of the speech—the results are almost always as the speaker had predicted, in spite of the fact that many of the proposals are highly complex and demand for their success a conjunction of numerous doubtful contingencies. This fact alone warns us that we are dealing with a highly tendentious version of history; as one scholar has said, "The thread of future probabilities is spun so fine that it becomes mere contrivance." [4]

These speeches deserve some comment, since they became the models for so much of later Chinese rhetoric. Though the form naturally varies, the speech usually begins with the state-ment of a general principle which the speaker intends to expound, introduced by the conventional phrase, "Your servant has heard." The general principle is often deliberately stated in a laconic or paradoxical form, presumably in order to arouse the hearer's interest and curiosity. Thus, to give an extreme example, a rhetorician who is attempting to dissuade a minor feudal lord from trying to fortify his city, states his principle as "Ocean big fish," explaining that the lord is like a fish in the ocean, and that his survival depends not upon fortifications, but upon the "sea around him," that is, the good will of the state of Ch'i in which his fief is situated (*Ch'i ts'e* 1). This fondness for express-ing or summing up political or philosophical principles in brief, enigmatic phrases is characteristic of Chinese rhetoric. The famous *Tao te ching* of Lao Tzu consists largely of such enig-matic phrases, and, much later, the "pure conversation" adepts of the Six Dynasties era or the leaders of Chinese Zen developed

---

[4] James I. Crump, "The Chan-kuo Ts'e and Its Fiction," *T'oung Pao*, XLVIII (nos. 4–5, 1960), 305–75; 315.

the technique to the point where doctrinal discussions and pronouncements are couched almost entirely in a private language of such phrases.[5]

Having enunciated his principle in some succinct and catchy form, the speaker then goes on to explain its meaning and its application to the present situation. These explanations are phrased in appropriately lucid and flowing language, usually made clearer and more effective by the use of rhythmical phrases, parallelism and other rhetorical flourishes. He is also almost certain to "prove" his point by reference to some historical event in the past, introducing into his speech anecdotes much like the one in which he himself is figuring. Occasionally, in order to break the flow of smooth, balanced phrases, he may inject a quotation from the Classics or a homey proverb, again something phrased in pithy or obscure language, to insure that his listener is still attentive and has not been lulled to sleep by the florid passages. He may conclude with a restatement of the original principle and, if he has several points to make, state a new principle and repeat the whole process, balancing principle against principle, historical example against historical example, trope against trope.

Sometimes the anecdote may involve several speeches giving different viewpoints on a particular problem. In *Chao ts'e* 2, we have an account of how King Wu-ling of Chao tries to persuade

[5] The *Han Fei Tzu*, a work contemporary with the *Intrigues* and sharing many of the same anecdotes, has an amusing story to tell about the origin of one such catch phrase. "Once a man of Ying wrote a letter to the prime minister of Yen. Since he was writing at night and the light was not very good, he told his torchbearer, "Hold up the torch!" At the same time he absent-mindedly wrote "Hold up the torch" in his letter, though it had nothing to do with what he was saying. When the prime minister of Yen received the letter, he was delighted. " 'Hold up the torch!' means to honor brightness. To honor brightness means to promote wise men and use them in the government!" When he reported this to the king, the king was greatly pleased and the state benefited from the suggestion." (*Han Fei Tzu* 11.)

his ministers and people to adopt barbarian dress, giving an impressive series of arguments to prove that barbarian dress is more suitable for the region of Chao than traditional Chinese robes. His ministers counter with a number of rather silly, ultraconservative arguments, including the assertion that "he who wears strange clothes will have licentious desires," and the anecdote develops into a full-fledged debate. In other cases we find a man not offering advice but attempting to talk his way out of a difficult situation, or someone trying to maneuver the downfall of a rival. But whatever the form, the emphasis is always upon clever words and clever schemes.

The *Tso chuan,* for all the sordidness of many of the incidents it recounts, is, as we have seen, a basically idealistic work: by conforming to correct ritual and moral principles one can hope confidently to achieve success, while any departure from them spells disaster. By contrast the *Intrigues,* in content and outlook, is the embodiment of cynicism. The old codes and forms of ritual behavior have by this time been so neglected and abused that an appeal to them would, one feels, bring only derision. There is no limit to the duplicity which the counselors will propose and the rulers employ; no scheme is too devious, vile, or underhanded if it will advance one's own interests and discomfit an enemy. The reader is reminded of Thucydides' famous description of the moral chaos that beset Greece during the Peloponnesian Wars when, "If pacts of mutual security were made, they were entered into by the parties only in order to meet some temporary difficulty, and remained in force only so long as there was no other weapon available. When the chance came, the one who first seized it boldly, catching his enemy off his guard, enjoyed a revenge that was all the sweeter from having been taken, not openly, but because of a breach of faith" (Book III, Rex Warner translation [*Penguin Classics* L39], p. 209).

The supernatural element so prominent in the *Tso chuan* is still present, but it is now only a device to dupe the credulous. We read in *Tung Chou ts'e* of how, after the ruler of Chao had seized some territory from the Chou court and later had fallen ill, the Chou court bribed the diviner of Chao to tell the king that his illness was due to a curse which could be exorcised only by returning the stolen territory.[6] Again, in *Wei ts'e* 2, we read that, when the ruler King Hui died and his son, the crown prince, was about to bury the body, there was a great blizzard and so much snow fell that it piled up "as high as the cows' eyes." The prince wished to go through with the burial anyway, but the high ministers, concerned about the cost and inconvenience of attempting to carry it out in such weather, opposed him. To get their way, they called in the philosopher Hui Shih, who explained to the prince that his father obviously desired to remain a little longer among his people and had therefore caused the snow to fall, supporting his argument with an example from ancient "history" of a similar incident. In other words, the appeal to the supernatural is simply another trick to bolster an argument or implement a scheme.

This extreme cynicism, unscrupulousness, and lack of concern for anything but motives of self-interest which characterizes so many of the anecdotes in the *Intrigues* has been a source of embarrassment to later scholars, who have been attracted to the book by its polished and engaging style but repelled by its contents. To justify their interest in it (since, according to Confucian teaching, all worthwhile literature must be literature of "uplift"), they have resorted to various arguments, among them that the work is valuable "as a picture of the age," or that it is always

[6] We read of a similar incident of bribery (*Tso*, Duke Hsi 28) which took place in 632 B.C., but this may be merely a projection back in time of the later cynicism.

wise to know the worst about human nature. The modern reader, uncommitted to the Confucian view, fortunately need not indulge in such soul-searching, but may read the *Intrigues* for what it is —a lively and often entertaining collection of anecdotes dealing with the age of political confusion and cutthroatery that led up to the unification of the empire under the Ch'in dynasty.

I say entertaining because one of the noteworthy characteristics of the *Intrigues* is the wit and humor displayed in many of the anecdotes. There are passages in the *Tso chuan* and *Kuo yü* that may strike us as humorous today, but it is doubtful that they were intended to be so. With the *Intrigues,* however, we find examples of obvious and conscious humor—of a wry and cynical variety, it is true, in keeping with the tone of the work, but humor nevertheless. The entire work, in fact, is dominated by an air of wit and sophistication, a reflection of the life and thought of the period. The anecdotes and speeches often have a clever twist to them, a subtle point that is not openly expressed but is left to the acute reader to perceive. I shall give a sample of the humor later, but first let me quote an example of the "pointed" story, so popular in later Chinese literature, in which the reader is left to divine the significance for himself.

It concerns the queen of Ch'i, consort of King Hsiang and mother of Crown Prince Chien, who became the last ruler of Ch'i. She was the daughter of an official of Ch'i and contracted a secret marriage with King Hsiang when he was still crown prince and was in hiding at her father's home from the rebels who assassinated his father. Later, when he became ruler, he made her his queen, though her father disowned her, declaring that "no daughter who would marry without a go-between is a child of mine!" She proved to be a wise aid to her husband, and to her son Chien when he succeeded to the throne. Among the many anecdotes concerning her virtue and political acumen is the following:

When the queen was ill and at the point of death, she admonished her son Chien, saying, "Among the various court officials, those who can be of use to you are So-and-so—"

"May I write that down?" asked the king.

"Fine!" replied the queen, but when the king had fetched a brush and writing tablet and was prepared to take down her words, she said, "I have already forgotten what I said." (*Ch'i ts'e* 6.)

Now what, one may ask, is the point of such a story? That even the wisest old ladies are subject to sudden lapses of memory? That a good politician never allows anything to be put in writing? The interpretation given by commentators, which is almost certainly correct, is that the queen concluded ruefully that if her son was not capable of remembering a few important names without writing them down there was no use in giving him the advice, and so she put him off with a profession of forgetfulness. But the text does not state the point, much less labor it. Rather it calls upon the reader to supply the interpretation himself, arousing his interest, taxing his powers of perception, and, when he has divined the meaning, making him party to a happy little conspiracy of the wise. It is a sophisticated device, representative of the degree of refinement which Chinese literature had achieved by the end of the Chou period.

To illustrate the clever way in which one reprimands an erring ruler and helps a friend out of a difficult situation, let us turn to another queen, this time an evil and foolish one, the consort of King Hui of Ch'in, who, at the time of the story, was long since dead.

The queen dowager Hsüan of Ch'in loved a man named Wei Ch'ou-fu. When she fell ill and was at the point of death, she issued an order saying, "At my burial, see to it that Master Wei is put to death and buried with me!"

Master Wei, deeply distressed, got Yung Jui to speak to the queen dowager on his behalf. "Do you believe that the dead have consciousness?" Yung Jui asked the queen.

"No, they have no consciousness."

"If Your Majesty is wise enough to understand that the dead have no consciousness, then why would you cause one whom you loved while you were alive to be buried in vain with an unconscious corpse? And should the dead perhaps have consciousness after all, then your husband, the late king, will have been piling up a store of jealous anger for a long time. Your Majesty will have all you can do trying to excuse your faults. What leisure could you expect to have for dalliance with Wei Ch'ou-fu?"

"You are right," said the queen dowager, and abandoned the idea. (*Ch'in ts'e* 2.)

The following is an example not of a clever speech, but of a clever and unscrupulous scheme, typical of the vicious court intrigues of the time.

The king of Wei sent the king of Ch'u [King Huai] a beautiful girl. The king was delighted with her, and his consort, Cheng Hsiu, aware of the king's infatuation, treated the girl with special affection. . . . When she was sure that the king would not suspect her of jealousy, she said to the new girl, "The king is much taken with your beauty, but he does not seem to care for your nose. When you go to see him, I suggest you always keep your nose covered." Accordingly, whenever the new girl visited the king, she would cover her nose.

"I notice," said the king to Cheng Hsiu, "that when the new girl is with me she covers her nose. Why is that, I wonder?"

"I could tell you why—" said Cheng Hsiu.

"If you know, then tell me, no matter how bad it is," the king insisted.

"It would seem," said Cheng Hsiu, "that she does not like the way you smell."

"What insolence!" exclaimed the king. "Let her nose be cut off at once!" he ordered. "See that there is no delay in carrying out the command!" (*Ch'u ts'e* 4.)

The following is an example of humor used not for its own sake but, as so often in early Chinese literature, to point a political moral.

Tsou Chi, the prime minister of Ch'i, was over eight feet tall and had a very handsome face and figure. One day as he was putting on his court robes and cap and looking at himself in the mirror, he said to his wife, "Who do you think is better looking, I or Lord Hsü of Ch'eng-pei?" His wife replied, "You are much better looking! How could Lord Hsü compare to you?" Lord Hsü of Ch'eng-pei was one of the handsomest men in the state of Ch'i.

Tsou Chi was not entirely confident, however, and so he put the same question to his concubine. "Who is better looking, I or Lord Hsü?" "Lord Hsü could never compare to you!" she replied.

The next morning a guest came to call and while Tsou Chi was sitting and chatting with him, he asked, "Who is better looking, Lord Hsü or I?" "Lord Hsü is nowhere near as good looking as you!" said the guest.

The following day Lord Hsü himself came to visit. Tsou Chi stared very hard at Lord Hsü and realized that his own looks could not compare, and when he went and looked in the mirror it was obvious that the difference between them was great indeed.

That night when he went to bed he thought over the incident. "My wife says I am better looking because she is partial to me, my concubine says I am better looking because she is afraid of me, and my guest says I am better looking because he hopes to get something out of me!" he declared.

The next time he went to court and had an audience with King Wei, he said, "I am certainly not as good looking as Lord Hsü. And yet my wife, who is partial to me, my concubine, who is afraid of me, and a guest of mine, who wants something from me, all have told me that I am better looking than Lord Hsü. Now the state of Ch'i is a thousand *li* square and contains a hundred and twenty cities. In this vast realm, there are none of the palace ladies and attendants who are not partial to Your Majesty, none of the court ministers who do not fear you, and no one within the four borders who does not hope to get something from you. If that is so, think how great must be the deception you face!"

"You are right," said the king, and issued a notice saying that, to any one of the officials or people of the state who would attack his faults to his face, he would give first prize; to anyone who would submit a letter of reprimand, he would give second prize; and to anyone who would spread critical rumors in the market so that they reached his ears, he would give third prize. When the notice was first issued, the officials who came forward with criticisms packed the gate of the palace until it looked like a market place. After several months, there were still people who came forward with criticisms from time to time. But by the end of a year, though men might wish to reprimand the king, no one could any longer find anything to criticize. (*Ch'i ts'e* I.)

I have not given any example of the formal speeches of the diplomats and advocates of alliances because they are, like most diplomatic speeches, long-winded and often maddeningly complex, following a pattern something like this: If A and B form an alliance with C and D against E, then F and G will attack C and D and H will come to their aid, etc., etc. The following excerpt, however, will show something of the style of the less formal speech or reprimand, with its characteristically homey details and appeal to the proof of history. It will also show the sophistication of the narrative style of the *Intrigues*. We have here not the lean, jerky narratives of the *Tso chuan* and *Kuo yü,* but a leisurely, detailed, and strikingly realistic description of a scene, with a subtle depiction of the psychological states of the characters suggestive of the modern novel. The queen dowager in this piece is the wife of King Hui-wen of Chao and the mother of King Hsiao-ch'eng. The lord of Ch'ang-an is her younger son, the brother of King Hsiao-ch'eng. At the time of the incident, King Hui-wen has just died and King Hsiao-ch'eng has succeeded to the throne; his mother is managing the affairs of state for him.

The queen dowager of Chao had just taken over the management of the state when Ch'in made a sudden attack on Chao. Chao sent a request to Ch'i asking for aid, but Ch'i replied, "We will dispatch our troops only on condition that you send the lord of Ch'ang-an to us as a hostage." The queen dowager refused to accept this condition, and when the high ministers strongly reprimanded her for her refusal, she told them in no uncertain terms, "I will spit in the face of the next person who tells me to send the lord of Ch'ang-an as a hostage!"

The high minister Ch'u Che requested an audience with the queen dowager. She was in a rage when he appeared and gave only a curt bow. He entered the room very slowly and, having taken his place before her, apologized, saying, "I'm afraid your old servant has a bad leg and cannot walk very fast. That is why I haven't been able to see you for such a long time. Considering the trouble I have had with my own health, I was wondering if perhaps Your Majesty might also be suffering from some infirmity and so I was hoping to be granted an audience."

"I myself can only get about in a palanquin," said the queen dowager.

"And is your appetite holding up these days?"

"I live on gruel and nothing else."

"I have had very little appetite myself lately. But I force myself to walk three or four *li* each day. As a result my appetite has improved somewhat and I feel better."

"I'm afraid that would be quite beyond me," said the queen dowager, her anger somewhat appeased.

"I have a son named Shu-ch'i," continued Ch'u Che, "my youngest child and a worthless one, but I am an old man and I confess I love him dearly. I wish that he could be granted the black robes and numbered among the guards in the king's palace. I would give anything to see such a request granted!"

"I will be happy to arrange it," said the queen dowager. "How old is he?"

"Only fifteen. I know that is very young, but I would like to see him taken care of before I die."

"Then do men also dote on their youngest sons?"

"Even more than women do!"

"Oh no," said the queen with a laugh. "When it comes to that, women are in a category by themselves!"

"If I may say so, however, it would seem that you love your daughter, the queen of Yen, better than you do your youngest son, the lord of Ch'ang-an."

"No, you are mistaken there," replied the queen. "I am much fonder of the lord of Ch'ang-an."

"If parents love their children, they plan carefully for their future. When you sent your daughter off to marry the king of Yen, I remember you clung to her heels and wept and, thinking sorrowfully of how far away she was going, you were filled with pity. After she had gone, you never ceased to think of her and whenever you offered a sacrifice you always prayed that the marriage might be successful and that she would not be sent home again. Was this not because you hoped that in the future her sons and grandsons would succeed to the throne of Yen?"

"Yes, you are right," said the queen.

"Think back over the years from the time when the Chao family first became rulers of this state until a few generations ago. During that period, were there any younger sons of the royal family who were enfeoffed as marquises whose descendants still hold the title today?"

"No, there are none."

"And not in Chao alone. Are there any noble families, founded by the younger sons of the rulers of other states, which are still in existence?"

"I have never heard of any."

"Some of the rulers' younger sons who were enfeoffed suffered disaster within their own lifetime, while in other cases it was their sons and grandsons who met misfortune. Could it have been because these younger sons who were enfeoffed were all worthless? I think not. Rather it was because they were granted great honors without having achieved any merit to deserve them, were given rich endowments without having labored for them, and were showered with treasures. Now you have honored your son with the title of lord of Ch'ang-an and enfeoffed him with rich and fertile lands, showering him with precious gifts, and yet up to now you have not let him do anything to win merit for the state of Chao. If you should one day pass away, how could he expect to enjoy any safety in Chao? It would seem to me, then, that you have not planned very carefully for his future, and that is why I say you do not care as much for him as you do for your daughter, the queen of Yen."

"You are right," said the queen dowager. "I will leave it to you to do as you see fit." (*Chao ts'e* 4.)

Almost all the anecdotes in the *Intrigues,* no matter how obviously fictionalized in content, are attributed to some historical person and place. In a few cases, however, even this mask of historicity is dropped and an anecdote is presented as a pure fable or parable like those used by Mencius, Chuang Tzu, or other philosophers of the time to illustrate their arguments. The following, in which there is no attempt to relate the incident to historical persons or events, is used to illustrate the folly of saying the right thing at the wrong time.

A man of Wei was getting married. When the bride climbed into the carriage that the groom had sent to fetch her, she asked, "Whose horses are these?"

The driver replied, "The two in the middle belong to the groom, but the other two are borrowed."

"You may strike the two on the outside, then, but don't whip the middle ones," she said.

When the carriage arrived at the gate of her new home and she had been helped down, she said to the old woman who had escorted her, "Put out the fire in that cooking stove before it sets something on fire!"

After she got in the house, she looked at the mortar and said, "Move that over there under the window! It's blocking the passage here!"

The groom burst out laughing.

All three of her remarks were perfectly apt in themselves, and yet people couldn't help laughing at her, since it was such an inappropriate time to make them. (*Sung Wei ts'e.*)

As a history of the period, the *Intrigues,* by modern critical standards, is of very limited value, while its form contributed nothing to the advancement of Chinese historiography. It was in fact never intended as a work of history, but as a collection of lessons on the art of political survival, a set of models on how to speak interestingly and effectively, a grab bag of ingenious and deadly schemes. The late Chou saw the appearance of numerous treatises on technical subjects: agriculture, medicine, warfare, divination. The *Intrigues* is in a sense such a treatise on the art of persuasive speaking, cast not in the form of general injunctions but in that of specific examples and anecdotes, designed to suggest to the reader that he too could, like the men described therein, win fame and fortune and command the ear of princes.

If the *Intrigues* is not a work of history, however, it did, in the matter of style, have an important influence on later historical writing. By the end of the Chou, the age of the *Han Fei Tzu,* the *Hsün Tzu,* the *Lü-shih ch'un-ch'iu,* and the *Intrigues,* Chinese prose had settled down to a fairly uniform style. It is a style which, from the point of view of later centuries, still retains a certain "antique" quality, but is by no means primitive or archaic sounding. On the contrary it is a facile and sophisticated instrument of expression, capable of a dignified, measured movement (which occasionally, in inept hands, lapses into monotony) and, as in the case of the *Intrigues,* of great wit and subtlety. It is the style which was inherited and used with such effectiveness by Ssu-ma Ch'ien, the author of the next major historical work to be considered, and which, with some modification, became the standard style of nearly all the important works of history down to the present century.

The *Shih chi* or *Records of the Historian*

So far we have described works whose authorship and date of compilation are unknown. With the *Shih chi* or *Records of the Historian* by Ssu-ma Ch'ien (145?–90? B.C.) we come to the first major historical work by a man whose identity and approximate dates are a matter not of legend but of attested fact. This is not the only way in which the *Shih chi* differs from the earlier works we have discussed, however. In its form, the span of its narrative, the variety of material embraced, and its general interest it represents an entirely new departure in Chinese historiography.

Ssu-ma Ch'ien was the son of Ssu-ma T'an, a scholar who served as grand historian at the court of Emperor Wu of the Han dynasty (reigned 140–88 B.C.). Though Ssu-ma T'an's official duties were confined to matters pertaining to astronomy and the calendar, so that the title grand historian is therefore somewhat misleading, he believed, as on his deathbed he told his son, that the ancestors of the Ssu-ma family in ancient times had been actual court chroniclers and that it was his duty to them and to his own age to compile a history of the famous men and great deeds of the past. He had in fact begun to gather material for such a work, though it is not certain whether he ever got around to any actual writing. It is also uncertain what the scope of his projected work was to have been—whether he intended to deal only with the Han dynasty, or to extend his account back to the point where the *Spring and Autumn Annals* had ended. At the time of his death in 110 B.C. he implored his son Ch'ien to complete the work he had begun.

Ssu-ma Ch'ien succeeded his father to the post of grand historian at Emperor Wu's court and, in obedience to his father's wishes, began work on the history. Midway in his labors, he incurred the displeasure of the emperor by speaking out in defense of a general who had failed in a campaign against the Hsiung-nu barbarians of the north and had been forced to surrender. As a result Ssu-ma Ch'ien was condemned to undergo castration, the severest penalty next to death. Rather than commit suicide, as was customary in such circumstances, he underwent the punishment in order to be able to finish his history, sacrificing honor and reputation for the sake of a work which he hoped would redeem his name in ages to come. His fortitude has been rewarded by,the acclaim of centuries.

Whatever sort of work his father may have envisioned, Ssu-ma Ch'ien stopped short of nothing less than a history of the entire knowable past, not only of China itself but of all the peoples and regions known to the Chinese of his time. Thus in scope the *Shih chi* far surpasses anything that had previously been attempted. To present such a wealth of material, Ssu-ma Ch'ien abandoned the simple chronological form of earlier works and created five large divisions under which he arranged the one hundred and thirty chapters of his work. First are the twelve *pen-chi* or Basic Annals which deal with ruling dynasties or individual rulers of the empire and are in many cases in the form of a year by year account of official acts of the ruler. These are followed by ten Chronological Tables listing in graph form the dates and principal events in the various fiefs and feudal states of the empire. Next are eight Treatises dealing with such subjects as rites, music, astronomy, economics, religious affairs, etc. Thirty chapters entitled Hereditary Houses follow, narrating the history of the feudal states of Chou times and the more important fiefs of the Han. The work ends with seventy chapters called *lieh chuan*: biographies of famous statesmen, generals, philosophers, etc., or accounts of foreign lands and peoples, closing with an autobiography of Ch'ien himself.

By creating such a form, Ssu-ma Ch'ien was able to impose a

hierarchical order on his material, suggesting by the place in which he presented a certain account something of his opinion of its importance and reliability. The form allowed him to focus, without the necessity of frequent digressions, upon the flow of events in those chapters devoted to the history of a state or a dynasty, upon the origin and development of institutions in the Treatises, and upon the life of the individual in the biographical sections. At the same time it made it necessary to scatter the material relating to a single period through a number of widely separated chapters and occasioned a certain amount of repetition. Because of this scattering of material, the work must be read in its entirety if the reader is to get a complete picture of any particular age.

In spite of these disadvantages, however, the form was acclaimed a masterpiece of organization and was adopted, with some changes, in the next major historical work, the *Han shu* or *History of the Former Han Dynasty,* and in all the succeeding dynastic histories down to the present.

It is the custom of Chinese historians when compiling their narrative to copy in their sources or the works of their predecessors almost verbatim, making some changes and abbreviations, perhaps, but usually sticking as closely as possible to the wording of the original. This practice, far from being considered plagiaristic, is taken as a sign of respect to one's predecessors in the field and an assurance of accurate transmission of the facts. Any personal remarks which the historian himself may have to make on the nature or interpretation of his material are generally placed at the beginning or end of a chapter and set off by some conventional phrase. In the present *Shih chi* text they are introduced by the word "The Grand Historian remarks"; in later works they are usually labeled "appraisals," "discussions," or "judgments."

Ssu-ma Ch'ien followed the usual practice in putting together his chapters on ancient history, copying in portions of the *Book of Documents* to fill out the genealogical accounts of early times. However, because the style of the *Documents* is so difficult, and was already considered so in his time, he frequently substituted a more common word for an obscure one in the original, and his version thus constitutes an important gloss on the way in which the text of the *Documents* was understood in early Han times. Little of what appears in Ssu-ma Ch'ien's chapters on high antiquity can be regarded as history. From late Chou times on, scholars had worked over the diverse and frequently contradictory legends of the past, attempting to fit the names of various ancient rulers and their ministers into neat genealogical and temporal sequence. The process is already apparent in the Yao and Shun sections of the *Book of Documents,* and was carried on enthusiastically by Han scholars, who had a passion for neatness and systematization. Ssu-ma Ch'ien accepted rather uncritically these systematized accounts and genealogies of what are actually no more than shadowy figures of legend. Though he warns that the age of the sage rulers is too far away to be described in detail, he seems to have felt that he was justified in giving a general outline of its history, and until the present century few scholars challenged his judgment. His opening chapters are valuable, therefore, not as a reliable account of high antiquity, but as a recital of the traditional Chinese version of the genesis of the Chinese culture and nation.

When dealing with the Spring and Autumn period, his practice is to present material selected from the *Tso chuan* or the *Kuo yü,* summarizing or adding connecting narrative where necessary. Sometimes he weaves together both the *Tso chuan* and the *Kuo yü* versions of a single event, selecting the most interesting details from each. As in the case of the *Documents,* he makes what changes are necessary to render the passage easily comprehensible to Han readers.

In dealing with the Warring States period, he does the same, reproducing large sections of the *Intrigues of the Warring States,* though in this case, since the style is so near to that of his own day, he seldom finds it necessary to reword. He seems to have had access to other works on the period, or perhaps other, orally transmitted, versions of the events, since his accounts often are different or more detailed than those in the *Intrigues,* though some of these differences may be due to literary embellishments of his own. What sources Ssu-ma Ch'ien had for the history of the brief but eventful Ch'in dynasty, other than the famous stone inscriptions of the First Emperor, which he copied into his text, we do not know.

In early Han times the statesman Lu Chia wrote a work entitled *Ch'u Han Ch'un-ch'iu* or *Spring and Autumn of Ch'u and Han,* an account of the struggle between Hsiang Yü, a general of the state of Ch'u who worked to overthrow the Ch'in dynasty and for a time made himself ruler of the empire, and his rival, Liu Pang or Han Kao-tsu, the founder of the Han dynasty. The book was lost in Sung times, but one reason for its disappearance may well be that most or all of the text was already preserved in the *Shih chi.* Ssu-ma Ch'ien states that he used it as a source for the period, and it is probable that the lively and dramatic accounts of the career of Hsiang Yü found in the Annals section of the *Shih chi* are actually the work of Lu Chia.

The remainder of the *Shih chi,* dealing with the reigns of Kao-tsu, Empress Lü, and Emperors Wen, Ching, and Wu, must be substantially, if not wholly, original with Ssu-ma Ch'ien, compiled by him on the basis of official files of documents preserved at court, speeches and writings of his contemporaries, and the accounts of men who witnessed the events described.

To summarize: the *Shih chi* consists of a highly idealized account of antiquity, a readable and convenient abbreviation of the material contained in the *Tso chuan,* the *Kuo yü,* and the *Chan-kuo ts'e,* and a long, detailed account, mainly the work of Ssu-ma Ch'ien himself, of the century or so from the unification of the empire by the First Emperor of the Ch'in to the historian's own time. Notwithstanding the intrinsic interest of some of the other material, it is this last section, dealing with the Ch'in and early Han, which is most reliable as history and which represents, along with the form of the *Shih chi,* Ssu-ma Ch'ien's most valuable contribution tŏ Chinese historiography.

In his autobiography Ssu-ma Ch'ien devotes considerable space to a discussion of the nature and purpose of the *Spring and Autumn Annals,* emphasizing the wonderful wisdom which the Classic imparts, the apt way this wisdom is conveyed in a record of historical fact, and the benefits which derive from a study of the work. In this he follows the interpretation of the *Annals* propounded by the *Kung yang Commentary* and generally accepted in his day. At the end of this passage he states that his own history, being a work of "transmission" rather than "creation," in no way bears comparison with the work of Confucius. This demurrer is no doubt intended to be sincere. He certainly did not expect posterity to tax the exact wording of the *Shih chi* in a search for hidden principles of "praise and blame," nor did he consider himself qualified to teach "the way of a true king," as Confucius was supposed to have done in the *Annals.* Yet there are indications that he did not believe his work to be wholly unrelated to that of the Sage. The function of history, for him as for Confucius (if·one accepts the traditional interpretation of the *Annals*), was still to teach moral lessons, to "censure evil and encourage good." He did not venture, indeed did not feel it necessary, to imbue the wording of his narrative with hidden moral judgments. His accounts, unlike the laconic notations of the *Annals,* are complete and detailed enough to reveal without further comment the consequences of good and evil action. He needed to be nothing more than a transmitter—and a highly skilled and readable one he is—to insure that the lessons of the past would be apparent to all thoughtful men.

Seeing that so much of his task consisted in compiling and weaving together accounts taken from earlier works, Ssu-ma Ch'ien could not help but be influenced in his thinking and writing by the ideas and forms of these works. From the *Documents* and other works he inherited the concept of periodic moral renascence and decay which explained the frequent dynastic changes of history. In addition he attempted, in good systematic Han fashion, to assign to each dynasty of the past a particular virtue which he believed had characterized the dynasty at its best, and a corresponding moral defect which derived from the decay of this virtue. There was no question but that the life of a dynasty was limited. The problem which should engage men's attentions, and was in fact a matter of serious thought and discussion in Ssu-ma Ch'ien's own time, was how to discover exactly where one stood in this process of growth and decay and how to determine what ritual steps, what policies, what moral attitudes were most appropriate to such a period in history.

In addition Ssu-ma Ch'ien inherited from earlier works the idea of classifying individuals into general categories on the basis of their actions and moral qualities. The *Documents,* the *Tso chuan,* the *Kuo yü* are full of sage rulers, wise ministers, evil counselors, pure-minded recluses, treacherous concubines, etc. These "types," and the formalized, often stereotyped anecdotes in which they appear, could not help being reflected in the *Shih chi.*

Like earlier historical works, Ssu-ma Ch'ien's narrative is almost always focused upon the life and deeds of the individual. He gives far more attention than his predecessors to the influence of geography, climate, economic factors, customs, and institutions upon the course of history. He is quick to give genealogical information where he feels that lineage may have some significance in explaining the character of an individual. But when all other factors have been noted, it is still primarily the will of the individual which, in his opinion, directs the course of history.

Though earlier works contained a great deal of biographical fact and anecdote, Ssu-ma Ch'ien was the first writer we know of to compile this information in the form of chapters devoted to the lives of single individuals or groups of individuals. In the *lieh-chuan* or biographical section of the *Shih chi,* he was clearly influenced by the old idea of "types," for often he groups together in a single chapter the lives of several men who, because of common interests or a common pattern to their lives and personalities, seem to him to be allied, much as Plutarch paired off the lives of Greeks and Romans who he felt belonged to the same category. Many of these groupings may seem forced and tenuous. We are sufficiently accustomed today to reading and assessing biographical works not to require neat moral labels affixed to them or implied in the form "wise but maligned statesman," "crafty counselor," "daring but imprudent general," or even to resent the attempt to affix such labels. It is interesting to note, however, that both Ssu-ma Ch'ien and Plutarch, the innovators of biographical writing in China and the Classical West, felt obliged to present their biographies in such a form, so strong was the didactic concept in the literatures of the two cultures.

Ssu-ma Ch'ien has a great deal to say in the way of personal comment upon the events he describes and the lives of the men he is dealing with. Many of these sections of personal comment add new material to the narrative, discuss its reliability, attempt to trace the cause of events, or describe the historian's own experiences as they relate to the subject. Many of them are given up to subjective moral judgments of the persons or events, or to expressions of admiration, censure, or pity. These passages are among the most interesting and lively in the *Shih chi,* and show Ssu-ma Ch'ien as a very human writer, deeply, often passionately, involved in his subject. But they do not reveal Ssu-ma Ch'ien as a systematic thinker or the propounder of a fixed philosophy of history. The efforts of scholars to sum up his personality in a conventional term—Taoist, Confucian, humanist, romanticist, hero of the people—are unconvincing. In Isaiah Berlin's terminology, he is a fox, and no attempts to make him out a hedgehog seem likely to succeed.

It is largely this variety and passion which account for the lasting interest of his work. His facts may be of dubious reliability at times, his biographies hardly more than a few dramatic anecdotes pieced together; but he is almost never dull. One expects to find rulers, statesmen, and military leaders figuring prominently in a history. But who but Ssu-ma Ch'ien would include chapters on the lives of fortunetellers, royal catamites, famous assassins (some of whom bungled the job at the crucial moment), humorists, big businessmen, or local bosses? In a way he seems to have been aiming at something like the modern social historian's "picture of an age." The core of his narrative is political history, since politics, in his view, was the highest among human activities. He is interested in individuals, not social classes as a whole, and so he seldom attempts to draw generalized pictures of the life of the farmers, the city dwellers, the merchants, or the artisans. But the range of individuals he is interested in and feels is worth writing about is far broader than in earlier works. He created for posterity not only a new form for the ordering and presentation of historical material, but a new concept of the breadth and complexity of history.

Among general readers, the *Shih chi* has been most widely read and admired for its succinct and penetrating biographies, sketched with a vividness and clarity of style that became models for all later biographical writing. Many of these are not rounded biographies in the modern sense; they are not so much catalogues of data on the life and career of an individual as collections of anecdotes designed to give insight into the personality and essential worth of the subject, evocations of particular human types and virtues. The following unusually brief biography will illustrate these qualities of form and style; retold from the *Chan-kuo ts'e,* it is one of five that make up Ssu-ma Ch'ien's chapter entitled "Biographies of Assassin-retainers" (*Shih chi* 86).

Yü Jang was a native of the state of Chin. He once served the Fan family, and later the Chung-hang family, but attracted no notice under either of them. He left and became a retainer of Chih Po, who treated him with great respect and honor. Later Chih Po attacked Hsiang-tzu, the lord of Chao. Hsiang-tzu plotted with the lords of Han and Wei, wiped out Chih Po and his heirs, and divided up his land among the three of them. Hsiang-tzu hated Chih Po intensely and had his skull lacquered and made into a drinking cup.[6]

Yü Jang fled and hid in the mountains. He sighed and said, "A man will die for one who understands him, as a woman will make herself beautiful for one who delights in her. Chih Po understood me. Before I die, I will repay him by destroying his enemy! Then my spirit need feel no shame in the world below."

He changed his name, became a convict laborer, and succeeded in entering the palace of the lord of Chao, where he was given the task

[6] Fan, Chung-hang, Chih, Chao, Han, and Wei were all high ministerial families of Chin. In the middle of the fifth century B.C., when these events took place, Chih Po wiped out the Fan and Chung-hang families and was in turn destroyed by Chao, Han, and Wei, who overthrew the ruling family of Chin and divided the state into three parts.

of replastering the privy. In his breast he concealed a dagger, hoping to stab Hsiang-tzu with it. Hsiang-tzu entered the privy but suddenly grew uneasy and ordered his men to seize and examine the convict laborer who was plastering the privy. It was Yü Jang who, clasping the knife to his breast, said, "I intended to avenge Chih Po's death!"

Hsiang-tzu's attendants were about to execute him on the spot, but Hsiang-tzu said, "He is a righteous man. From now on I will simply take care to keep him at a distance. Chih Po and his heirs were all wiped out. If one of his retainers feels compelled to try to avenge his death, he must be a worthy man." So he pardoned Yü Jang and sent him away.

After some time, Yü Jang painted his body with lacquer to induce sores like those of a leper, destroyed his voice by drinking lye, and completely changed his appearance until no one could recognize him. When he went begging in the market place, even his wife did not know him. But as he was going along, he met a friend who recognized him and asked, "Aren't you Yü Jang?"

"I am," he said.

His friend began to weep. "With your talent, you could swear allegiance and take service under Hsiang-tzu, and he would be sure to make you one of his close associates. Once you got close to him, you would have a chance to accomplish your aim. Would that not be easier? Destroying your body and inflicting pain on yourself in order to carry out your revenge—is this not doing it the hard way?"

Yü Jang replied, "To seek to kill a man after you have sworn allegiance and taken service with him amounts to harboring traitorous thoughts against your own lord. I have chosen the hard way, it is true. But I have done so in order to bring shame to all men in future generations who think to serve their lords with treacherous intentions!" Then he took leave of his friend.

Sometime later, word got about that Hsiang-tzu was going out on an excursion, and Yü Jang accordingly went and hid under the bridge he was to pass over. When Hsiang-tzu came to the bridge, his horse suddenly shied. "This must be Yü Jang!" he said, and sent one of his men to investigate. It was indeed Yü Jang.

Hsiang-tzu began to berate him. "You once served both the Fan and Chung-hang families, did you not? And yet when Chih Po wiped them out, you made no move to avenge their deaths, but instead swore allegiance and took service under Chih Po. Now that Chih Po too is dead, why are you suddenly so determined to avenge his death?"

Yü Jang replied, "I served both the Fan and Chung-hang families, and both of them treated me as an ordinary man; therefore I repaid them as an ordinary man would. But when I served Chih Po, he treated me as one of the finest men of the land, and so I have determined to repay him in the same spirit."

Hsiang-tzu sighed a deep sigh and tears came to his eyes. "Ah, Yü Jang," he said, "the world already knows of your loyalty to Chih Po, and I have already pardoned you all I need to. You had best take thought for your end. I can pardon you no more!" He ordered his men to surround Yü Jang.

"They say that a wise ruler does not hide the good deeds of others," said Yü Jang, "and a loyal subject is bound to die for his honor. Formerly you were gracious enough to pardon me, and all the world praised you as a worthy man. For today's business I have no doubt that I deserve to be executed. But I beg you to give me your robe so that I may at least strike at it and fulfill my determination for revenge. Then I may die without regret. It is more than I dare hope for, yet I am bold to speak what is in my heart."

Hsiang-tzu, filled with admiration at Yü Jang's sense of duty, took off his robe and instructed his attendants to hand it to Yü Jang. Yü Jang drew his sword, leaped three times into the air, and slashed at the robe, crying, "Now I can go to the world below and report to Chih Po!" Then he fell on his sword and died. That day, when men of true determination in the state of Chao heard what he had done, they all wept for him.

The *Han shu* or *History of the Former Han*

Just when Ssu-ma Ch'ien stopped writing and when he died we shall probably never know. His narrative seems to stop around the year 100 B.C.; though there are passages in the *Shih chi* dealing with events after that date, they appear to be later additions. Some half century later, a court scholar named Ch'u

Shao-sun took it upon himself to add further material to Ssu-ma Ch'ien's narrative. The passages which he wrote, undistinguished in style and of dubious value, are appended here and there to the ends of chapters in the present *Shih chi* text and duly marked with Ch'u's name. Though his intentions may have been sincere, he has won only scorn from later critics by this attempt to link his own pedestrian accounts with the work of a master.

Other scholars of the late years of the Former Han made similar attempts to compile material that would serve as a continuation of the *Shih chi,* but their efforts also, we are told, "were common and tasteless and completely unworthy to act as a continuation of Ssu-ma Ch'ien's work" (*Hou Han shu* 40A). It remained for the Pan family of the Latter Han to do the job.

In A.D. 9, a high court minister named Wang Mang deposed the infant emperor and ascended the throne as the founder of a new dynasty, the Hsin, and with this the Han dynasty was officially declared at an end. His success was short-lived, however, and in A.D. 25 the Han dynasty was restored and the period known as the Latter, or Eastern, Han began. Pan Piao (A.D. 3–54), a scholar who lived through this period of political unrest, worked over the material of his predecessors and compiled a series of chapters on the history of the latter part of the Former Han to act as a continuation of the *Shih chi.* On his death, his son, Pan Ku (A.D. 32–92) took over the work. But he decided that a mere continuation of the *Shih chi* narrative was not sufficient to convey the glory of a dynasty which, after a period of eclipse, had returned to its former position as ruler of the empire. He therefore determined to compile a history covering the entire Former Han period and the reign of the usurper Wang Mang, that is, the period from 209 B.C. to A.D. 25. His work, in one hundred chapters and entitled *Han shu* or *History of the Former Han,* thus became the first of the so-called dynastic histories.

Pan Ku utilized the form created by Ssu-ma Ch'ien, dividing his material into Annals, Treatises, Chronological Tables, and Biographies. His only major change was to eliminate the *Shih-chia* or Hereditary House section, which he believed was no longer needed in dealing with a period of strong central government. When he adapted material from the *Shih chi* Hereditary House section, he shifted it to the Biography section. He also added some new topics to the Treatise section, among them geography and bibliography, the last being an invaluable list of the books in the Imperial Archives.

Nearly half of Pan Ku's history consists of material copied almost verbatim from the *Shih chi*. As we have seen, there is nothing reprehensible about this fact in Chinese eyes. It shows the degree to which Pan Ku admired and trusted Ssu-ma Ch'ien's work and wished to see it widely disseminated. In adapting material from the *Shih chi* he occasionally added a few new facts or anecdotes. But for the most part he was content merely to brush up the style to conform to his own tastes, rewriting sentences which are obscure or clumsy in the *Shih chi* and cutting out what he believed to be unnecessary words here and there.

In the later parts of his history he was presumably drawing frequently upon material compiled by his father, as well as, in the Treatise section, by other scholars of the preceding century such as Liu Hsiang and Liu Hsin. At the time of his death (he died in prison, where he had been sent for investigation because of his association with a general accused of treason) it is said that parts of the Treatises and Chronological Tables were still incomplete. His sister Pan Chao (d. *ca.* A.D. 116) was summoned by the emperor to complete the work and make sure that the text was properly received and understood by scholars of the time. Thus it is impossible to say just what portions of the present text are the work of which members of the Pan family.

Pan Ku, however, was the compiler of the work, and for all practical purposes may be regarded as the author.

Discussions of the relative merits of Ssu-ma Ch'ien and Pan Ku, like discussions of those of Herodotus and Thucydides, tend to be highly partisan; scholars who champion one author are likely to find little to praise in the other. Certainly much credit must go to the pioneer in both cases. Ssu-ma Ch'ien created the form which Pan Ku utilized and demonstrated its possibilities, in addition to providing Pan Ku with a great deal of actual material. Pan Ku shines not as an innovator but as a judicious follower and adapter of earlier models. His approach to history is less subjective and passionate than that of Ssu-ma Ch'ien. He seldom indulges in personal remarks or expressions of feeling and his opinions conform to the orthodox Confucian doctrines which dominated his age. His prose is stately, ordered, even a trifle archaic; on the whole, it is conventional, easier to read than the sometimes rather erratic and personal style of Ssu-ma Ch'ien, but seldom as interesting.

Since his work is confined almost wholly to a well-documented period and does not attempt to deal with the shadowy ages of antiquity, it is more reliable than much of what is found in the *Shih chi*. This does not necessarily mean, however, that Pan Ku had a keener critical sense than his predecessor. On the contrary, in the few passages where he does deal with the history of the legendary or semilegendary rulers of high antiquity, his accounts are even more idealized and systematized than those of Ssu-ma Ch'ien. Thus, for example, the earliest date given in the *Shih chi* is one equivalent to 842 B.C.; in dealing with periods previous to this, says Ssu-ma Ch'ien, one can reckon only in rough terms of generations. But Pan Ku, following Liu Hsiang and his son Liu Hsin, claims to be able to give the exact date of King Ch'eng T'ang's attack upon the last ruler of the Hsia dynasty, a date equivalent to 1751 B.C.! In this he reflects the tendency of scholars of his time to fill in the outline of ancient history found in the *Shih chi* and other earlier works with more and more detail based upon legend and conjecture. Ssu-ma Ch'ien had done just this, beginning his account of antiquity farther back than many of the scholars of his day believed could be reliably known. This process continued unabated until, by T'ang times, we find one commentator on the *Shih chi* compiling and adding a whole new chapter to the *Shih chi* to cover the history of the period *before* Ssu-ma Ch'ien's account begins. Thus the farther removed they are from antiquity, the more volubly are the scholars able to describe it.

Pan Ku's history, focused upon a single dynasty, is a much neater and more manageable work than the *Shih chi,* whose narrative begins at an arbitrary point in the legendary past and straggles to an end in the middle of Emperor Wu's reign. Moreover, whereas at least ten of the *Shih chi*'s one hundred and thirty chapters seem to be in unfinished or faulty condition, the text of the *Han shu* is in all but perfect condition. Finally, Pan Ku is on the whole more careful than his predecessor about giving the full name and place of birth of the subject in his biographies, and deals with several important topics that Ssu-ma Ch'ien did not deal with. His work, however, precisely because it is limited to the history of a single dynasty, has often been criticized by later scholars who argue that the really important lessons of history are to be found not within the history of a single dynasty, but in the history of the change of dynasties, the crucial period when one regime is faltering to an end and a new and more vigorous one is rising to replace it. The *Shih chi,* they argue, because it is a continuous history, does justice to these critical periods of change, whereas the *Han shu,* by its arbitrary time limitation, obscures them. In spite of the facts, therefore,

that the *Han shu* has always been read and admired, and that it
became the model for a series of dynastic histories covering all
the reigns down to the present century, there have from time to
time been historians who preferred to cast their work in the
"continuous history" form of the *Shih chi.*

The *Han chi* or *Records of the Former Han*

The *Han shu* is a long and by no means easy work. One scholar
of the fourth century A.D., a champion of the *Shih chi,* pointed
out disapprovingly that Pan Ku took almost twice as much space
to cover the history of two hundred odd years as Ssu-ma Ch'ien
had taken to cover that of three thousand. Such an observation,
if it merits serious consideration at all, will serve at least to show
the value Chinese historiography placed upon mere brevity. It is
not surprising, therefore, that some hundred years after the *Han
shu* appeared, a work called the *Han chi* or *Records of the
Former Han,* was compiled which rearranged the *Han shu*
material into year by year chronicle form and, more important,
condensed it to a handy thirty chapters.

The work was compiled by a court scholar named Hsün Yüeh
(148–209), according to tradition at the order of an emperor who
found the *Han shu* itself too bulky and difficult for his taste. In
addition to weaving material from various sections of the *Han
shu* into a continuous narrative, greatly condensing it, and adding
a small amount of new material, Hsün Yüeh inserted a number
of short essays on the political and moral questions raised by
the events described—little "lessons from history" whose form
and style were to be imitated by countless later writers. He thus
not only spares the reader the task of plodding through Pan
Ku's lengthy narrative, but saves him the trouble of discovering
for himself the significance of the events described. Because of
its convenient chronological form, which was hailed as a con-

tinuation of the *Tso chuan* tradition, the elegance of its prose, and its self-proclaimed didactic value, it won considerable popularity and was for many centuries honored and studied along with the *Shih chi* and *Han shu* themselves. Fortunately it did not, like so many of the epitomes of Greece and Rome, bring about the eclipse and disappearance of the work it was derived from. Scholars were wise enough to see that, whatever the *Han chi*'s convenience as a summary of the period and didactic worth, it was no substitute for a knowledge of Pan Ku's work.

COMPARISON OF THE HISTORIOGRAPHY OF ANCIENT CHINA WITH THAT OF GREECE AND ROME

By the end of the Latter Han dynasty in A.D. 220, the Chinese tradition of historical writing was firmly established. Among the books of the Confucian canon, which had assumed definitive shape by this time, were included several works—the *Documents*, the *Spring and Autumn Annals*, and the *Tso chuan*—which, if their reliability as history seems questionable to us today, were nevertheless studied and revered at the time as records of the distant past and embodiments of moral principles which were still applicable. These were followed by the *Conversations from the States* and the *Intrigues of the Warring States*, and the two Han masterpieces, the *Shih chi* and the *Han shu*, the latter with its satellite, the *Han chi*. Historians now had two forms to choose from, the simple year by year chronicle form of the *Tso chuan* and the more complex Annal and Biography form of the *Shih chi* and the *Han shu*; in imitation of the latter, they could limit their narrative to the history of a single dynasty; in imitation of the former, they could deal with a longer span of time. By studying these works, particularly the *Shih chi* and *Han shu*, they could acquire a concise, dramatic, and highly effective narrative style, though as literary fashion changed in the succeeding centuries, historians departed farther and farther from the simplicity of the Han prose style. A bureau of official historiographers was now a recognized institution at the court of the ruler, and from the Latter Han on, secretaries were customarily assigned the duty of keeping a day by day record of the emperor's official acts and pronouncements in order to provide reliable source material for future historians. These institutions did not always function ideally in the chaotic age which followed the breakup of the Latter Han empire, and it took many years and the efforts of a number of historians before a satisfactory history of the Latter Han itself could be produced. Nevertheless, Chinese historical writing was now firmly launched on its course and whatever the difficulties succeeding historians had to labor under they were able to produce some account of every period down to the present.

This group of Chinese historical works corresponds in time with the great histories of the Classical West, and in closing it may be of some interest to note the ways in which the two literatures resemble and differ from each other.

It is the similarities which at first glance are most striking, and this is the more surprising considering the very real differences between the societies and cultures of ancient China and ancient Greece and Rome. Greece and Rome were only two among many highly developed civilizations in the Mediterranean and Middle Eastern areas. They were in frequent contact with nations that spoke different languages, that had different systems of writing, and that in many cases were much older than Greece or Rome. Ancient China, on the other hand, was surrounded by tribes of nomads or primitive agricultural peoples who possessed no system of writing and whose level of material civilization was decidedly inferior to that of the Chinese people. It was only in Ssu-ma Ch'ien's day that the Chinese first gained any real knowledge of the more highly developed civilizations of India and Central Asia, and even then the contacts were too slight to have much immediate influence on Chinese life and thought, though the influence may have been greater than has generally been recognized. In any event, there is nothing in early Chinese history to match the geographical and cultural breadth and variety we find described in Herodotus or Polybius. On the other hand, neither do we find in early Chinese history anything to match the detailedness of Thucydides' day by day, hoplite by hoplite account of the Peloponnesian War. Chinese history falls somewhere in between these two extremes, giving a general account of events taking place in the broad expanse of the Chinese empire, but seldom mentioning events beyond the borders of the empire (for, it was assumed, there was little going on there that was worthy of the historian's attention).

It is a foregone conclusion in the works of both East and West that the primary purpose of history is to teach lessons that will be of value to men of later times. This is so obvious to anyone reading the historical literature of China or the Classical West that it needs no discussion here. Closely allied to this didactic function is the particular duty of the historian to praise good men in his works by recording their names and deeds for posterity to see. This "special virtue of history," as Polybius calls it (Book II [Loeb Classics], I, 391), is often mentioned in Chinese literature in connection with the *Spring and Autumn Annals,* which is said to take particular pains to record the full names of good men as a form of reward for their virtue (the reward of evil being oblivion).

A second conviction shared by East and West alike is that history moves by cycles. "Every body or state or action has its natural period first of growth, then of prime, and finally of decay," writes Polybius (Book VI [Loeb Classics], III, 385), and the same concept is stated or implied in all early Chinese historical works. Polybius, applying the concept to the world he knew, stated, following the Stoics, that monarchy regularly evolved, or rather degenerated, into tyranny, aristocracy into oligarchy, and democracy into mob rule, concluding, "Such is the cycle of political revolution, the course appointed by nature in which constitutions change, disappear, and finally return to the point from which they started" (Book VI [Loeb Classics], III, 289). In like manner Ssu-ma Ch'ien saw the dynasties of the past as evolving in a fixed progression of moral characteristics: from the virtue of good faith to its corrupted form, rusticity; from piety to its corruption, superstition; and from refinement, to its corruption, hollow show, "a cycle which, when it ends, must begin over again" (*Shih chi* 8).

In the best historians of both East and West we find a relatively small element of the clearly supernatural or miraculous. Occasionally in Greek or Roman works the gods or Fate, in Chinese works Heaven, will seem to intervene in human affairs, though such interventions are generally treated as a matter of doubt or conjecture only. That is, there *seems* to be some force outside of human actions which is influencing the course of events, the historians imply. Though they themselves may take a neutral or actually skeptical attitude toward such an interpretation, it is clear that many of the men they are describing believed firmly in divine intervention, and so we find them giving much attention to divination and the interpretation of portents and prodigies. Eclipses, sudden storms, unseasonable weather, and the strange behavior of birds or beasts are carefully recorded by both Western and Chinese historians, for such events often had great political significance in the eyes of the men of the time and are therefore as much a part of the history of the period as the most overtly human acts.

If the histories of early China and those of Greece and Rome resemble each other in content and purpose, they are less alike in manner of treatment. Greek and Roman historical writing was from its origin closely related to and influenced by epic poetry and drama, two literary forms which scarcely existed in ancient China. Moreover, Greek and Roman histories were customarily written to be recited aloud, and were often presented to the public in this fashion, whereas Chinese histories were designed to be read. This may account for the very striking brevity and restraint of the Chinese historians in comparison with their Western counterparts, who were often writing more for the ear than for the eye. Ssu-ma Ch'ien in his introduction to the Chronological Table of the Six Kingdoms (*Shih chi* 15), describes a state of political and moral chaos much like that described by Thucydides in the famous passage on the revolution in Corcyra in Book Three. But Ssu-ma Ch'ien condenses into a few sentences what Thucydides elaborates on for two or three pages. Similarly, in the *Intrigues of the Warring States* (*Chao ts'e* 1) we have a description of the suffering of a besieged city, but it is a mere outline compared to the agonizingly detailed descriptions of similar suffering in an author like Josephus. And, as already mentioned, battle scenes in Chinese history, upon which Greek and Roman historians expend so much space and loving care, are merely sketched out, lucidly and vividly but with the utmost economy, in a matter of a hundred or two hundred written characters. There is no lingering over the din and horror of the battle, no gore simply for the sake of gore. Massacres, lavish banquets, the sexual extravagances of rulers, and other sensational events of like nature are accorded the same restrained treatment, are briefly and frankly described but never lingered over.

The Chinese historian's account is focused upon a narrative of events, with frequent insertions of speeches, conversations, letters, memorials to the throne, edicts, and other papers of historical importance. But he has little time for painting word pictures or composing descriptive passages for their own sake, particularly when the subject of the description is intrinsically horrible or squalid. Such brevity and economy have their own beauty and may even come as a relief to one wearied of the sprawling, discursive volumes of Western historiography. But it is beauty bought at a price, and our picture of ancient China will never be as rich and well-rounded, as full of the actual sight and smell and feel of the time, as our pictures of ancient Greece and Rome.

HAN PROSE

Chou dynasty prose, often rather stark and elliptical, though at times a brilliant and expressive medium in the hands of a master, is marked by regional differences and the eccentricities of individual writers. With the unification of China under the Ch'in and Han, such regional differences largely disappear and Chinese prose achieves a unity of style and diction at the same time that it develops new power and subtlety of expression. The Han is one of the great periods of Chinese prose, and the dignity, vigor, and simplicity of its characteristic style were admired and often imitated in later centuries.

Actually there were two styles in common use in the Han. The first, the narrative style, is best exemplified by the great histories of Ssu-ma Ch'ien and Pan Ku. Deriving from the anecdotal, often novelistic style of works like the *Intrigues of the Warring States,* with something of the economy of the old Chou chronicles, it is marked by simplicity and directness. Except in rare passages of introduction or summary, it carefully eschews all rhetorical flourishes and ornaments and, though its phrases often fall into units of equal length, it never strains for such verbal regularity but follows what we may suppose were the ordinary speech rhythms of the time.

The second style, employed for argumentative writing, derives from the speeches and writings of the late Chou rhetoricians and philosophers and is characterized by assiduous attention to rhetorical effect. The sentences and clauses are again and again tailored in balanced and uniform patterns, at times to the detriment of clarity and logic. There is a tendency to pile up clauses into lengthy and complex thought units, and then break the rhythm with an abrupt, one- or two-word exclamation or question. Historical allusions abound, as well as proverbs, similes, and quotations from the Classics and other early works. This was the style employed in memorials to the throne, numerous examples of which are preserved in the histories of the period, as well as in formal essays and philosophical treatises.[7]

Judging from the examples we have, it was also used to a large extent in letter writing, though this may be due partly to the fact that only the most elegant and polished letters were deemed worthy of preservation. Unfortunately we have few letters from the Han period, the small number that exist being preserved in the histories. Presumably a group as cultured and literary-minded as the Han ruling class must have carried on a voluminous correspondence. But if Cicero had his counterparts among his contemporaries on the other side of the globe, their letters did not enjoy as good fortune in the hands of time as those of the Roman statesman, and we can only guess from the few surviving examples what epistolary riches may have existed.

One letter by the historian Ssu-ma Ch'ien, in which he explains the circumstances of his fall from favor and the reason why he

---

[7] For typical examples, see *Sources of Chinese Tradition*, p. 166: Chia I's "The Faults of Ch'in," and p. 192: Pan Piao's "On the Destiny of Kings."

chose to suffer punishment rather than commit suicide, has been
preserved in his biography in the *Han shu*.[8] The following letter,
which will serve to illustrate Han epistolary style, is by Yang
Yün, the son of Ssu-ma Ch'ien's daughter and only child. It too
is preserved in the *Han shu,* ch. 66, the biography of Yang Yün.
Yang Yün's father was a high ranking statesman, and Yang Yün
likewise rose to a position of prominence at the court of Emperor
Hsüan (74–48 B.C.); because of the part he played in exposing the
plot of the Ho family to dethrone the emperor, he was enfeoffed
as a marquis. He made many enemies at court, however, and
was in time accused by a rival of various treasonable acts and
utterances. The emperor spared Yang the death sentence but
stripped him of his position and title. Yang retired to the country,
where he devoted himself to farming and speculating in grain.
Sometime later he received a letter from a friend, Sun Hui-tsung,
reprimanding him for his way of life. A gentleman in disgrace,
Sun is reported to have written, should live in humble and ab-
ject seclusion instead of entertaining friends and engaging in that
most degrading of human activities, the pursuit of material gain.
The following is Yang's reply. Couched in the terms of elaborate
humility required by Han epistolary etiquette and employing
many of the rhetorical devices of argumentative style, it nevertheless makes its point with unmistakable clarity.

I am a man of paltry talent and unworthy actions, possessing
neither refinement nor native ability. Yet I was fortunate enough, because of my father's achievements, to win a post in the palace guard,
and later, happening upon a time of plotted disaffection, I gained
the title of marquis. But I deserved neither of these, and so in the
end I met with misfortune. Moved to pity by my stupidity, you have
been good enough to write me a letter teaching me my shortcomings
and how to correct them. Your heartfelt concern is truly generous. I

[8] It is translated in Watson, *Ssu-ma Ch'ien: Grand Historian of China,* pp.
57–67.

am disturbed that, because you have perhaps not examined deeply enough into the circumstances of my case, you may be misled by the judgments of the common run of people, though I realize that if I speak my unworthy thoughts too frankly I may appear to be contradicting you and attempting to gloss over my own errors. Nevertheless, if I were to remain silent, I fear I would be ignoring Confucius' injunction to let "each man speak his mind" [*Analects* XI, 25]. Therefore I have ventured briefly to set forth my ideas in the hope that you will give them your consideration.

When my family was at the height of its power, ten of us rode about in the vermilion-wheeled carriages of high officials. I held a place in the ranks of ministers and was enfeoffed as a marquis. I had charge of the officials who waited upon the emperor and I took part in the handling of affairs of state. And yet at that time I was unable to contribute anything to the advancement and glorification of imperial rule, nor did I succeed in joining my efforts with those of my fellow officials in repairing defects and oversights in the government. For a long time I was guilty rather of stealing a post I did not deserve and enjoying a salary I had not earned, coveting my stipend, greedy for power, and quite unable to check myself. Then I met with a sudden change of fortune and found myself faced with unbridled accusations. I was confined to the North Tower of the palace and my wife and children were thrown into prison. At that time I concluded that even the death penalty would be insufficient to atone for my guilt. Surely I never thought that I could keep head and body together and serve once more the grave mound of my father. And yet the mercy of our sage ruler knows no bounds!

The superior man practices the Way and delights in forgetting his cares. The mean man seeks to prolong his life and loves to forget his faults. Considering that my errors had been great and my actions far from what they should have been, I decided that it was best for me to end my days as a farmer. So I took my wife and family to the country where, pooling our strength, we plow, tend the mulberries, water the garden, and so produce enough to pay our taxes to the state. It never occurred to me, however, that such activities might arouse your censure.

One cannot put a stop to human emotions: even sages do not try.

Therefore although rulers or fathers command the greatest honor and affection, when they die the period of mourning for them must eventually come to an end. And it has already been three years since I incurred disgrace.[9]

My family and I work hard in our fields, and when the summer and winter holidays come we boil a sheep, roast a young lamb, bring out a measure of wine, and rest from our labors. My own family came originally from Ch'in and so I can make music in the Ch'in style, while my wife is from Chao and consequently plays the lute very well. In addition we have several maidservants who sing. After I have had something to drink and my ears are beginning to burn, I gaze up at the sky and, thumping on a crock to keep time, I give a great "ya-a!" and sing this song:

> I sowed the southern hill
> But I could not keep back the weeds.
> I planted an acre of beans
> But they fell off the vine, leaving empty stems.
> Man's life should be spent in joy.
> Why wait in vain for wealth and honor? [10]

At such times I flap my robes in delight, wave my sleeves up and down, stamp my feet, and dance about. Indeed it is a wild and unconventional way to behave, and yet I cannot say that I see anything wrong in it.

I was lucky enough to have a little of my stipend left over, and with the amount I bought up grain cheap and sold it dear, making a ten percent profit. This is a vile and merchantly thing to do, a sordid undertaking, and for me to engage in it personally places me among the lowest ranks of society and makes me the butt of censure. Though the weather is not cold, I shiver to think of the disgrace. Even you, who know me so well, appear to have followed along with

[9] I.e., as it would be unnatural to expect a person to mourn more than three years (actually twenty-five months) even over the death of a father, so it is unreasonable for people to expect him to continue to mope three years after his dismissal from office.

[10] The song is a veiled attack on the corrupt political situation of the time. The letter, along with other evidence, eventually led to Yang's execution in 55 B.C. on charges of treason. He had committed the unpardonable sin, it would seem, of abandoning and even ridiculing the ideals of his class.

the rest in reprimanding me. Under such circumstances, what business would I have trying to win a fair reputation?

The philosopher Tung Chung-shu[11] has said, has he not: "To strive with all one's might for benevolence and righteousness, fearful always lest one fail to educate the people—this is the ambition of a statesman. To strive with all one's might for goods and profit, fearful always of poverty and want—this is the business of ordinary people." So, as Confucius said, "those who do not follow the same road cannot lay plans for each other" [*Analects* XV, 39]. Why, then, do you come with the ideals of the statesman and use them to censure a person like *me*?

The old region of Wei west of the Yellow River, where you are from, prospered under the rule of Marquis Wen, and its people still retain something of the ways of the sages Tuan Kan-mu and T'ien Tzu-fang. All of them are men of the most lofty virtue, capable of clearly distinguishing right from wrong. Now, however, you have left your native land and are acting as governor of An-Ting. An-Ting is a mountainous region, the old home of the K'un-i barbarians, and its sons are greedy and uncouth. But how could you be changed by the customs and habits of such peoples?

I fully understand from your letter what your ambitions are. Now, when the Han is at the height of its glory, I hope you will pursue them with utmost diligence and not spend too much time talking. (*Han shu* 66; *Wen hsüan* 41.)

[11] See below, p. 135.

SUGGESTED READINGS

GENERAL WORKS

William Theodore de Bary, *et al. Sources of Chinese Tradition*. 1960.
Charles S. Gardiner. *Traditional Chinese Historiography*. Rev. ed.,
    1961.
Herbert A. Giles. *A History of Chinese Literature*. 1923; reprint,
    1958.
James Robert Hightower. *Topics in Chinese Literature*. Rev. ed.,
    1953.
Burton Watson. *Ssu-ma Ch'ien: Grand Historian of China*. 1958.

TRANSLATIONS

   Shu ching

Bernhard Karlgren. *The Book of Documents*. 1950.
James Legge. *The Shoo King*. (Vol. 3 in *The Chinese Classics*.)
    1865.

   Ch'un ch'iu and *Tso chuan*

James Legge. *The Ch'un Ts'ew, with Tso Chuen*. (Vol. 5 in *The
    Chinese Classics*.) 1872.

   Shih chi

Derk Bodde. *Statesman, Patriot and General in Ancient China*. 1940.
    A translation of three biographies pertaining to the Ch'in dynasty.
Burton Watson. *Records of the Grand Historian of China*. 2 vols.
    1961. A translation of the chapters pertaining to the Han dynasty.

   Han shu

Homer H. Dubs. *History of the Former Han Dynasty*. 3 vols. 1938,
    1940, 1955. A translation of the Annals section and the biography
    of Wang Mang.

PHILOSOPHY

T HE NEXT WRITINGS to be discussed are the philosophical works; mixtures of expository prose, dialogue, and historical or pseudohistorical anecdotes whose aim is to expound the doctrines of one or another of the thinkers or schools of thought of early China. This group contains some of the most famous and important of all Chinese books, such works as the Confucian *Analects,* the *Mencius,* the *Lao Tzu,* and the *Chuang Tzu,* which have been an invariable part of the education of cultured Chinese up to the present day and whose stories and sayings have become a part of the language itself. Unlike the early historical writings, which have been somewhat neglected by Western translators, most of the major works in this group have been translated into English or other European languages, one of them—the *Tao te ching* of Lao Tzu—so many times that bibliographers have all but lost count. In many cases, therefore, the reader unfamiliar with Chinese may turn directly to a translation of the work for his own verification of the remarks which will be made hereafter.

I shall not attempt to give a systematic analysis of the ideas expressed in these works. There are a number of excellent histories of early Chinese thought in Western languages, some of them listed in the bibliography at the end of this section, which deal at length with this aspect of the subject. Rather I shall concentrate here upon a description of the form, style, and literary interest of the works themselves, though this will necessarily involve at times a consideration of the principal ideas expressed in them. Nor shall I attempt in most cases to give biographical information on the reputed authors of the works. Certain of the Han works may be largely or entirely from the hand of the author to whom they are attributed, a figure about whom we have biographical information of reasonable reliability. But most of the pre-Han works, though they bear the name of a particular thinker, are in fact collections of writings from different hands and different periods. Though they may include some passages actually written by the nominal author, they are more in the nature of expositions of his ideas, or the ideas associated with his name, put together in later years by his followers. Biographical information about the reputed author of the book, often confused and interwoven with legend, may therefore actually give a false impression of the antiquity of the work which bears his name. The pre-Han philosophers are at best shadowy figures. But the books, regardless of how and when they were put together, exist today, and it is upon them that I shall concentrate my discussion.

THE CONFUCIAN WRITINGS

The most important group of writings is undoubtedly that associated with the Confucian school. Confucius and his followers, more than the men of any other school of thought, made themselves the special guardians of the ancient literature of China. Thus such pre-Confucian works as the *Book of Documents,* the *Book of Odes,* and even to some extent the *Book of Changes,* in time came to be regarded as the exclusive property of the Confucian school, and its scholars the sole transmitters and interpreters of the ancient texts. When Confucianism won out over its rivals and was made the official doctrine of the state at the end of the second century B.C., these texts, along with later works such as the *Spring and Autumn Annals* and its commentaries, the collection of writings on ritual and ethics known as the *Li chi* or *Book of Rites*, the *Analects*, and the short *Classic of Filial Piety*, became the sole basis for an officially recognized education. Scholars from that time to the present were free to read or study the texts of the other schools of thought, or of Buddhism after it was introduced in the early centuries of the Christian era. But they could seldom hope to win a post in the government—the ordinary goal of all learning—if they were not thoroughly conversant first of all with the Confucian texts. It is these texts, therefore, which have played the largest part in molding later Chinese culture and thought.

Of the so-called Five Classics, I have dealt with the *Book of Documents* and the *Spring and Autumn Annals* in the preceding section, and shall deal with the *Book of Odes* in the section on poetry which follows. I shall postpone the discussion of the other two, the *Book of Changes* and the collections of ritual texts, until later in this section and begin with a consideration of the most widely read of all Confucian works, the *Analects*.

The *Lun yü* or *Analects*

Confucius is believed to have died in 479 B.C. It was probably a hundred years or more before the *Analects*, the earliest work we have on his life and teachings, attained anything like its present form. It consists of twenty chapters, divided into 497 sections, some of them no more than the briefest pronouncements. There is no order to the chapters nor continuity to the sections. What we have in the *Analects* is not a book in the modern sense, but a collection of fragments, of varying dates and degrees of reliability,[1] united only by the fact that they all deal with Confucius and his teachings. Imagine a handful of earnest scholars

---

[1] The last ten chapters of the *Analects* differ in grammar from the first ten and have long been recognized as being of somewhat later date.

working through the years to contact the former students of the late Professor So and so, or the students of his students, collecting their reminiscences of the professor and his sayings, and finally pasting together the results in a book. Allow for the special difficulties of such a procedure in the China of twenty-five hundred years ago, and you will have an idea of how the *Analects* was most likely formed.

This fragmentary, disarranged form of the work is one thing that makes the *Analects* difficult to appreciate on first reading. A second difficulty is posed by the nature of the fragments themselves. Anyone hoping to find in the *Analects* a clear or systematic statement of Confucius' thought will be greatly disappointed. It is true that most of the concepts that were to become important in later Confucian thinking are already expressed or hinted at here—the fundamental humanism of Confucius' teachings, the emphasis upon moral education as a means of reforming the state, the concern for ritual and correct behavior, the insistence that conduct and not birth is what distinguises a man. But all these ideas are expressed in the form of brief conversations between Confucius and his disciples, answers to specific questions, or sometimes simply isolated pronouncements. Nowhere do we find Confucius discoursing at length on philosophical principles or attempting to formulate detailed rules for a way of life. He seldom defines his terms or tries to weave his ideas together into a unified system of thought. He merely comments on a specific problem or situation, endeavoring to give whatever suggestion will be most applicable to the circumstances and the capacities of his hearers. Where some of his pronouncements stand alone, without qualification or context, it is likely that the original setting has been lost, not that they were intended from the first as universal truths.

Confucius, it should be recalled, was primarily interested in becoming a statesman so that he could put his ideas for reform into actual practice. Failing to achieve this goal himself, he turned his attention to the training of young men who he hoped would be able to win posts in the governments of his time and apply his teachings. But the last thing he was interested in, one may surmise, was the formulation and propagation of an abstract system of philosophy.

Obviously the reader, in order to understand the force of Confucius' various remarks, must therefore understand the specific problems and situations which evoked them, which means understanding something of the society of the time and the men with whom Confucius was associated. Much information on these subjects, of reasonable reliability, it would seem, can be gleaned from works of the period such as the *Tso chuan,* and scholars have duly gathered it together in their notes and exegeses on the *Analects.* Such information will help one to understand and appreciate the historical Confucius, the importance of the man in his time, and the novelty of many of his ideas.

The degree to which such an historical approach can be used to unlock the secrets of the *Analects* should not be overestimated, however. The *Analects,* as I have said, is a collection of fragmentary dialogues and sayings, couched in what appears to be the conversational style of the period, simple in diction and forceful in expression. But the conversations are too often like those overheard from the house next door—scraps and unrelated utterances whose full import can only be guessed at. Contexts for such remarks supplied by works written centuries later can hardly be accepted as reliable, while works contemporary with the *Analects* make no mention of the book. So if we follow the historical method rigorously, we find our text reduced to a few anecdotes, a few descriptive passages, and a number of brief logia whose exact significance is now lost beyond recovery. We cannot even say with any certainty whether any of these represents the actual words or ideas of the man named Confucius.

The historical approach will therefore serve to indicate to the student what can be known today about the original meaning of the *Analects* and inform him of the boundaries to our understanding marked out by modern critical scholarship. But it is only in recent years that the *Analects* has been read with such sharp and skeptical eyes. What the modern historical approach cannot explain, therefore, is what the *Analects* has meant to readers in China, and later in Korea and Japan, over two thousand years and why it has won from them such extravagant respect and admiration. What, for example, is the Western reader to make of the statement by the Neo-Confucian scholar Ch'eng I (1033–1107) that at times when he reads the *Analects* his hands unconsciously begin to dance and his feet to stamp, or the assertion by the Japanese Confucianist Itō Jinsai (1627–1705) that the *Analects* "is the greatest and most profound book in the universe"?

The *Analects,* along with the Five Classics, had always been read and studied by educated Chinese, and from the Han dynasty on we find constant allusions to or echoes of its phraseology in literary works of all kinds. But the Sung Neo-Confucian philosopher Chu Hsi (1130–1200) accorded it even greater importance by making it, along with the *Mencius,* the *Ta hsüeh* or *Great Learning* and the *Chung yung* or *Doctrine of the Mean* (two short texts from the *Book of Rites*), a primer of Confucian education. From his time on, therefore, these four texts, called the *Ssu shu* or *Four Books,* were used in China and, to a lesser extent, in the countries under Chinese influence, as a school book for children. Before they were able even to comprehend the difficult, archaic language of the *Analects,* much less its ideas, children were obliged to commit the text to memory. There it remained, stored in their minds, to be gradually illumined by later study and experience. Having mastered the words of the text, they could spend the rest of their lives, if they were so disposed, pondering and savoring its meaning and finding ways in which its words were applicable to their own situation.

To understand the appeal of the *Analects* to later Chinese readers, its scriptural significance as opposed to its historical significance, it would probably be necessary for the Western reader to adopt something like the Chinese approach: if not actually memorizing the text, at least reading it often enough to have a firm grasp of its contents and the ways they have customarily been interpreted.

When the reader has done this, he might then begin to consider the brief pronouncements of the text as a series of mottoes such as he would copy out and hang on his wall (as is so often done in China and Japan), or as a series of texts for sermons or opening lines for essays. Since there is so little context or explanation included in the *Analects* itself, he may proceed to construct his own explanations of what the passage means to him and how it tallies with his own experience. Some passages dealing with specific details of the life of ancient China may never have anything more than historical interest for the modern reader. Some passages may come to life only when he has read farther in Confucian thought and seen how the hint given in the *Analects* has been elaborated and expanded by later writers. Some passages can perhaps not be fully appreciated until the reader himself has undergone experiences similar to those referred to in the text. But, if Chinese and Japanese scholars are to be believed, the meager sayings of the *Analects,* when so studied and contemplated over the years, will take on deeper and deeper meaning the older one grows. As one's own experience broadens to match that of Confucius and his disciples, the pronouncements of the *Analects* will one by one light up with the light of personal recognition. Once this has happened, the words of the *Analects* will become for him the most succinct and poignant summation of that particular idea or experience, and he will understand to some degree why they have been regarded with such reverence.

This may seem a fanciful and irresponsible way to approach a classic of a foreign culture, and I do not suggest that the reader adopt it until he has first mastered what can be known of the historical meaning of the text. But unless he also somehow goes beyond the historical meaning of the text, he can never understand the importance of the *Analects* in later Chinese culture as an educational and devotional work, any more than he can understand the importance of the Bible in the West if he approaches it merely as an historical record of early Jewish and Christian religious teachings. It is the mark of a great book that it can outlive the time and place of its beginning and continue to be meaningful to readers of other times and places. The *Analects* is such a book, and its importance lies not only in what it meant to the men who first compiled it, but what it has meant to readers of later times and can still mean to readers today.

The *Meng Tzu* or *Mencius*

The *Mencius,* a work in seven chapters dealing with the teachings of the Confucian philosopher Mencius (372–289 B.C.), resembles the *Analects* in many ways. It too was probably compiled by the philosopher's disciples after his death, though tradition credits Mencius himself with a part in the work of compilation. As in the case of the *Analects,* there is little suggestion of system or order in the arrangement of the material. However, though some of the pronouncements are presented without context, many of them are given a fairly elaborate anecdotal setting, usually in the form of an interview between Mencius and one of the feudal rulers of the time. This is a stock literary device in the philosophical works of the period and it is useless to inquire whether such descriptions of interviews have any basis in historical fact. The important thing to note is that in the *Mencius* these anecdotes have a remarkably realistic tone. Mencius does not always preach the same sermon and the rulers do not invariably respond in the same way, as happens so often in the anecdotes of other works of the period such as the *Yen Tzu ch'un-ch'iu.* The conversations frequently take sudden, unexpected turns and there are little graphic details or psychological touches that bring the narrative to life. The style is clear and straightforward. The conversations, like those of the *Analects,* have an easy, natural air and, since the *Mencius* was probably compiled a century or so later than the *Analects,* are a good deal easier to read. The writers have taken care to vary the sentence patterns and thus to avoid the tediously formal and balanced style that makes works such as the *Mo Tzu* or *Kuan Tzu* a burden to read.

The *Mencius* was always read and admired in early times as one of the important texts of the Confucian school. But from the time when Chu Hsi included it in his *Four Books* as one of the foundations of a Confucian education, it acquired a position of honor and importance second only to that of the *Analects* itself. The Western reader, however, will probably have less difficulty understanding the appeal of the *Mencius* than he will that of the *Analects.* Some passages, such as the famous pronouncement: "All things are complete in me" (*Mencius* VIIA, 4), are so vague as to be almost meaningless. But on the whole there is sufficient background and continuity to allow one to form a fairly concrete idea of Mencius' views.

Like Confucius, Mencius traveled from one feudal state to another seeking a hearing for his ideas on government. He was granted hearings, which are described in the *Mencius,* but there the matter usually ended. None of the rulers seems to have seriously considered putting his ideas into practice; as the historian Ssu-ma Ch'ien remarks in his biography of Mencius (*Shih chi* 74), "they regarded him as hopelessly impractical and out of touch with the facts of life." When we recall the avarice, deceit, and ruthlessness that characterized the political life of the age, the vicious dog-eat-dog atmosphere so vividly conveyed in the *Intrigues of the Warring States,* this is hardly surprising. Faced with such an age, Mencius nevertheless insisted that men are basically good by nature, the evil they commit being due only to an obfuscation of their original goodness. In a world where economic and military power seemed to be the sole deciding factors in the struggle for political survival, he nevertheless counseled rulers to forget all else in the pursuit of virtuous and benevolent government, assuring them that "the benevolent man has no enemies" (IA, 5). Mencius has specific suggestions on how to recover one's original goodness and how to insure prosperity and good government in the state. His arguments are interesting, though not always logically convincing, and at times he achieves passages of eloquent and poetic beauty. And, whatever one thinks of his ideas, the text leaves one with a deep impression of his sincerity in putting them forward.

His thought is admirable precisely because it does not compromise with the harsh realities, the corruption and evil of his time. It is easy enough to make fun of the apparent impracticability of such lofty and mystic idealism, as Mencius' contemporaries were quick to do. But, as in the case of the Sermon on the Mount, the practicability or impracticability of such ethical teachings can never really be settled until someone sincerely endeavors to put them into effect. Till then one may presumably suspend judgment on their ultimate utility and admire the faith and persistence of a man who clung so tenaciously to such beliefs.

The *Hsün Tzu*

Before Chu Hsi made Mencius' interpretation of Confucianism the only orthodox one, the *Mencius* was read as merely one of several Confucian works, among which the collection of essays known as the *Hsün Tzu* was perhaps more influential in early centuries. This work, in thirty-two sections, is attributed to a statesman and thinker named Hsün Ch'ing who was born around 300 B.C. Many of the essays may actually be from his hand, though some of the latter portions of the book were probably added by his followers in the Han. Here for the first time in Confucianism, therefore, we have not a fragmentary collection of logia and anecdotes put together after the death of the teacher but essays written by the man himself for the express purpose of expounding his ideas. In this respect the *Hsün Tzu* marks a definite advance in the development of expository prose.

These expository chapters of the *Hsün Tzu* are among the earliest examples we have of the essay form. Unlike the sections of the *Analects* and the *Mencius,* whose titles are taken from the opening words of the section and bear no relation to the contents, the essays in the *Hsün Tzu* have titles which state the theme of the chapter. The theme is developed in an orderly, logical fashion, with frequent quotations from the *Odes,* the *Documents,* or other early works introduced to illustrate a point. Unlike most other philosophical works of the period, the *Hsün Tzu* contains relatively few anecdotes and makes very little use of the dialogue form. The style is much more consciously literary than that of the *Mencius,* the diction is richer, and the sentences are more often cast in balanced, symmetrical forms. The reader may at times be disturbed by repetitiousness and a tendency to belabor the obvious. Yet some sections of the work, such as that on the nature of Heaven (sec. 17) or the evilness of human nature (sec. 23) are among the most lucid, cogent, and effective passages in all early expository prose. Parts of the work were apparently so much admired that they were copied almost verbatim into the *Book of Rites* (though with no acknowledgment of the source) and have thus become part of the Five Classics, an honor not accorded even to the *Analects* or the *Mencius*.

In spite of his general felicity of style, however, some of Hsün Tzu's ideas have long troubled Chinese readers and prevented him from enjoying the favor and honor accorded Mencius. For, unlike Mencius' lofty idealism, the thought of Hsün Tzu is deeply colored by the cynicism and stern authoritarianism of his age. Some critics have even questioned whether he deserves to be regarded as a true Confucian, though this is simply to follow Chu Hsi in regarding Mencius' interpretation of the teachings of Confucius as the only orthodox one.

The greatest stumbling block is Hsün Tzu's flat assertion, diametrically opposed to that of Mencius, that all men are by nature basically evil. Naturally no thinker is going to affirm such a dismal concept unless he has some mode of salvation to suggest, and Hsün Tzu is quick to offer his. Though men are born evil, they are all capable (that is, all except an incorrigible few) of becoming good through education. Confucius himself seems to have had great faith in the efficacy of education, and Hsün Tzu is even more optimistic than the Master about the results which can be attained through proper moral training. But the harshness of Hsün Tzu's first premise and his insistence that without the authority and guidance of a good teacher one can never rise above the level of a beast have struck many readers as betrayals of the essential warmth and humanity of Confucius' teachings.

Because for Hsün Tzu education is man's only salvation; because the intellect and all its products—crafts and scholarship, the rites and laws which govern society, the hierarchical distinctions proper in human relations—are what distinguish mankind from lower forms of life, he attacks every idea or superstition, such as the belief in portents or the art of physiognomy, that would distract men from the use of their own reasoning power and make them turn their attention to the supernatural. He even reinterprets the ancient mourning and sacrificial rites in such a way as to purge them of any element of supernatural significance or efficacy and make them no more than exercises for the moral edification of the living. This side of his thought, his uncompromising rationalism and insistence that men confine their search for knowledge to human affairs, had a great influence on the thought of the Han period, though it was not long before scholars, impatient of such restrictions, began seeking knowledge in precisely those spheres that Hsün Tzu had warned them away from. Such a one was the early Han Confucian, Tung Chung-shu (179?–104? B.C.), whose book, the *Ch'un-chiu fan-lu,* is the next important work in the Confucian tradition to be considered.

The *Ch'un-ch'iu fan-lu* of Tung Chung-shu

The *Ch'un-ch'iu fan-lu* is a work in eighty-two sections, most of them very brief, attributed to the Confucian scholar Tung Chung-shu. The title, literally "Abundant Dew of the *Spring and Autumn,"* can perhaps be paraphrased as "The Deep Significance of the *Spring and Autumn Annals,"* since some of the sections deal with the profound moral lessons to be learned from the *Annals,* which Tung interprets in the light of the *Kung yang Commentary.* Other essays deal with the function and duties of the ruler, sacrifices, portents, human nature, and the Yin-yang and Five Elements theories. It is probable that most, if not all, of the work is actually from Tung's own hand. It is written in the rather ornate style typical of Han expository prose, with its neat numerical categories, balanced phrases, and long thought units varied at times by brief, staccato sentences.

Hsün Tzu's thought, though basically Confucian, already shows signs of eclecticism: a strain of quietism reminiscent of Taoism, an appreciation for the practical value of strict law and authority that resembles Legalist thinking, though he is careful to insist that laws must always be regarded as less important in governing than the moral qualities of the ruler. When we turn to Tung Chung-shu we find other elements, originally quite foreign to Confucian thought, incorporated into Confucianism, notably the cosmological theories of the Yin-yang and Five Elements schools. His work represents a synthesis intended to provide the ruler with all the wisdom he needs to understand not only the affairs of man but those of heaven and earth as well, the three members of the eternal triad so beloved by Han thinkers. In his attempt to create a comprehensive system of thought that would embrace the human, natural, and supernatural worlds, Tung Chung-shu often resorts to reasoning that is forced and fanciful. He can never compare to Mencius or Hsün Tzu in depth and originality, and many of his ideas are of only historical interest today. Yet his work obviously filled a need that could not be met by the simpler and more limited doctrines of his predecessors in the Confucian school. Though he abandoned Hsün Tzu's stern rationalism to the extent of prescribing ceremonies to produce rain or make it stop, he did much to win recognition for Confucianism and was influential in having it declared the orthodox doctrine of the Han state.

The *Fa yen* of Yang Hsiung

More directly in the line of traditional Confucian thought is the scholar, statesman, and poet Yang Hsiung (53 B.C.–A.D. 18), who attempted to combat the extraneous elements which had crept into the Confucianism of his day and to return to the rationalism and humanism of former times. He wrote a work in thirteen sections called the *Fa yen* or *Model Words* in which he expounded his ideas in the form of dialogues between himself and an anonymous questioner. Yang Hsiung explains this choice of the dialogue rather than the essay form by stating that he deliberately patterned his work on the *Analects,* an indication of the sincere reverence which he felt for Confucius and his teachings. Unfortunately he copied not only the fragmentary, conversational tone of the *Analects,* but also its actual style and diction, which by his own day were far removed from the ordinary language of the time. His *Fa yen* is thus a rare example of a work written in a consciously archaic style.

This fact, which gives the work a somewhat stiff, pretentious tone, helps to account for its lack of general appeal, as well as the fact that, though Yang Hsiung at times deals with serious philosophical questions, he at other times wanders off into a kind of pedantic chitchat on the intellectual and literary figures of his time.

Nevertheless his work has often been read along with the *Mencius* and the *Hsün Tzu* as a sincere and valuable interpretation of Confucian principles. The great Sung historian Ssu-ma Kuang (1019–86), in the preface to his commentary on the *Fa yen,* writes: "The style of Mencius is direct and clear; that of Hsün Tzu is rich and elegant; that of Yang Hsiung is simple and profound." It is interesting that he should choose the adjectives "simple and profound" to describe a work which Westerners, on first reading at least, would more likely call sententious and obscure. It is an indication of the fondness, evident in so much Chinese philosophical writing, for aphoristic pronouncements over detailed and lengthy exposition, the conviction that the deepest and most complex ideas can eventually be reduced to and expressed adequately in a few well-chosen words.

Even less inviting to the general reader is another work by Yang Hsiung, the *T'ai-hsüan-ching* or *Classic of the Great Mystery,* which he wrote in imitation of the *Book of Changes* and which Hightower aptly describes as being "as murky and impenetrable as its prototype" (*Topics in Chinese Literature,* p. 10). Unlike the *Fa yen,* it was little appreciated by Yang Hsiung's contemporaries, one of whom suggested that posterity might conveniently use its pages to cover sauce jars. If the work has not actually met such a fate, it has suffered one almost as sad, that of being seldom read and even less admired.

Like many other eminent men of his time, Yang Hsiung served, in his later years, in the government of Wang Mang, the usurper who for a brief period succeeded in overthrowing the Han dynasty, though he seems to have been uneasy in his post and once reached the point of attempting suicide by throwing himself from the window of the court library where he was working. For a thousand or more years after his death scholars, sensible of the circumstances which may oblige a man to serve under a sovereign he does not approve of, or at least charitable enough to distinguish between the man and his works, were willing to wink at Yang's later political career and admire his writings for what they were worth. But when Chu Hsi and his disciples compiled their highly moralistic summary of history, the *T'ung-chien kang-mu,* they insisted upon identifying Yang Hsiung in no uncertain terms as a minister of Wang Mang (*T'ung-chien kang-mu, T'ien-feng* 5th year [A.D. 18]). This served effectively to throw a pall of guilt not only over his name but over his works as well, and they remained in general disrepute as long as Chu Hsi's ideas retained their grip on the minds of the Chinese literati. In Confucian thought literature and politics not only mix; they often become inextricably fused.

THE RITUAL TEXTS

The works described above are all written by, or closely associated with the name of, a single Confucian thinker. Of major importance in the Confucian tradition is another group of works, of uncertain date and authorship, which from early times have been regarded as a part of the Confucian literature: the ritual texts. Three of these, the *Chou li*, the *I li*, and the *Li chi*, counted as one work, are numbered among the Five Classics;[2] a fourth, the *Ta-Tai li-chi*, though not a recognized part of the canon, was of considerable influence in Han times.

The *Chou li* or *Rites of Chou*, also known as the *Chou kuan* or *Institutes of Chou*, is an idealized description of the bureaucratic system which was supposed to have been in effect during the Chou dynasty. Though of dubious historical value, it has often been utilized by statesmen looking for an appropriately ancient and scriptural "authority" to justify reforms they wished to make in the governmental systems of later times.

The *I li* or *Ceremonial* contains minute and systematic descriptions of the etiquette to be followed at weddings, banquets, sacrifices, funerals, archery contests, and other ceremonial occasions in the life of the feudal aristocracy. As in the case of the *Chou li*, it is not clear how far the descriptions are mere idealization and how far they represent actual Chou dynasty practices. Neither text contains any dialogue or anecdotal material; the treatment of the subject is orderly, factual, and devoid of literary embellishment.

[2] In Chin and early Han times only the *I li* was counted among the Classics. Later the *Chou li* was lumped with it, and still later the *Li chi*, though the last was regarded more as a commentary on the other two than as a ritual text in its own right.

The *Li chi* or *Book of Rites*

Of much greater interest is the lengthy *Li chi* or *Book of Rites,* in forty-nine sections. The work in its present form was put together in the early part of the first century B.C. from various texts of late Chou, Ch'in, and Han times. Some of the sections have traditionally been attributed to immediate disciples of Confucius, but such attributions are rejected by modern scholarship.

It is difficult to make general comments on an assortment of texts as heterogeneous as those in the *Li chi*. Some of them resemble the *Chou li* and *I li,* being descriptions of government regulations or detailed instructions on how to manage a household, cook, behave at a dinner party or a funeral, drive a carriage, name a baby, etc. Some, such as the treatises on education, music, and rites, reflect the thinking of Hsün Tzu and embody quotations from his work. Two short philosophical chapters, the *Ta hsüeh* or *Great Learning* and the *Chung yung* or *Doctrine of the Mean,* have acquired enormous fame and influence—more, perhaps, than their intrinsic interest merits—because of the fact that they were included by Chu Hsi in his *Four Books*. Others, such as the *Ju hsing* or "Behavior of a Confucian," a lofty and independent-minded statement of the ideals that should guide a true Confucian gentleman, have received somewhat less attention than they deserve. Most of the ideas expressed are those of early Confucianism, especially as represented in the school of Hsün Tzu, though borrowings from Taoism and Yin-yang and Five Elements thought are occasionally discernible.

The style and literary interest of the texts tends to be as heterogeneous as their contents. Some are as tedious as the Levitical sections of the Bible, which they call to mind, while others, such as the chapters on music and the evolution and significance of ritual, contain passages which are justly renowned for their beauty and dignity of expression. Dialogue and anecdote are widely used throughout the work, some chapters consisting entirely of anecdotes about Confucius and his disciples, in which the Master is portrayed as expounding his views on proper ritual practice. The expository sections make generous use of simile and metaphor, sometimes containing extended metaphorical passages.

Perhaps most interesting to Western readers are the sections on the significance and purpose of the mourning and sacrificial rites, which follow but greatly elaborate the ideas of Hsün Tzu on the subject. The scholars of the Confucian school were often criticized for their conservative devotion to the practices of the past and their overnice attention to detail. Certainly in the chapters of the *Li chi* we can see their earnest concern to preserve and propagate the ancient ceremonies, particularly those relating to mourning and sacrifice. But at the same time they realized that such ancient ceremonies would eventually become meaningless and pass out of existence entirely, unless somehow reinterpreted to accord with the thinking of a more sophisticated and enlightened age. They therefore worked to imbue the rites with new meaning, purging them of all the superstitious fear of the dead that had originally called them into being.

In this new interpretation of the funeral rites, for example, there is no longer any suggestion that the spirit of the dead can actually be summoned back to the body by the custom of ascending the roof of the house and calling to the dead man to return; there is no suggestion that the vessels and musical instruments buried with the dead man can actually be of any use to him. Yet, according to the Confucian scholars, the mourner deeply *wishes* that the dead could be recalled or that they could be comforted and aided by the articles interred with them. And in Confucian teaching one must never attempt forcefully to repress a wish, a sincere human desire, but only to guide and channel it in a socially acceptable direction. Thus, though the mourner knows intellectually that such practices are not efficacious (as they were believed to have been in earlier times), he yet performs them in order to assuage his own feelings of grief. As Confucius is made to express it (*Li chi* sec. 3, *T'an Kung* A), "To treat the dead as dead would show a lack of love and therefore cannot be done; to treat the dead as living would show a lack of wisdom and likewise cannot be done." The Confucians in their interpretation seek a compromise between the conflicting claims of love and wisdom, recognizing that the mourning rites have no real effect upon the dead, but urging that they be carried out as a means of paying respect to the departed and regulating the emotions of the living, insuring that the expression of grief will be neither too perfunctory nor too fervid and prolonged.

Followers of other schools frequently condemned the mourning practices of the Confucians as expensive and troublesome and complained that they were too often used merely as occasions for hypocritical display. This may at times have been true in practice. Yet the *Li chi* and other Confucian works repeatedly stress that it is not the rites themselves that are important, but the sincerity with which they are performed, and they specifically condemn any ascetic practices that might endanger the health of the mourner.

The chapters of the *Li chi* devote particular attention to the *ming ch'i* or "spirit articles," the vessels and other objects interred with the dead, specifying that they should be *like* those used by living men (the claim of love), but at the same time somehow different and useless (the claim of wisdom)—pots that are crude and unfinished, lutes, pipes, and bell stands that cannot be played upon. In other words, that which is intended for the dead must never be confused with that which serves the living. The reason for this insistence is not difficult to guess. Rulers in the Chou not only consigned much of their wealth to the graves of deceased kin, but on occasion even slaughtered the concubines and officials of the deceased so that their spirits might accompany their master in death. The custom of interring treasures with the dead continued in the Han, in spite of the protests of enlightened men, making grave robbing a lucrative enterprise. That of "following in death," the offering of human sacrifices on the death of a ruler, mercifully ceased. But the Confucian scholars were deeply concerned that, if men did not once and for all learn to distinguish between the needs of the living and the needs of the dead, the gruesome practice might someday be revived.

The interpretation of the sacrificial rites expounded in the *Li chi* is similar to that of the mourning rites. Ordinary men believe that at a sacrifice the spirit of the dead partakes of the offerings and, pleased and satiated, then confers blessings upon the sacrificer. In reality, the *Li chi* insists, there is no "spirit" involved other than the spirit of reverence and piety born and nurtured in the heart of the sacrificer himself as he performs the ritual, and the "blessing" which he receives is simply the moral training and excellence derived from the experience. As in the case of the mourning rites, the important thing is not the outward actions and accouterments of the ceremony, but the emotional purity of the participant. Thus the rituals themselves, as well as the sentiments which prompt them and the effects which they produce, "are not something which comes down from Heaven, not something which springs up from earth, but only a matter of human feeling" (sec. 35, *Wen sang*).

As I have said, many of the ideas of the *Li chi* are expressed or illustrated in the form of anecdotes about Confucius and his disciples. There is little likelihood that these have much sound historical basis. Some of them were probably invented in order to give a setting to pronouncements of Confucius which in the

Analects lack any context; others simply borrow his name for the sake of authority. Some of them, such as those in the important *T'an Kung* chapter, are probably genuine products of late Chou times and as such are valuable in showing the image of Confucius and his teachings which the men of the Confucian school held at that time and which became so influential in later centuries. It is an image somewhat different from that built up in the *Analects* alone. Confucius has become much more of a scholar, able to speak with authority on all manner of difficult and technical points of ritual and ancient history. Yet he remains a warm, human figure, nothing like the divine hero or omniscient, infallible sage he sometimes became in later periods of Chinese thought.

Since anecdotes lend themselves to quotation better than lengthy philosophical exposition, I shall quote a few of these to illustrate the style and content of the *Li chi* and to show something of the image of Confucius revealed in its pages. The first of these is found not in the *Li chi* but near the end of the *Hsün Tzu*. The chapter which contains it is almost certainly not by Hsün Tzu himself but by his later followers, and the form and style of the anecdote are exactly like those of similar anecdotes contained in the *Li chi*. The remaining three are from the *Li chi* itself.

Duke Ai of Lu was questioning Confucius. "I was born," he said, "in the depths of palace chambers and raised by the hands of women. So I have never known sorrow, I have never known anxiety, I have never known trouble, fear, or danger."

. . .

Confucius said, "When you enter the gate of the ancestral temple and turn to the right, when you ascend its eastern steps and gaze up at the beams and ridgepole, when you look down at the tables and mats, you see the possessions of your ancestors still there, and yet they themselves are gone, and so your thoughts grow sorrowful. How then can you say that sorrow never comes to you?

"When the first light begins to break, you comb your hair and put on your cap, and at dawn you listen to the reports of your ministers at court. You know that if one single detail is not properly attended to, it may become the seed of confusion and disaster. At that time your thoughts are filled with anxiety. How then can you say that anxiety never visits you?

"At dawn you go to court, and only when the sun is declining in the west do you retire, and you know that in the outer court wait the sons and grandsons of other feudal lords [who have been forced by rebellion and internal disorder to flee from their own states and seek refuge in Lu]. At that time you think of their troubles. How then can you say that no thought of trouble ever comes?

"When you go out of the four gates of the capital of Lu and gaze across the suburbs in each direction at the sites of ancient states that have perished, you find them numerous indeed. At such a time your thoughts are filled with fear. How then can you say that fear never comes?

"I have heard it said that the ruler is a boat and the common people are the water. It is the water that bears the boat up, and it is the water that capsizes it. When you think of this you are filled with a sense of danger. How then can you say that no thought of danger ever comes to you?" (*Hsün Tzu*, sec. 31, *Ai Kung*.)

When Confucius' pet dog died, he instructed Tzu-kung to bury it. "I have heard it said that one should not throw away a worn curtain, for it will serve to bury a horse in," said Confucius, "and one should not throw away a worn carriage cover, for it will serve to bury a dog in. I am too poor to own a carriage cover, but when you make the grave mound for my dog, lay a mat under his head so that it will not sink down into the earth." (*Li chi*, sec. 4, *T'an Kung* B.)

Confucius had an old friend named Yüan Jang. When the latter's mother died, Confucius helped him prepare the outer coffin. The task finished, Yüan Jang climbed up on the coffin shell and said, "What a long time it's been since I expressed myself in song," and [beating time on the coffin] he sang:

> Wood dappled like the wildcat's head,
> Soft to touch like a maiden's hand—

Confucius pretended not to notice and went on his way.

One of Confúcius' followers [appalled by such behavior] said, "Isn't it time to break off with such a fellow?"

"I have heard," said Confucius, "that in the case of kin you must never forget that they are kin, and in the case of old friends you must never forget that they are old friends." (*Ibid.*)

The last anecdote concerns the *la* or winter sacrifice, a festival held in the twelfth month, just after the winter solstice, when the work of the fields had been completed for the year. Sacrifices were offered to the gods and the people spent the day feasting and drinking.

Tzu-kung was watching the winter sacrifice. "Well, Tzu-kung, are you enjoying yourself?" asked Confucius.

"Everyone in the whole country seems to have gone mad!" said Tzu-kung. "I fail to see anything enjoyable about it!"

"After a hundred days of labor comes the winter sacrifice, one whole day of the lord's bounty!" said Confucius. "But then, you wouldn't understand. To keep the people always taut and never relaxed—even the sage kings Wen and Wu could not have done that. To keep them always relaxed and never taut—that they *would* not have done. A period of tautness followed by a period of relaxation—that was their way!" (*Li chi*, sec. 21, *Tsa chi* B.)

The *Ta-Tai li-chi*

The *Li chi*, which was said to have been compiled by a scholar named Tai Sheng in the first part of the first century B.C., was not the only such collection of ritual texts. There was another, compiled by his older cousin Tai Te, known as the *Ta-Tai li-chi* or *Book of Rites of the Elder Tai*. Originally much larger than the *Li chi*, it now contains only thirty some sections, most of them quite brief. All the portions of Tai Te's collection which were considered really valuable were apparently copied into the *Li chi*: what we have in the present *Ta-Tai li-chi* is simply what was left over—the chapters that were rejected as being too similar to texts preserved elsewhere, or as intrinsically worthless or unreliable. One must not judge the work of the Elder Tai too harshly, therefore, on the grounds of these remnants alone.

In most cases it is not difficult to understand why these sections were rejected from the *Li chi,* and hence from the Confucian canon. Some of the ideas expressed are at variance with the rationalism of Hsün Tzu which forms the basis of much of the thinking of the *Li chi.* Such for example is the assertion (*Ta-Tai li-chi, Sheng-te*) that the prayers of the people can directly influence the gods to reward or punish the rulers of the time. Some chapters are systematized genealogies and accounts of the rulers of high antiquity, no more dubious, perhaps, than many such accounts included within the Confucian canon itself, but more patently of late date. Most of the texts appear to be by Han scholars and deal with typically Han concepts, some being almost identical with works attributed to the early Han statesman Chia I (201–169 B.C.). Though one encounters occasional passages of interest, there is no single outstanding chapter, and the style is often overpoweringly tedious and uninspired. It is not difficult to see, therefore, why the *Ta-Tai li-chi* has generally been neglected by Chinese readers. Among the work's few surprises for the Western reader is the fact that it contains what, allowing for the distortions involved in the transition through several languages, seems to be the *locus classicus* for the inscription on Madame Butterfly's sword, "Con onor muore chi non può serbar vita con onore" (Cf. *Tseng Tzu chih-yen*).[3]

---

[3] Though the same maxim is found in *Shih chi* 79, which may be the source from which it passed into popular parlance.

The *Hsiao ching* or *Classic of Filial Piety*

One brief text, the *Hsiao ching* or *Classic of Filial Piety,* closely resembles the texts contained in the *Li chi* in style and content and might very well have been incorporated in that collection. Instead it has been transmitted separately and stands as one of the Thirteen Classics.[4] It is an extremely brief text, in the form of a colloquy between Confucius and his disciple Tseng Tzu, in which Confucius expounds the view that a proper understanding of filial piety is the foundation of all moral knowledge and action.

This ideal of filial piety is perhaps one of the most difficult aspects of Confucian thought for readers of today to appreciate. By many of the younger generation in the Far East at present it is regarded as a tiresome and outmoded remnant of feudal thinking, to be ignored or even openly condemned, while in most modern Western countries, if contemporary literature is any indication, love for a parent is considered the mark of a neurotic and maladjusted personality. To readers of such opinions, the Confucian writings on filial piety are bound to seem remote and difficult to comprehend. Yet the effort must be made if one is to understand Confucianism and, through Confucianism, the traditional culture of China.

The ideal of filial piety, that children should love, serve, and obey their parents, is common enough in many societies. Its development in China was undoubtedly aided by the ancient

---

[4] The *Book of Changes, Book of Odes, Book of Documents, Spring and Autumn Annals,* and the ritual texts made up the so-called Five Classics referred to in late Chou and Han literature. By Han times, however, there were three commentaries on the *Spring and Autumn,* each with its own slightly different version of the text, and three ritual works, and the *Analects* and *Filial Piety* were already being raised to canonical status alongside the older works. The number of works in the canon was therefore actually eleven. When the *Erh ya,* a brief lexical work, was added to the canon in the T'ang, and the *Mencius* in the Sung, the number was increased to thirteen. The term "Thirteen Classics" seems to have been used first in a work of the thirteenth century.

belief that the spirits of the dead, if not regularly sacrificed to, would literally suffer from hunger. Aging parents, we may surmise, were therefore particularly assiduous in urging their children to serve and remember them in death as well as in life. By the time the texts of the *Li chi* were written, however, the mourning and sacrificial rites were no longer believed, at least by educated men, to have any power to affect the welfare of the departed. As we have seen, they were rather a means for the living to express their love and devotion to the memory of the dead, in particular to their deceased parents.

It should be noted, however, that in Confucian literature there is never any question as to whether children should have, or actually do have, such a deep and abiding love for their parents. As in the case of the literature of romantic love in the West, the emotion itself is taken for granted, and the only question is how it is to be guided and expressed. Both assumptions are of course idealizations. There have undoubtedly been millions of Chinese who felt quite indifferent toward their parents, as there have been millions of Westerners who have never been swept by the fires of romantic passion. Both are poetic exaggerations and must be understood as such.

Sometimes the Confucian ideal of filial piety is expressed in terms that are poignant and perfectly understandable to readers today. Thus we read in the *Li chi* (sec. 13, *Yü-tsao*) that a filial son, "when his father has died, cannot bear to read his father's books, for the mark of his father's hand is still upon them; when his mother has died, he cannot bear to drink from her wine ladle, for the stain of her lips still clings to it." In another chapter, however (sec. 7, *Tseng Tzu wen*), we find Confucius declaring, "When a bride has been taken into the household, there shall be no music played for three days, for one then thinks of the fact that one has succeeded as heir to one's parents." Here we almost suspect we have misread the text, so far removed in our minds are weddings and new families from the idea of sorrowful reflection. Yet the commentators remind us that one's wedding is a sign that one's parents have grown old and that their day is past, hence a time for sadness. To such an extent is Confucian thought centered about the figure of the parent.

Like all such idealizations, the concept of filial piety at times tends towards an unwholesome parody of itself, as in the famous story of the elderly man who wore children's clothes and behaved like a little boy before his parents so that they would forget their own advanced age.[5] At its best, however, it is a sincere and poignant ideal, and at the same time serves as a foundation for the other ideals of social behavior. As the *Classic of Filial Piety* points out, filial piety is not something confined to one's own family, to be observed only at home: "The Confucian gentleman . . . in teaching filial piety shows respect to all the fathers in the world, and in teaching brotherly affection, he shows respect to all the brothers in the world." That is, by learning to honor the members of one's own family, one learns to do the same to all other men.

The philosopher Mo Tzu and his followers preached universal love but offered few suggestions as to how this ideal was to be achieved. The Confucians repeatedly attacked this doctrine of the Mohists, insisting that it was unnatural to expect men to love other men's parents as much as their own. But they realized that family affection, once firmly established, could to some degree be extended to other members of society. In their concept of moral training through the mourning and sacrificial rites, they thus had a means for attaining, at least in part, the goal which the Mohists proclaimed. But for the Confucians, love, good faith, a sense of

---

[5] This story, I am happy to say, is not from the *Li chi* but from a far less reputable work, the *Kao-shih chuan* by Huang-fu Mi (215–82).

duty, cannot be applied universally until one has first learned to apply them to particular persons. That is why, for them, filial piety is the cornerstone and beginning of all moral action.

The *I ching* or *Book of Changes*

The *I ching* or *Book of Changes,* though originally not connected with Confucianism, in time was accepted as one of the Five Classics of the Confucian canon. In its present form the work consists of a manual of divination, which was probably already in existence by the time of Confucius, and a number of later "wings" or commentaries. The divination manual was traditionally said to have been the work of King Wen, the sage founder of the Chou dynasty.

The manual section consists of short oracles arranged under sixty-four hexagrams, symbols made up of combinations of broken and unbroken lines in groups of six. Using the so-called divining stalks, the diviners of the Chou period, and those who still use the work today, cast a series of lots, even numbers representing broken lines and odd numbers unbroken, until they arrived at a particular hexagram, and then proceeded to interpret the oracular formula recorded under it in the *Changes.*

These formulas are extremely terse and cryptic—somewhat like the jingle, "Step on a crack, break your mother's back," which we used to chant as children when we walked down the sidewalk. In a work on divination, this is all to the good, of course, since they can usually be interpreted to mean almost anything one wishes. Many of them are interesting for the incidental light which they shed on the life of the early Chou period, but it is questionable whether their original meaning can ever be established with any certainty.

The commentaries appear to be the work of late Chou and early Han scholars, though some have traditionally been attributed to

Confucius. Their aim is not so much to explain the exact meaning of the oracular formulas as to invest the work as a whole with a profound and far-reaching cosmological significance. The entire universe, according to the interpretation of the commentaries, is characterized by a process of constant change. To achieve success, therefore, the wise man must understand this process, know in what direction it is moving at any given moment, and adapt his own actions accordingly. In this he is aided by the hexagrams, which describe to him symbolically the steps in the process of change. By divining to discover which hexagrams is descriptive of the present moment, he may therefore determine the appropriate course of action.

The commentaries, particularly the longest, the *Hsi tz'u* or *Appended Words,* are interesting in themselves as examples of early cosmological and metaphysical speculation, written in the elaborately balanced and parallelistic style of late Chou and Han. The fact that they are so closely tied to the cryptic formulas of the divination manual, however, often blurs their intelligibility, and the same may be said for the volumes of later metaphysical writing which use the same formulas as their point of departure. The murky language of the formulas, and the hardly less murky language of the commentaries, endlessly reinterpreted and expanded, has in fact not only dominated almost all later Chinese metaphysical and cosmological writing, but has even been employed in such unrelated fields as literary criticism, to the great detriment of clarity and good sense. Thus, for example, when the Ch'ing scholar Chang Hsüeh-ch'eng (1738–1801), in discussing early historiography, informs us that the work of the historian Ssu-ma Ch'ien is "round and spiritual" while that of Pan Ku is "square and sagacious" (*Wen-shih t'ung-i,* ch. 1, *Chiao shu* III), we may recognize that he is borrowing phrases from the *Ap-*

pended Words, but our understanding of his views on the two historians is not remarkably aided.

Nevertheless, the *Book of Changes* has filled a need in Confucian thought that could not be met by the other four Classics or the texts of the philosophers. The great mass of early Confucian literature is concerned almost entirely with ethical and political problems, doggedly humanistic and full of sound advice and good common sense. The *Book of Changes* is the great exception, a work written in arcane and antique language and dealing not with human affairs alone but with the mystic working of the universe as a whole (or so it was believed). It thus provided an opportunity for scholars with a more metaphysical and transcendental bent of mind to indulge their tastes without going outside the realm of the Five Classics, and the endless volumes of commentary on the hidden meaning of the *Changes* are the result. Had there been no such text in the Confucian canon, it is likely that such men would have abandoned Confucianism entirely in favor of the Taoists, who from the beginning interested themselves in mystical and cosmological speculation. It was probably to preclude just such an eventuality that the early Confucian scholars took over the *Book of Changes* and made it a part of their literature.

THE MOHIST WRITINGS

The philosopher Mo Ti or Mo Tzu (470–391 B.C.?) was born shortly after the death of Confucius and died a few years before the birth of Mencius. The school which he founded was of considerable importance in late Chou times—Mencius specifically attacks its teachings in several ill-tempered passages—and may for a while have posed a serious challenge to the doctrines of the Confucians and Taoists. By Han times, however, it had all but dropped out of sight and was of little significance in the history of Chinese thought thereafter.

Though typically Mohist ideas are occasionally found in other works, we have only one work that belongs specifically to the school, the text known as the *Mo Tzu*. The Han version of the work is said to have contained seventy-one sections, though eighteen of these are now lost. Parts of the work are by later followers of the school, but it seems likely that some chapters represent the ideas, if not indeed the actual words, of Mo Tzu himself. A few of the chapters are in the form of dialogue between Mo Tzu and various contemporaries. Most, however, are essays dealing with particular points of doctrine, the topic being stated in the title of the chapter, and as such represent the earliest examples we have of expository essays.

Many of Mo Tzu's doctrines—universal love, nonaggression, free will—sound attractive enough when one first hears of them. Unfortunately one is almost certain to be disappointed when one becomes acquainted with the way in which Mo Tzu expounds them. His arguments are uninspired, his logic shaky, and his style of presentation unbelievably flat and repetitious. Though the *Mo Tzu* makes use of the standard literary devices of the period —anecdotes, dialogues, proverbs, quotations from the Classics— it is, as Arthur Waley has said, "devoid of a single passage that could possibly be said to have wit, beauty or force" (*Three Ways of Thought in Ancient China*, p. 163).

Chinese literary historians usually describe the style of the *Mo Tzu* as "logical." This is somewhat misleading, since Mo Tzu's arguments are often far from logical; if one is determined to be charitable, "lucid" would perhaps be a more appropriate epithet. The reader never has any difficulty following Mo Tzu's arguments, since he insists upon spelling out every step of his reasoning process with frequent recapitulations no matter how tedious or repetitious the result may be. When so many early Chinese works are characterized by maddening ellipsis, it may seem ungrateful to complain of such painstaking clarity. Yet one has only to read the *Mo Tzu* to realize that if there is anything in Chinese worse than too much ellipsis it is none at all.

A Japanese friend once remarked that the *Mo Tzu* reminded him of the sermons of a country priest. Certainly there is much of this tone in Mo Tzu's writing—a deep and earnest piety combined with a singularly graceless manner of expression. Compared with the writings of the other schools, his ideas often seem naïve and old-fashioned—his insistence, for example, that Heaven punishes every evil deed of man or that the ghosts of the dead can come back to take revenge on people who had harmed them. In his attacks on the Confucians for their expensive burials and their music and dances, his insistence that all emotions must be got rid of and pure utilitarianism be made the only criterion of worth, he shows a rather cold and dour attitude rare in Chinese thought. He was said to have been a selfless and devoted man, deeply concerned about the evils of his time and ready to journey anywhere to gain a hearing for his doctrines or aid in the defense of a state which was under attack. No doubt he had much of the simple piety and dedication of a country priest or preacher, and it is unfortunate that he or his disciples lacked the literary talent to give his ideas a more attractive form. It is possible, of course, that they deliberately eschewed all literary embellishment in the hope of rendering their message more lucid and compelling, but they have paid the price which that decision, except in the case of a master stylist, almost always entails: posterity has left them unread.

The latter chapters of the *Mo Tzu,* probably written by later followers of Mohism, deal in considerable detail with questions of logic and military defense. The adherents of the Mohist school were a close-knit, disciplined band, obeying in all things the command of their leader. Following the example of Mo Tzu himself, they often assisted states which were being attacked and acted as advisers on techniques of warfare. These chapters contain a great deal of valuable information on early Chinese warfare, including descriptions of the types of battlements, scaling ladders, missiles, weapons, etc. to be used in laying siege to or defending a city. The chapters on logic are of less general interest and are extremely difficult to make out, partly due to the faulty state of the text. Waley makes the suggestion that the followers of the Mohist school took up the study of logic not out of any intrinsic interest in the subject, but "in the same way that some Church-men today have taken up psycho-analysis, in order to arm them-selves against modernist attack" (*The Way and Its Power,* p. 65). Certainly it seems unlikely that men of such practical bent would have interested themselves in these subtleties of language and thought except for some such reason as Waley suggests. Whatever the motive, their chapters on the subject, along with some passages in the *Chuang tzu* and one brief and badly corrupted text, the *Kung-sun Lung tzu,* constitute the only examples still extant of early Chinese writings on logic.

THE TAOIST WRITINGS

The works of the early Taoist philosophers have enjoyed a popularity and exercised an influence in Chinese culture second only to those of the Confucian texts. While the works of other ancient thinkers sank into obscurity or retained only a limited appeal, the Taoist writings, from the time they became known until the present, have constituted an indispensable part of the education of every cultured Chinese. The reasons for this un-diminishing popularity are easy to perceive. While some of the Taoist texts deal with problems of government and can be interpreted as expositions of political philosophy, they are nevertheless far more concerned with the nature of the universe and man's place in it as an individual rather than as a social being. Thus, during the extensive periods when Confucianism was acknowledged to have supplied all the answers to political and social problems, it was still possible to read and enjoy the Taoist writings for the light they shed upon problems outside the sphere of Confucian interest. Again, during the long age when Buddhism was a vital force in Chinese intellectual life, the Taoist texts were even more avidly read because of the resemblances between Buddhist and Taoist thought and the fact that much of the vocabulary of early Chinese Buddhism was borrowed from Taoism. Finally, and perhaps most important, the Taoist writings have been read because they are witty, spirited, and imaginative and because they contain some of the most beautiful and compelling passages in all Chinese literature. Had the ideas of the Taoists been as drably expressed as those of the Mohists, they would still undoubtedly have attracted considerable attention. The fact that they are set forth in superlative language assures them a place of prime importance not only in Chinese literature but in the literature of the world.

The *Lao Tzu* or *Tao te ching*

Of the three most famous Taoist texts, the *Lao Tzu,* the *Chuang Tzu,* and the *Lieh Tzu,* the *Lao Tzu* or *Tao te ching* has traditionally been accepted as the oldest. It was attributed to a sage and recluse named Lao Tan who was supposed to have been a contemporary of Confucius. Scholars now generally agree that the biographical accounts of Lao Tan are no more than a jumble of confused legends, and that the text called *Lao Tzu* is probably no older than the fourth or third century B.C., though it may incorporate older material. It is impossible to say anything about its authorship other than that it may well have been the work of a single writer.

The work as we have it at present is in eighty-one brief paragraphs or stanzas. There is little formal structure to the work or systematic development of ideas. Much of it is made up of what appear to be ancient maxims, often rhymed, interspersed with passages of interpretation in verse or prose. The style is highly formal and parallelistic like that of much late Chou literature.

What distinguishes the *Lao Tzu* so sharply from other works of the period is its mystical, rhapsodic tone. Not only is much of it in verse, but it is dominated throughout by a poetic and highly symbolic manner of expression. The ideas are not explained or elaborated, but rather flung in the reader's face. "Truth sounds like its opposite!" proclaims the author (sec. 78), and he proceeds to lay before the world his own perception of truth, couched in as bold and paradoxical language as he can devise. The rhythm and balance of the sentences drum the reader on his way, the trenchant symbolism draws him along, and he may go for pages before he wakes with a start to realize that he has only a hazy idea of what is being said.

This is of course the secret of the work's inexhaustible charm. To render the *Lao Tzu* into another language, the translator must always be more explicit than the original; he must choose one of a number of possible meanings before he can produce any kind of coherent version. Yet the original remains magnificently elusive and suggestive, which is no doubt why it has been translated so many times. Each new translator of the work is fired with a determination to bring out hidden beauties and subtleties which his predecessors have overlooked.

Though isolated passages are scarcely intelligible, it is nevertheless possible to make out the general meaning of the text. It begins by postulating a great first principle or Absolute: the Tao, which precedes and informs all other beings in the universe. Since this Tao is basically indescribable, the author can only hint at its nature through the use of poetic epithets. While extolling the Tao, the author also describes the type of action and attitude which one must adopt to put oneself into harmony with its workings: an attitude of passivity, of yielding, of doing nothing that is forced, unnatural, or purposive. Specifically he suggests ways in which this quietistic attitude can be applied to the ruling of the state.

It is when one comes to the question of whom the book is addressing, of whom these injunctions are intended for, that interpretations differ. I am inclined to feel that it is a good deal more political than is generally realized, or than is brought out in most translations; that it is essentially a treatise on laissez-faire government, expressed in mystic and transcendental language, but expounding principles that are intended to be translated into specific political measures by the rulers of the time. I see it as the Taoist reply to the busy do-goodism of the Confucians and Mohists; an attack on the state planners, the empire builders, and the aggressive, grasping rulers of the Warring States period; and a plea for greater mercy and restraint in the exercise of political power. But this may indicate only that, with a text of such initial vagueness, each reader will discover in it only those ideas which interest him personally.[6] Certainly the *Lao Tzu* can be, and has been, interpreted to be much more than this; to be, in fact, not a theory of government but a creed for the Taoist sage who, as in the *Chuang Tzu,* is indifferent to and infinitely above mere political concerns. Like the *Book of Changes,* which it resembles in many ways, its brief, laconic utterances may be made to yield

---

[6] The philosopher Han Fei Tzu (see below, p. 175), in his comments on the *Lao Tzu* (*Han Fei Tzu,* secs. 20 and 21), certainly gives it a strongly political interpretation, but this again may reflect merely what he himself found, or wished to find, in the work.

up many meanings. And, unlike the oracular formulas of the *Changes,* the *Lao Tzu* has the great advantage of being couched in consciously poetic and arresting language. Thus, when one tires of attempting to make out its exact meaning, he may still read it with pleasure for its beautiful music and imagery.

The *Chuang Tzu*

The *Chuang Tzu,* a work in thirty-three chapters, was said to have been written by Chuang Chou, a philosopher whose dates are tentatively given as 369–286 B.C. It is divided into three sections: seven "inner chapters," fifteen "outer chapters," and eleven "miscellaneous chapters." The "inner chapters" may indeed be from the hand of Chuang Chou; they contain most of the basic ideas of the work and are in a vigorous, individual style. The remaining chapters for the most part expand and elaborate on these ideas; the style is more flowing and conventional, making them easier to read but less vivid and powerful.

The *Chuang Tzu* is unique in early Chinese literature for two reasons. One is that it is the only prose work of the ancient period which does not, at least in part, deal with questions of politics and statecraft. Chuang Tzu has little advice for the rulers of his time outside of the advice he has for all other men as well; unlike Confucius, Mencius, Mo Tzu, or the Legalist philosophers, he expounds no program for political reform. He is concerned only with the life and freedom of the individual.

Freedom is the central theme of the work—not political, social, or economic freedom, but spiritual freedom, freedom of the mind. While the Confucians labored to define virtue and social responsibility, the Mohists to abolish war and material want, and the Logicians to pin down the meanings of words, Chuang Tzu seeks to lift men's minds to a plane which is above all such, to him, petty and fallacious concepts. The popular distinctions between good and bad, right and wrong, are based upon narrow and purely relative viewpoints; the emotions of ordinary men spring from fear and misunderstanding; the words of daily life are powerless to describe the really important levels of experience. One must therefore transcend all these to gain true freedom. He must break away to another realm of thought and experience and unite himself with the Tao—the mystical working of the universe. When he has reached this realm of understanding, he will be indifferent to the values of the world. He may remain in society or he may withdraw and become a recluse. In either case his only concern will be his own freedom and integrity. The claims and ills of society as a whole will no longer touch him. Such is the uniquely apolitical philosophy of the *Chuang Tzu*.

The second thing which makes the *Chuang Tzu* unique is the remarkable wit and imagination with which this philosophy is expounded. Other works of Chinese history and philosophy abound in anecdotes that are obviously based on no more than myth or legend, but are always put forward in a solemn, pseudo-historical manner. The *Chuang Tzu*, on the contrary, deals in deliberate and unabashed fantasy. Sometimes the reader is introduced to gods, immortal spirits, or mythical creatures of fabulous size and nature; sometimes he is let in on the conversations of birds and insects; sometimes he is confronted with real historical figures, such as Confucius and his disciples, who are made to behave ridiculously or to express ideas outrageously at variance with their actual teachings. Nowhere else in early Chinese literature do we encounter such a wealth of satire, allegory, and poetic fancy. No single work of any other school of thought can approach the *Chuang Tzu* for sheer literary brilliance.

In keeping with the unconventional nature of his thought, Chuang Tzu's anecdotes and parables linger lovingly over everything that ordinary men regard as ugly, useless, or bizarre—

grotesquely deformed cripples, fierce bandits, maimed criminals, creatures of ungainly size and shape. His technique is seldom to argue or persuade, but to shock the reader into awareness of his own narrow conventionalism and coax him out of it with visions of the realm beyond, usually couched in the metaphor of a mystic, soaring journey through boundless space.

Chuang Tzu opens breath-taking vistas for the reader, though these are often rather cold and uninviting, since they are founded upon the rejection of ordinary human values and emotions. Certainly it would be difficult for all men to live by such a philosophy, and fortunately the Chinese have never tried. Nevertheless Taoism, and particularly the Taoism of the *Chuang Tzu,* has provided a useful complement to the doggedly commonsensical, this-worldly doctrines of the Confucians, an antidote to their often narrow and convention-ridden morality. The *Chuang Tzu* added a whole new dimension to Chinese thought, and a whole new world of wit and fantasy to Chinese literature. When Buddhism was introduced into China, it brought with it metaphysical doctrines more vast, elaborate, and systematic than anything Chuang Tzu ever dreamed of. But it possessed in its canon nothing to rival the literary sparkle and incisiveness of the *Chuang Tzu,* nor did it inspire any such work in China. The *Chuang Tzu,* along with the *Lao Tzu,* thus remains the most brilliant expressions of mystic thought in the Chinese language.

I would like to close this discussion of the *Chuang Tzu* with a few short selections. This is no easy task, however, since the work is of such charm that, unless one exercises firm restraint, he will quickly find himself quoting whole chapters. Instead of attempting to indicate the entire range of Chuang Tzu's ideas, I shall restrict myself to a few quotations illustrative of one of the most important themes of the work, Chuang Tzu's view of death, trusting that at the same time they will illustrate some of the literary qualities I have mentioned. All are from the "inner chapters," the most difficult section of the work. Because of the richness of Chuang Tzu's vocabulary, the unconventional nature of his anecdotes, and his fondness for leaping from one idea or image to another, the exact sense is not always easy to make out, and the text in places appears to be in faulty condition. In spite of these difficulties, however, the general meaning is clear enough.

How do I know that loving life is not a delusion? How do I know that in hating death I am not like a man who, having left home in his youth, has forgotten the way back?

Lady Li was the daughter of the border guard of Ai.[7] When she was first taken captive and brought to the state of Chin, she wept until her tears drenched the collar of her robe. But later when she went to live in the palace of the king, shared his couch with him, and tasted the delicious meats of his table, she wondered why she had ever wept. How do I know that the dead do not in the same way wonder why they ever longed for life? (*Chuang Tzu*, ch. 2.)

Master Ssu, Master Yü, Master Li, and Master Lai were all four talking together. "Who can look upon nonbeing as his head, on life as his back, and on death as his rump?" they said. "Who knows that life and death, existence and annihilation, are all parts of a single body? I will be his friend!"

The four men looked at each other and smiled. There was no disagreement in their hearts and so the four of them became friends.

All at once Master Yü fell ill. Master Ssu went to ask how he was. "Amazing!" exclaimed Master Yü. "The Creator is making me all crookedy like this! My back sticks up like a hunchback so that my vital organs are on the top of me. My chin is hidden down around my navel, my shoulders are up above my head, and my pigtail points at the sky. It must be due to some dislocation of the forces of the yin and the yang!"

Yet he seemed quite calm at heart and unconcerned. Dragging

[7] Presumably the same Lady Li, daughter of a barbarian chief, who figures in the selection from the *Kuo yü*, p. 69, above.

himself haltingly to the edge of a well, he looked at his reflection and cried, "My! my! So the Creator is making me all crookedy like this!"

"Do you resent it?" asked Master Ssu.

"Why no," replied Master Yü. "What is there to resent? If the process continues, perhaps in time he'll transform my left arm into a rooster. In that case I'll herald the dawn with my crowing. Or in time he may transform my right arm into a crossbow pellet and I'll shoot down an owl for roasting. Or perhaps he will even transform my buttocks into cartwheels. Then with my spirit for a horse, I'll climb up and go for a ride. What need will I ever have for a carriage again?

"I received life because the time had come; I will lose it because the order of things passes on. If only one will be content with this time and dwell in this order, then neither sorrow nor joy can touch him. In ancient times this was called the 'freeing of the bound.' Yet there are those who cannot free themselves, because they are bound by mere things. Creatures such as I can never win against Heaven. That's the way it has always been. What is there to resent?"

Suddenly Master Lai grew ill. Gasping for breath, he lay at the point of death. His wife and children gathered round in a circle and began to cry. Master Li, who had come to find out how he was, said to the wife and children, "Shoo! Get back! Don't disturb the process of change!"

Then he leaned against the doorway and talked to Master Lai. "How marvelous the Creator is!" he exclaimed. "What is he going to make out of you next? Where is he going to send you? Will he make you into a rat's liver? Will he make you into a bug's arm?"

"A child, obeying his father and mother, goes wherever he is told, east or west, south or north," said Master Lai. "And the yin and the yang—how much more are they to a man than father or mother! Now that they have brought me to the verge of death, if I should refuse to obey them, how perverse I would be! What fault is it of theirs? The Great Clod burdens me with form, labors me with life, eases me in old age, and rests me in death. So if I think well of my life, for the same reason I must think well of my death. When a skilled smith is casting metal, if the metal should leap up and cry,

'I insist upon being made into a famous sword like Mu-yeh of old!', he would surely regard it as very inauspicious metal indeed. In the same way, having had the audacity to take on human form once, if I should now cry, 'I don't want to be anything but a man! Nothing but a man!', the Creator would surely consider me a most inauspicious sort of person. So now I think of heaven and earth as a great furnace, and the Creator as a skilled smith. What place could he send me that would not be all right? I will go off to sleep peacefully, and then with a start I will wake up."

Master Sang-hu, Meng-tzu Fan, and Master Ch'in-chang, three friends, said to each other, "Who can join with others without joining with others? Who can do with others without doing with others? Who can climb up to heaven and revel in the mists, roam the infinite, and forget life forever and forever?" The three men looked at each other and smiled. There was no disagreement in their hearts and so they became friends.

After some time had passed without event, Master Sang-hu died. He had not yet been buried when Confucius, hearing of his death, sent his disciple Tzu-kung to assist at the funeral. When Tzu-kung arrived, he found one of the dead man's friends weaving frames for silkworms, while the other strummed a lute. Joining their voices, they sang this song:

> Ah, Sang-hu!
> Ah, Sang-hu!
> You have gone back to your true form,
> While we must remain as men, O!

Tzu-kung hastened forward and said, "May I be so bold as to ask what sort of ceremony this is—singing in the very presence of the corpse?"

The two men looked at each other and laughed. "What does this man know of the meaning of ceremony?" they said.

Tzu-kung returned and reported to Confucius what had happened. "What sort of men are they anyway?" he asked. "They pay no attention to proper behavior, disregard their personal appearance and, without so much as changing the expression on their faces, sing in the very presence of the corpse! I am at a loss to know what to call such conduct! What sort of men are they anyway?"

"Such men as they," replied Confucius, "roam beyond the border; men like myself roam within it. Beyond and within can never meet. It was stupid of me to send you to offer condolences. Even now they have joined with the Creator as men to roam in the single breath of heaven and earth. They look upon life as a swelling tumor, a protruding wen, and upon death as the draining of a sore or the bursting of a boil. To men such as these, how could there be any question of putting life first or death last? They borrow the forms of different creatures to house the same body. They forget liver and gall, cast aside ears and eyes, turning and revolving, ending and beginning again, knowing no final limit. Idly they wander beyond the dust of the world, they roam at will in the service of inaction. Why should they trouble themselves about the ceremonies of the vulgar world which are good only for filling the ears and eyes of the common herd?" (*Chuang Tzu,* ch. 6.)

This is not the place for a lengthy discussion of traditional Chinese attitudes toward death, but a few remarks may help to give some context to the views of Chuang Tzu quoted above. Judging from excavations of burial sites, the Chinese of the Yin or Shang dynasty (traditionally dated 1766–1123 B.C.) seem to have believed in some sort of life after death. They sacrificed little children at the graves of their rulers, presumably so that their spirits might rejuvenate the dead, and killed and buried human beings, dogs, and horses with the dead to give them added power or to attend them in the afterworld. This grisly custom of providing the ruler with "followers in death" was continued sporadically, as we have seen, until late Chou times.

The attitudes toward death expressed in Chou literature often seem confused and contradictory; no doubt they varied widely with different parts of the country and different social classes. Usually the spirits of the dead are pictured as going down into the earth, to some vague dwelling place called the Yellow Springs, where they maintain for a time a shadowy existence, like the shades of the Greek Hades, until eventually they fade away entirely; occasionally there seems also to be a second soul, or part of the soul, which ascends to the sky on death. Like the Greeks and Romans, the Chinese were deeply concerned that their dead receive a proper burial, and were horrified by disrespectful treatment of corpses. See, for example, *Tso chuan,* Duke Hsi 28th year, where the people of Ts'ao, besieged by the army of Chin, expose the corpses of the Chin dead on their city wall, and the Chin army, infuriated by this outrage, threatens to desecrate the graves of Ts'ao; or Duke Wen 3rd year, where Duke Mu of Ch'in stops in Chin to bury the remains of his soldiers who had fallen three years before at the battle of Yao. No doubt such actions were based partly on primitive fear of the dead, and indeed in the *Tso chuan* we occasionally meet with angry spirits who return to haunt the living. More often, however, the attitude expressed is one of uncertainty: one cannot say for sure whether the dead have any consciousness or not, as in *Kuo yü* ch. 9, *Wu yü*: "If the dead have no consciousness, then there is an end to the matter, but if they do . . .", a formula repeated in *Mo Tzu,* sec. 31, *Kuan Tzu,* sec. 32, and elsewhere in the literature of the period.[8]

This is essentially the attitude of the Confucian scholars, who refused to commit themselves on the question of whether the dead have consciousness; they insisted only that one must serve the dead with all the respect and piety (but not fear) one would show if one were sure that they had consciousness. Mo Tzu, on the other hand, attempted to uphold the earlier conviction that

[8] Compare the words of Pompey's wife in Lucan's *Pharsalia*: "But soon I shall pursue him [Pompey] through empty space and through the dark Underworld— if there is any such place." (Book 9, Robert Graves translation, Penguin Classics ed., p. 199.)

the dead had knowledge and power to reward or punish the living, using it in his teaching as a moral sanction.

Chuang Tzu, who obviously had no patience with the Confucian view, did not even deign to notice that of the Mohists. He wished men to rise above such distinctions as life and death and the emotional involvements which they engender, and in his eagerness to combat the conventional view, he is led into an almost morbid glorification of death, the cure to the sickness which is life. His view is completely new and without precedent in the literature before his time.

In a description of the collapse of traditional values which accompanied the break-up of the Old Kingdom in Egypt, a poetic work of the period is quoted:

> Death (stands) before me today
>   (Like) the recovery of a sick man,
>   Like going out-doors (again) after being confined.
>
> Death (stands) before me today
>   Like the fragrance of myrrh,
>   Like sitting under a shade on a breezy day.
>
> Death (stands) before me today
>   As a man longs to see his house,
>   After he has spent many years held in captivity.[9]

The verbal resemblance between this and Chuang Tzu's pronouncements is obvious and striking, yet there is one great difference which separates the two views. The Egyptian poet craves death because he is convinced that it will carry him to another world where he will live more happily and fully than he can in this one; Chuang Tzu's dead, far from moving on to a better world, cease to exist as entities, melted down in the great furnace

---

[9] *The Intellectual Adventure of Ancient Man,* by Henri Frankfort *et al.* (Univ. of Chicago Press, 1946), p. 103.

of the Creator. The house which the Egyptian longs to see is essentially like the one he dwells in on earth, only incomparably finer; the Taoist house—to "return to one's original home" is a standard Taoist expression for death—is nature itself, which swallows up the identity and material of the dead man and fashions something else out of it. It is one thing to despair of life, as the Egyptian does, but another to face with equanimity the prospect of annihilation. The Taoists faced it not only with equanimity, but, as Waley says, with "a lyrical, almost ecstatic acceptance" (*The Way and Its Power*, p. 54). They delighted in the prospect of becoming a rat's liver or a bug's arm, because they were convinced that no state of being is more precious or desirable than any other. This is one of the most remarkable aspects of the Taoist writings, setting them off sharply from the rest of early Chinese literature, and for that reason I have chosen to illustrate it above.

The *Lieh Tzu*

The *Lieh Tzu*, a Taoist work in eight chapters, has traditionally been attributed to a philosopher named Lieh Yü-k'ou (*c*. 450–375 B.C.). This attribution probably merits no more serious consideration than similar ones concerning other philosophical works of the late Chou. The work appears to be later than the *Chuang Tzu*, from which it borrows not only its ideas and form, but many passages. The style is simpler and more conventional than that of the "inner chapters" of the *Chuang Tzu*, but there is much of the same wit and fondness for fantasy. The ideas, expressed usually in the form of anecdotes, differ little from those of the *Chuang Tzu*, except that chapter 7, which supposedly represents the view of the philosopher Yang Chu, expounds a hedonistic doctrine not typical of Taoism as a whole. In addition the *Lieh Tzu* seems to be less original and incisive than the

Chuang Tzu, and at the same time to possess a certain melancholy and tenderness which the *Chuang Tzu* lacks, though this is no more than a personal impression.

Chinese scholars have long eyed the *Lieh Tzu* with suspicion, and in recent years it has become customary to regard it as a forgery of the third or fourth centuries A.D. Certainly it cannot all be a forgery, since over half of the text is duplicated in genuine works of the earlier period. Part of the reason for the suspicion which surrounds it is the presence of a few scattered passages which suggest Buddhist influence. There seems to be little doubt that these passages are indeed late—one of them appears to have been taken from a collection of Indian Buddhist tales translated into Chinese in A.D. 285—but their presence can hardly brand the whole work as a forgery. Probably they were inserted into the text sometime before its redaction around the middle of the fourth century.[10] With the exception of such passages, the work as a whole, both in the ideas which it expounds and in its lively and imaginative manner of presentation, shows a close affinity with the *Lao Tzu* and the *Chuang Tzu* and ranks with them as a masterpiece of Taoist literature.

I shall close with two anecdotes from the *Lieh Tzu,* illustrating the Taoist concept of the fatuity of conventional emotions and values. It is interesting to note that the second anecdote, though it is intended to make us laugh at the folly of the deceived man, comes perilously near to enlisting our sympathies on his side.

A man named Master Hua of Yang-li in Sung, having reached middle age, began to suffer from forgetfulness. If he acquired something in the morning, he would forget about it by evening; if he gave something away in the evening, he would forget it by morning. Out on the street he forgot to walk; in a room he forgot to sit down. At one moment he had no idea what he was going to do next; in

---

[10] See E. Zücher, *The Buddhist Conquest of China* (Sinica Leidensia series, Vol. XI, Leiden, 1959), pp. 274–76; see also A. C. Graham, "The Date and Composition of Liehtzyy," *Asia Major,* VIII (No. 2, 1961), 139–98.

the next moment he would have forgotten what he had done the moment before.

His family was very upset and called in a diviner to see if he could find out what was wrong, but the diviner was unable to discover anything. They called in a sorcerer to see if prayers would help, but they had no effect. They sent for a doctor to treat him, but it was useless.

There was a Confucian scholar of Lu, however, who let it be known that he could cure the man. Master Hua's wife and children offered half their possessions if he would give them a remedy. The Confucian said, "This is not a matter which can be handled by divination, influenced by prayer, or treated with medicine. I will try to change his heart and alter his way of thinking, and perhaps he will get well."

As an experiment, he tried stripping Master Hua naked to see if he would ask for clothes, starving him to see if he would ask for food, and putting him in a dark place to see if he would try to get to the light. "The disease can be cured!" he announced to the family with delight. "But my remedies are handed down in secret from generation to generation and must not be divulged to others. Let me try dismissing everyone else and staying in a room alone with him for seven days."

The family consented, and as a result, although no one knew what measures the Confucian took, Master Hua's illness, which had been growing steadily worse for years, was completely dispelled in one morning.

When Master Hua came to his senses again, he was furious. He berated his wife, railed at his children, and, seizing a spear, drove the Confucian from the house. The people of Sung rushed forward to restrain him, asking why he was behaving in this way.

"Formerly," said Master Hua, "I had forgotten everything. In a state of wonderful vastness, I wasn't even conscious of whether heaven and earth existed or not. Now suddenly I have regained awareness, and all the gains and losses, all the hits and misses, all the joys and sorrows, loves and hates of the past thirty or forty years have come swarming in upon me to plague me with their coils. I am terrified to think that in the future too these emotions will distract my heart like this. If I could only regain a moment of my former forgetfulness!"

Tzu-kung heard of the incident and, thinking it very strange, reported it to Confucius. "This is not the sort of thing you would understand," said Confucius, and then, turning to Yen Hui, he told him to make a note of it.

Once there was a man who had been born in the state of Yen, in the far north, but brought up in Ch'u in the south. When he grew old, he determined to return to his native land. As he was passing through the state of Chin, one of his traveling companions decided to play a joke on him. Pointing to a city, he said, "This is the capital of Yen!"

The man immediately assumed a solemn expression.

Pointing to a shrine, the fellow traveler said, "This is the shrine of your native village!"

The man gave a deep sigh.

Pointing to some cottages, he said, "These are the homes of your ancestors!"

The man burst into tears.

Finally, pointing to some mounds of earth, he said, "And these are your ancestors' graves!"

With this the man began to weep uncontrollably.

His companion roared with laughter. "I was just fooling you," he said. "This is only the state of Chin!"

The man was overwhelmed with shame, and when he finally did reach Yen and saw the real cities and shrines of Yen and the real houses and graves of his ancestors, he could not feel as deeply moved by the sight as he had felt before. (*Lieh Tzu,* ch. 3.)

THE LEGALIST WRITINGS

China in the fourth and third centuries B.C. was undergoing a painful process of social and political change. The spread of the use of iron had revolutionized agricultural and warfare techniques; the growth of the merchant class, the increasing affluence of urban life, and the diffusion of learning were breaking down the rigidity of the old social order. The Chou court no longer retained any semblance of power and prestige, and China was divided among a handful of states whose boundaries and spheres of influence fluctuated wildly in the incessant wars and diplomatic intrigues. If the literature of the period is any indication, the problem of political survival and advancement was uppermost in men's minds.

The philosophical schools of the time, rising in response to this problem, offered their panaceas: the Mohists a call for thrift, universal love, and nonaggression; the Confucians a program of social reform based upon education and the moral suasion of the ruler; the Taoists, in so far as they interested themselves in political matters, a doctrine of laissez-faire that they hoped would somehow bring about a return to the simple life of antiquity.

Such proposals, however, proved to have little attraction for most of the rulers of the day, who were seeking hardheaded, practical means by which they might strengthen the economic and military power of their domains and further their private interests. It was not long, therefore, before another political doctrine began to take shape which catered more directly to their needs, the doctrine known in the history of Chinese thought as *fa-chia,* the Legalist or Realist school.

The *Shang-chün shu* or *Book of Lord Shang*

The *Book of Lord Shang,* in twenty-four short sections, has been attributed to a statesman named Wei Yang or Kung-sun Yang (d. 338 B.C.), who served as adviser to Duke Hsiao of the state of Ch'in and was enfeoffed with the title of Lord Shang. Although the policies advocated may in fact be those of the historical Lord Shang, the book itself was probably put together some years after his death. It contains a few dialogues between Lord Shang and Duke Hsiao, but most of it is in essay form. The style is simple, straightforward, and undistinguished.

The sole concern of the book is the condition of the state, how to keep it strong, how to make it stronger. To achieve this end, says Lord Shang, the ruler must do everything he can to encourage agriculture and aggressive warfare, the two keys to prosperity and power. An elaborate and rigidly enforced system of rewards and punishments, not education or guidance, will insure the cooperation of the people, while trade, learning, art, anything that may distract their energies from the pursuit of these goals are to be suppressed. The ruler must lay aside all moral scruples, for, as Lord Shang assures us, "mercy and benevolence are the mother of error" (*Shang-chün shu,* sec. 5).

I shall not elaborate this description, since the twentieth-century reader is familiar enough with totalitarianism to know what this type of thinking implies. On the whole, the *Book of Lord Shang* is as grim as the doctrine it preaches, pounding over and over at the basic principles of its system, heavy and repetitious, though often capable of gripping the reader with a kind of horrid fascination. The rulers of the time, particularly those of the state of Ch'in, may have welcomed its ideas, but they could hardly have been captivated by so blatant and heavy-handed a presentation of them, nor would they have dared openly to espouse a work that represented such an affront to traditional morality. The First Emperor of the Ch'in, who led his state to supreme power and united China under one rule, made use of many of the ideas and policies suggested by Lord Shang. But when he set up steles here and there about the country extolling his achievements, though he emphasized the law, order, and uniformity which his rule had brought to China, he did not neglect to praise himself in older and more conventional terms as a "sage ruler of benevolence and righteousness . . . who cares for and pities the common people" (*Shih chi* 6).

The *Han Fei Tzu*

Essentially the same philosophy of government is stated, less harshly and in far more engaging form, in a longer work, the *Han Fei Tzu* in fifty-five sections. A large part of it is undoubtedly from the hand of Han Fei Tzu himself, a highly educated thinker, writer, and would-be statesman, who attracted the attention of the king of Ch'in but was immediately forced by a political rival to commit suicide in 233 B.C. Some sections, however, may be by later writers of the Legalist school.

The *Han Fei Tzu* dates from the same period as the *Chan-kuo ts'e* or *Intrigues of the Warring States*. The two works share many of the same anecdotes and are marked by the same air of urbanity, wit, and pervading cynicism. Both show a keen interest in rhetoric, the *Han Fei Tzu* actually containing an essay devoted to the subject of persuasive speaking.

The *Han Fei Tzu*, however one reacts to the ideas expressed, is almost always a delight to read. Lucidly and cogently argued, it is couched in a clear, balanced, yet seldom monotonous style, and enlivened by ancedotes and parables which, though they do not match those of the *Chuang Tzu* in originality, are often witty and incisive. I shall give two examples, the first an apology for the *Mo Tzu*, which shows the *Han Fei Tzu*'s interest in rhetoric and questions of style, the second a biting attack on the Confucian scholars and their intellectual mud pies. Only a lengthy excerpt could do justice to the brilliance of Han Fei Tzu's argumentative writing, but these passages may suggest some of the discursive charm of his work.

The king of Ch'u remarked to T'ien Chiu, a follower of the Mohist school, "Mo Tzu was an eminent scholar and I approve of his actions. But his words are often lacking in eloquence. Why is that?"

T'ien Chiu replied, "In Ch'u there was once a man who sold pearls to the people of Cheng. He made cases of magnolia wood and little boxes for the pearls, fashioned of fragrant laurel and pepperwood, tied with strands of pearls and jade, decorated with carnelians, and trimmed with kingfisher feathers. The people of Cheng bought the boxes but returned the pearls. No one can say he wasn't good at selling boxes, but he can hardly be said to have been good at peddling pearls. Speakers these days all use rhetorical flourishes and fine phrases in their discourses. The rulers take note of their style but forget the usefulness of their words. In his teachings, Mo Tzu related the Way of the former kings and discussed the sayings of the sages, proclaiming them to men. He was afraid that if he used a lot of fancy rhetoric men would be enchanted by the style but forget the substance of his words. If he had allowed the style to obscure the usefulness of what he was saying, he would have been the same as the pearl-peddler of Ch'u. Therefore his words are often lacking in eloquence." (*Han Fei Tzu,* sec. 32.)

When little children play house together, they use dirt for rice, mud for soup, and bits of wood for slices of meat. But when sundown comes they all have to go home to eat supper. Dirt rice and mud soup are all right to play with, but they are no good to eat. Those who preach and praise the ways of high antiquity do so with much eloquence but little sincerity. They can discourse on the benevolence and righteousness of the former kings but they cannot put the country on its feet again. Their doctrines are all right to play with too, but they cannot be used in governing. (*Ibid.*)

Han Fei Tzu is said to have studied for a while under the Confucian thinker Hsün Tzu, and many of his principles, as well as the insistence with which he reiterates ideas that strike Western readers as too commonplace to need comment, cannot be understood without reference to the Confucianism of his day. Few readers today would question his assertion that the nation should be governed by detailed laws, impartially applied and published and made known to the people at large. Yet this assertion flies in the face of the Confucian doctrine that it is the moral suasion and example of the ruler and his ministers, rather than a fixed code of laws, that insures order in the state. (See *Tso chuan,* Duke Chao 6th year, where a statesman of Chin criticizes the people of Cheng for casting tripods with the criminal code of the state inscribed on them, insisting that such action will only incite the people's minds to contentiousness and disrespect for their rulers.) Again, his bitter condemnation of men who undertake private vendettas seems ordinary enough, but we should recall before passing over it too lightly the old Confucian injunction that "a man must not dwell under the same sky with his father's enemy!" (*Li chi,* sec. 1, *Ch'ü li* A.)

When Confucianism became the official philosophy of the Han state, it was forced to abandon some of its outmoded ideas, such as the ideal of private revenge, and compromise to some extent with Legalist policies, which were in some ways much better adapted to the ruling of a vast empire. From that time until the present day in China, Confucian and Legalist thought have remained uneasy bedfellows, the former providing a lofty and impressive theory of rule, the latter more often dictating the actual policies of government.

But though the two doctrines have often been combined in practice, they remain utterly unreconcilable on the theoretical level. Much of the *Han Fei Tzu* is devoted to attacks on Confucian concepts; much of later Confucian writing, particularly during the Han, is given up to attacks on Legalism. Yet though the two schools seem to be speaking a common language in their attacks and rebuttals, the meaning and value which they attach to such key words as "law," "virtue," or "benevolence" are in fact so different that their arguments never so much as make contact, but simply whirl about in space like fiercely opposing windmills. Thus, for example, the *Han Fei Tzu,* in a passage calling for severer penal laws, urges the ruler to cast aside benevolence in his government because it leads to nothing more than a coddling of the people that is eventually injurious to both them and the state (sec. 46). No true Confucian, however, could be expected even to grasp the meaning of this assertion, since in Confucian terminology benevolence is a goal in itself, the pursuit of which transcends all demands of the state and society at large. So with all the other countless opposing dicta of the two schools.

The Confucians believed that the life of a dynasty was dependent upon the personal virtue of the ruler and his ministers, and all their literature implies that they assumed no ruling house could produce an unbroken succession of virtuous heirs for more than three or four centuries at a time: hence the periodic changes of dynasty. The Legalists maintained, on the contrary, that with a proper set of laws regulating the state, the personality of the ruler would cease to be of importance, and they therefore optimistically foresaw dynasties which would endure indefinitely. When the king of Ch'in, a believer in Legalist principles, conquered all of China and set himself up as supreme ruler, he took the title of First Emperor, announcing that his heirs would be called Second Emperor, Third Emperor, "and so on endlessly for a thousand or ten thousand generations" (*Shih chi* ch. 6). In 207 B.C., two years after his death, his successor, the Second Emperor, was forced by a eunuch official to commit suicide, and a month or so later the dynasty came to an end. No one in China ever forgot this fact, and it explains why, though Legalist ideas have remained of vital importance in Chinese political theory and practice up to the present day, self-proclaimed Legalist literature ends with the *Han Fei Tzu.*

THE ECLECTIC WRITINGS

I shall close this section on the philosophical writings with a discussion of a number of works which, because of the special or heterogeneous nature of their contents, are not closely allied to any of the particular schools of philosophy, though they have often been assigned to one or another.

The *Kuan Tzu*

The work called the *Kuan Tzu* takes its name from Kuan Chung or Kuan I-wu, a statesman who died in the middle of the seventh century B.C. He is mentioned in the *Tso chuan*, where he is said to have become minister to Duke Huan of Ch'i and, by his astute advice, enabled Duke Huan to achieve a position of leadership among the feudal lords of his time. The work itself is a great hodgepodge of texts of very disparate contents, style, and date. How or why they all happened to end up together in one book is not known. The work originally consisted of eighty-six sections, of which ten are now lost. Considering the dull and hackneyed content of many of the extant sections, it is remarkable that this much of the work has survived.

The various sections which make up the work may be divided into several categories on the basis of their contents. First, and perhaps most interesting and valuable, are the sections on Kuan Tzu and Duke Huan. Some of these are in the form of historical narratives which borrow heavily from the *Tso chuan*, or from the mass of history and legend upon which the *Tso* itself is based. Others are dialogues in which Kuan Tzu advises the duke to adopt some particular political or economic policy. Kuan Tzu's aim is to strengthen the power of the state of Ch'i, and the measures he proposes are usually typically Legalist in nature, including such cutthroat economic practices as deliberately creating a demand for a particular article produced in a neighboring state and then, when the neighbor has geared its economy to the production of that article, suddenly cutting off the demand and utilizing the resulting economic chaos to further one's own interests. These chapters contain a good deal of invaluable information on early Chinese economic life and thought, though the difficult terminology employed, the faulty state of the text in many places, and the uncertainty of its date make the data difficult to utilize.

Another small group of texts attempts to describe the activities appropriate to the government in each season of the year. The idea of such a calendar of religious, educational, and political activities to be carried out by the government was a common one in late Chou times and resulted eventually in the detailed "monthly ordinances" type of text found in the *Lü shih ch'un-ch'iu*, the *Huai-nan Tzu*, and the *Li chi*. These in the *Kuan Tzu*, arranged not by months but by seasons, seem to represent earlier and cruder treatments of the subject.

Other sections of the work deal with principles of government or ideal systems of political and social organization. Some of these are strongly Legalist in flavor, some abound in Confucian concepts, and others are clearly Taoist in inspiration. When these sections deign to deal with concrete matters—types of charitable institutions to be set up by the government, village organization, water control, forestration, what types of grain to grow in what soils—they are very interesting and valuable, though difficult enough. More often, however, they confine themselves to purely abstract statements of principles, phrased in a monotonously formal and repetitious style: a handful of late Chou political platitudes expressed in a hundred drab and uninspired ways.

Finally there are a few sections which do not seem to fall into any of these categories. One is section 39, a little Taoist essay that on the surface seems to be extolling the metaphysical properties of water, jade, etc., but is perhaps in fact dealing in some sort of sexual symbolism. Another is section 59, "The Duties of a Student," a very brief but vivid and concrete description of how to behave in school ("If there is something you are in doubt about, raise your hand and ask a question"), how to wait on one's teacher at meals, clean the dormitory rooms, tend the torches at night, etc.—a gem of pedagogical, or rather pupillary, literature.

It is obviously impossible to select a quotation that will be representative of such a conglomeration of texts. The selection which follows, a translation of section 54 (with a few minor cuts to avoid repetition), represents the type of specific information which makes the *Kuan Tzu* valuable. Confucian writers are forever enjoining the ruler in vague terms to "care for the aged and pity the weak and orphaned." Here for once we have a concrete, detailed proposal on how this lofty ideal may be translated into action. We have no idea whether any early Chinese ruler ever attempted such an ambitious program of social aid. The fact that such a program is outlined, however, in a work which we may suppose dates largely, if not entirely, from late Chou or Ch'in times, sheds important light, I believe, on the development of Chinese political institutions and ideals.

TAKING OVER THE RULE OF THE STATE

On entering the capital and taking over the government, a new ruler shall, after forty days, take steps to set up the Nine Missions of Mercy. These are: (1) honoring the aged; (2) taking pity on the young; (3) aiding the orphaned; (4) caring for the disabled; (5) bringing together the single; (6) inquiring about the sick; (7) helping the poor; (8) assisting the needy; (9) maintaining sacrifices that would otherwise come to an end.

Honoring the aged. In all cities throughout the country, officials shall be appointed to look out for the aged. Persons over seventy shall have one son exempted from government service and shall receive a gift of meat every three months. Those over eighty shall have two sons exempted and receive meat every month. Those over ninety shall have their entire family exempted and receive meat and wine every day. The young men of their families shall be urged to feed them the finest food, inquire what they wish to eat, and make every effort to please their tastes. When they die, the authorities shall provide inner and outer coffins for them. This is called honoring the aged.

Taking pity on the young. In all cities throughout the country officials shall be appointed to look out for the young. It often happens that the people, in bearing children, find themselves burdened with more infants than they are able to care for. In families with three little children the wife shall be exempted from government taxes. In families with four the entire family shall be exempted. In families with five the goverment shall provide a nursemaid and food for two persons. This shall continue until the children are old enough to take care of themselves.

Aiding the orphaned. In all cities throughout the country officials shall be appointed to look out for orphans. People often die and leave behind little children who, having no parents to look after them, are unable to live alone and must be taken in by friends of the family or people of the village. Families taking care of one orphan shall have one son exempted from government service. Those taking care of two shall have two sons exempted; those taking care of three shall have their entire family exempted. The officials in charge of orphans shall visit the families from time to time to determine if the orphans are getting proper food and clothing, see whether they are plump or skinny, and look out for their needs.

Caring for the disabled. In all cities officials shall be appointed to look out for the disabled. Those who are deaf, blind, dumb, lame, partially paralyzed, or have deformed hands cannot make a living for themselves. The authorities shall gather such persons together and house them in institutions for the disabled, providing them with food and clothing until their death.

Bringing together the single. In all cities officials shall be appointed to act as matchmakers. Men without wives are called bachelors or widowers; women without husbands are called spinsters or widows. The officials shall bring the bachelors and spinsters together and unite them, giving them land and houses to live in. Only after three years shall they be required to render government service.

Inquiring about the sick. In all cities officials shall be appointed to look out for the sick. When a person is sick, the official charged with looking out for the sick shall inquire about his illness in the name of the authorities. In the case of persons over ninety, inquiry shall be made every day; for persons over eighty, every other day; for persons over seventy, every third day; for all others, every fifth day. If the illness is critical, this shall be reported and the head of the office shall call on the sick man in person. The officials in charge of such affairs shall make it their business to travel throughout the country inquiring about the sick.

Helping the poor. In all cities officials shall be appointed to help the poor. If there are poor men and women who have no place to live, or poor visitors from other states who have run out of provisions, the people living in the same village who report the fact to the authorities shall be rewarded and those who fail to report it shall be punished.

Assisting the needy. When the year is bad, the crops are poor, and the people are suffering from disease or plague so that many of them die, the ordinary penalties for misconduct shall be eased, offenses pardoned, and grain distributed to feed the sufferers.

Maintaining sacrifices that would otherwise come to an end. When men die in government service or in battle, some friend or acquaintance of theirs shall be designated to receive funds from the authorities in order to perform sacrifices to their spirits.[11]

The *Yen Tzu ch'un-ch'iu*

The *Yen Tzu ch'un-ch'iu* or *Spring and Autumn of Master Yen*, in eight chapters, consists of anecdotes about the life and policies of Yen Ying, a contemporary of Confucius who served as adviser to Dukes Ling, Chuang, and Ching of the state of Ch'i. Because Yen Ying lived later than Kuan Chung (according to *Shih chi* 32, he died in 500 B.C.), I have chosen to treat the work after the *Kuan Tzu*, though there is no evidence of when either work was compiled or which took form first.

Like Kuan Chung, Yen Ying figures in the *Tso chuan*, being noted from early times for his frugal ways, and frugality is one of the principal themes of the anecdotes which make up the *Yen*

---

[11] The assumption is that the deceased have left no families that could carry on this important function.

Tzu ch'un-ch'iu. The other main theme is the importance of selecting worthy men and employing them in the government. These are standard Mohist principles, and much of the material in the *Yen Tzu ch'un-ch'iu* may well be of Mohist inspiration. The last chapter, which consists of anecdotes specifically attacking Confucius and the Confucian fondness for lengthy and elaborate mourning practices and musical performances, is almost certainly the work of Mohist writers.

Most of the anecdotes are in the form of admonitions by Yen Tzu to his sovereign, Duke Ching. The duke is pictured as being inordinately fond of luxurious and riotous living, and is egged on in his pursuit of sensual pleasure by two stock "evil advisers," Liang Ch'iu-chü and I K'uan. In addition he has an unhealthy interest in supernatural happenings and portents. Yen Tzu, in anecdote after anecdote, explains why such tastes are unbecoming in a ruler and injurious to the people, often dramatically threatening to resign, leave the court, or submit to execution if his censures are not heeded. Almost invariably the duke admits his folly and agrees to reform. Yet in the following anecdote we find him right back at his old mischief.

Much of the material is taken from the *Tso chuan,* and the authors have obviously been at pains to give the anecdotes a convincingly "historical" air—which is probably the reason for the words "Spring and Autumn" in the title. Yet their efforts are defeated by the stereotyped nature of the anecdotes, the pious but hardly convincing arguments which Yen Tzu employs, and the improbable alacrity with which the duke capitulates to them. The reader is expected, of course, to admire Yen Tzu for the sincerity and frankness with which he admonishes the ruler, heedless of the danger to himself. Actually one finds one's sympathies shifting quickly to the duke, who is not only chastised for the usual royal failings, such as undue fondness for wine, women, and hunts, but is not even permitted to wear fancy clothes, furs, or decorated shoes, or to enjoy his gardens, lakes, palaces, or musical performances without the ubiquitous carpings of his chief minister. Surely only the dour Mohists would have thought of making life so difficult for a ruler.

Some of the anecdotes picture Yen Tzu in conversation with other men or acting as foreign representative of his state, and we get glimpses of a wry sense of humor, for instance, when Yen Tzu, sent as envoy to the court of Ch'u, is asked by the king of Ch'u if Ch'i has no worthier man to employ as its envoy, and Yen Tzu replies that it is the policy of Ch'i to send worthy envoys only to the courts of worthy rulers.

The *Yen Tzu ch'un-ch'iu* has sometimes been cited as the earliest example of Chinese biography. Certainly it contains much biographical or pseudobiographical information on Yen Ying, though the material is not in most cases even arranged in chronological order. But one cannot believe that the authors or compilers of these anecdotes had any interest in Yen Tzu outside of the doctrines which he is made to preach. The anecdote form is simply a literary device, rather crudely and naïvely employed, to give the doctrines a setting. As one cannot conceive of a ruler possessed of so many failings as Duke Ching and yet so amenable to reprimand, so one cannot for a moment believe in a man like Yen Tzu who could spend his life mouthing these pious platitudes in the face of continual disappointment. It is not until the *Shih chi,* where the emphasis shifts from doctrine to the actual personality of the individual, that we encounter true biography in Chinese literature.

The following is an example of one of the less stereotyped anecdotes concerning Yen Tzu and the duke, a rare treatment of the theme of conjugal devotion.

Duke Ching had a favorite daughter whom he wished to give in marriage to Yen Tzu. Accordingly he went to a feast at Yen Tzu's house and, when the drinking had reached its height, glanced at Yen Tzu's wife and asked, "Is that your wife?"

"It is," replied Yen Tzu.

"My, how old and ugly she is!" exclaimed the duke. "I happen to have a young and attractive daughter. I beg to present her to you to complete your household."

Yen Tzu respectfully moved off his mat onto the floor and replied, "My wife is indeed old and ugly, as you see, for she has lived with me a long time. But I have known her when she was young and beautiful. Moreover, it is natural for people, while they are young and in their prime, to take thought for their old age, and while they are still attractive, to provide for the time when they will be ugly. She made such provisions by entrusting herself to me, and I accepted her. Now though you wish to bestow this honor upon me, My Lord, surely you would not force me to turn against her in her old age!"

Bowing twice, he declined the duke's offer. (Ch. 6, no. 24.)

The *Lü shih ch'un-ch'iu*

Another work which bears the title "Spring and Autumn," though in content it more closely resembles the *Kuan Tzu,* is the *Lü shih ch'un-ch'iu* or *Spring and Autumn of Mr. Lü*. It was said to have been compiled by scholars working under the patronage of Lü Pu-wei (d. 235 B.C.), a merchant turned statesman who served as minister to the ruler who became First Emperor of the Ch'in dynasty.

The book is interesting first of all because it is the earliest work in Chinese literature whose form is obviously intended to convey some meaning. It is divided into three large sections, called Prescriptions, Considerations, and Discussions, and representing the trinity of heaven, earth, and man. The first section is divided into twelve chapters, each beginning with a description of one month of the year and the activities of the government appropriate to it. Each of the twelve chapters is further divided into five smaller sections. The Considerations consist of eight chapters divided into eight smaller sections, the number eight being symbolic of earth; while the Discussions are made up of six chapters with six smaller sections, six being symbolic of man. In form, therefore, the work suggests that it is a compendium of knowledge embracing the celestial, natural, and human worlds. Except for the sections on the twelve months, however, the contents seem to have little or no relation to this elaborate formal structure. All of the smaller sections within one chapter may deal with a single subject—scholarship, music, warfare, funerals, etc. —but there appears to be no particular reason for the selection of subjects or the order in which they are treated.

Most of the chapters deal with political problems. One short section gives some fairly specific information on agriculture, but on the whole the work is concerned with general principles rather than specific details of the subjects treated. Like so much of late Chou literature, it devotes considerable space to the question of how to judge men's abilities, how to select able men for government service, how to avoid being deceived by flatterers, and similar questions of vital concern to the rulers of the time. The philosophical outlook varies with the different chapters, and there seems to have been no effort by the compilers to avoid inconsistencies. On the whole the chapters are strongly Confucian or Mohist in tone, though there are occasional Taoistic sections, some perhaps the work of the egoist philosopher Yang Chu, whose writings were long believed to be lost.[12] Surprisingly enough, since the work was supposedly compiled under the auspices of the prime minister of Ch'in, Legalist ideas are scarcely represented at all, and one section (chap. 19, sec. 3, *Shang te*), specifically attacks the Legalist concept of government by harsh laws and rich rewards.

[12] The sections identified by modern scholars as excerpts from the lost *Yang Chu* are ch. 1, secs. 2, 3, 7, and 8.

The *Lü shih ch'un-ch'iu* displays little originality; with the exception of a few legends not preserved elsewhere, it is made up almost entirely of ideas and anecdotes borrowed from earlier works, though among such compilations of earlier material it is perhaps the most readable. Like other works of this period, it is written in a clear, dignified style, marked by wit and sophistication. The following quotation, while illustrating these qualities, at the same time shows the critical spirit with which scholars of the time were beginning to eye the legends of the past.

EXAMINING TRADITIONS

One must be critical when dealing with words. When a story has been passed along from one person to another a number of times, white often turns into black and black becomes white. A dog resembles a baboon, a baboon resembles an ape, and an ape resembles a man, but a man is a long way from a dog. This is just how fools are led into serious error. If people stop to consider what they hear, they will win good fortune; but if they fail to do so, it would be better that they didn't hear anything at all. . . .

Duke Ai of Lu asked Confucius, "Is it true that the Music Master K'uei had only one leg?"

Confucius replied, "In ancient times Emperor Shun wanted to employ music to spread his virtue throughout the world. He therefore ordered Chung Li to select K'uei from among the common people and present him at court, where Shun appointed him music master. K'uei corrected the six pitch pipes, harmonized the five tones, and opened up the eight winds, and the whole world was filled with admiration. Shun said, 'Music is the soul of heaven and earth and the regulator of gain and loss. Therefore only a sage is capable of ordering it. Harmony is the basis of music. K'uei has been able to bring harmony to music and thereby pacify the world!' Chung Li then wanted to look about for other men like K'uei to employ, but Emperor Shun said, 'With a man like K'uei, one is enough!' Hence the phrase 'K'uei—one is enough.' It does not mean that he had only 'one leg!' " [13]

[13] The word *tsu* means both "leg" and "enough"; hence the phrase can be interpreted as "K'uei one enough" or "K'uei one leg."

The Ting family of Sung had no well in their house, but had to go outside to draw water, so that one member of the family was kept busy every day going out to fetch it. Later, when they dug a well within the grounds, they told someone, "We dug a well and got a man." The person then went and told the story to someone else: "The Ting family dug a well and got a man!" Presently everyone in the state was talking about it and it even came to the ears of the ruler. The ruler of Sung sent someone to ask the Ting family if the story was true. "What we meant," they explained, "was that we saved the services of one man by digging a well. We didn't mean we actually got a man out of the well!" If people are going to go about telling stories like this, it would be better to have no stories at all.

When Confucius' disciple Tzu-hsia was on his way to Chin, he passed through the state of Wei. Someone was reading from the records of the court historian and remarked, "It says here that the Chin army and three pigs crossed the Yellow River."

"That can't be right," said Tzu-hsia. "Three pigs must be a mistake for the date *chi-hai*. The character for 'three' looks like the character for *chi*, and 'pig' and *hai* are very much alike." When he got to Chin and asked about it, he found that the correct reading was in fact: "The Chin army on the day *chi-hai* crossed the Yellow River."

Words often seem to be wrong when they are actually right, and often seem to be right when they are actually wrong. Thus one must distinguish between what is really right and really wrong. A sage is very careful to do so. And how does one go about being careful? Only if one examines what he hears in the light of the logic of things and the common sense of human affairs will he get at the truth. (*Lü shih ch'un-ch'iu*, ch. 22, sec. 6, *Ch'a chuan.*)

The *Huai-nan Tzu*

Similar to the *Lü shih ch'un-ch'iu* in many ways is the *Huai-nan Tzu*, a work in twenty-one sections compiled by scholars at the court of Liu An (d. 122 B.C.), king of Huai-nan and grandson of the founder of the Han dynasty. Like the *Lü shih ch'un-ch'iu*, it is an eclectic work covering a variety of topics, and contains the same month by month almanac of government activities found in the *Lü shih ch'un-ch'iu* and the *Li chi*. The emphasis, however, is strongly on Taoist teachings. Many ideas, terms, and anecdotes are borrowed from the *Chuang Tzu* and *Lao Tzu,* and the work is therefore valuable as an exposition of early Han Taoism. One of its few original contributions is a brief description of the creation of the universe out of a primal state of emptiness and "unwrought simplicity." The mystical, poetic language of Taoism, so effective in a short work like the *Lao Tzu,* often tends to sound merely turgid and obscure when extended over long passages, and the *Huai-nan Tzu* does not always escape this defect. Usually, however, it manages to redeem itself by the insertion of some lively anecdote or legend, which serves to bring the thought into focus and saves the reader from drowning in generalities.

The following anecdote, one of the few that does not seem to have been culled from earlier works, is taken from a chapter of anecdotes (Ch. 12) arranged so as to function as glosses on passages in the *Lao Tzu.*

The Ch'u general Tzu-fa liked to search for men with unusual talents. In the state of Ch'u there was a man who was good at breaking into houses, and he went to call on Tzu-fa, sending in this message: "I hear that you are looking for men with unusual talents. I am a housebreaker, and I would like to offer my services and become one of your soldiers."

When Tzu-fa received the message, he did not take time even to put on his sash or straighten his hat, but immediately rushed out to receive the visitor with all due courtesy. Those about him objected, saying, "A housebreaker is nothing but a common thief! Why should you be polite to a man like that?" But Tzu-fa replied, "You don't know anything about such matters!"

Not long afterwards, the state of Ch'i called up its troops and attacked Ch'u. Tzu-fa led his army to meet the attack, but his men were three times driven back. The wise statesmen of Ch'u exhausted their supply of stratagems and wore out their brains, but the Ch'i forces only grew stronger. The housebreaker then stepped forward and said, "Paltry though my talents are, I beg to put them to work for my commander." "You may," said Tzu-fa and, without asking what he intended to do, sent the man on his way.

That night the housebreaker sneaked into the Ch'i camp, stole the draperies from the general's tent, and presented them to Tzu-fa. Tzu-fa then dispatched an envoy to return them to the enemy with this message: "One of my men was out gathering firewood and came into possession of your general's draperies. I am hereby returning them to the proper authorities."

The next evening the housebreaker went out and came back with the Ch'i general's pillow; Tzu-fa returned it with the same message. The evening after, he went out once more and came back with the general's hairpin, which Tzu-fa likewise returned.

When the Ch'i army learned what was happening, they were filled with astonishment. The Ch'i general summoned his officers into conference and said, "If we don't get away from here today, I'm afraid the Ch'u army will make off with my head!" He thereupon ordered his troops to turn around and march home.

So we see that there is no such thing as a talent that is too insignificant or paltry to bother about. Everything depends on how the ruler makes use of it. Hence Lao Tzu [sec. 27] has said: "The not-so-good man is raw material for the good man."

The *Yen t'ieh lun* or *Debates on Salt and Iron*

Emperor Wu (r. 140–87 B.C.) of the Han dynasty, a dynamic and strong-willed ruler, expanded the borders of the empire, dispatched armies to break the power of the Hsiung-nu tribes to the north, built roads and canals, and undertook many other projects to strengthen the nation and impress neighboring states with the power and glory of China. In order to finance these costly undertakings, he resorted to a number of typically Legalist measures, including the setting up of government monopolies in the salt and iron industries.

In 81 B.C., shortly after his death, a debate was held at court between the Legalist-minded officials in charge of these monopo-

lies and a group of Confucian literati, who opposed such measures
and who had been selected to voice the complaints of the common
people against them. The *Yen t'ieh lun* or *Debates on Salt and
Iron,* a work in sixty sections compiled by a scholar of the first
century B.C. named Huan K'uan, is supposedly a record of these
discussions. The arguments put forward by the two parties probably represent the actual arguments used in the controversy,
though the speeches in which they are presented have most likely
been given a considerable amount of literary polish by the compiler. Yet, for all the intricate rhetoric, there is a vivid, realistic
air to the *Debates*: points and key phrases are picked up and
carried on from one speech to the next, insult answers insult,
and occasionally, as tempers wear thin, a session breaks down in
spluttering abuse.

As might be expected with two philosophies so diametrically
opposed as Legalism and Confucianism, the two views collide
head on. The Confucians attack the foreign wars and entangle-
ments of the ruler; the government spokesmen declare that such
wars bring exotic goods to the capital and lend prestige to the
dynasty. The officials shout that the Hsiung-nu must be conquered; the literati retort that "all men are brothers!" (sec. 48)
and, laying the blame for Hsiung-nu hostility upon Chinese
aggression and bad faith, insist that the loyalty of the barbarians
be won by friendship instead of arms. The Confucians describe
the misery of the common people and call for government aid;
the officials assert that relief measures only make the people soft
and encourage the lazy. Both parties are given equal opportunity
to express their views, which they do in equally colorful and
impressive rhetoric: the Legalists advocate government by force
and terror, the Confucians government by moral suasion; the
Legalists demand that the common people be held in check by
stern and detailed laws, the Confucians urge that they be taught

and led to virtue. Neither side moves an inch toward compromise, and the discussions end exactly where they began, with the two parties, the two views, adamantly opposed.

There is no room here to give an entire section of the *Debates*, but I would like to quote briefly from one of the many speeches of the Confucian scholars which depict the sharp social and economic differences separating the upper and lower classes during the Han. In a long, keening passage of parallel sentences, the speaker draws a series of bitter contrasts between the lives of the rich and the poor, the ruler and the ruled, and points up the melancholy lack of understanding that exists between the two groups.

Those who live in high halls and spreading mansions, broad chambers and deep rooms, know nothing of the discomforts of one-room huts and narrow hovels, of roofs that leak and floors that sweat. Those with a hundred teams of horses tethered in their stables and wealth heaped in their storehouses, who hoard up the old and stow away the new, do not know the anxiety of facing days that have a beginning but no end, of weighing goods by the pennyworth. . . . Those whose pastured horses cover the hills, whose oxen and sheep fill the valleys, cannot understand the wretchedness of those who do not have even one suckling pig or a single scrawny calf. . . . Those who recline on soft couches or felt mats, with servants and attendants crowding about them, know nothing of the hardships of the cart-puller or the boat-hauler, straining up the hills, dragging against the current. Those who wear light warm garments, furs and patterned silks, who live in heated rooms and ride in comfortable carriages, do not comprehend the danger and cold of those who must mount the border defenses to gaze across the barbarian wastes or face into the icy wind. . . . Those who sit in the place of authority and lean on their writing desks, examine criminal charges brought before them and scribble their decisions, know nothing of the terror of canques and bonds, the pain of whips and rods (sec. 41).

Huan K'uan, the compiler of the *Debates,* is clearly sympathetic ·

to the Confucian party, and ends his work with a postface prais-
ing them. Even without his pleading, however, it is almost impossible, in spite of the cogent arguments of the government
spokesmen, to read the *Debates* without being won by the
warmth and humanity of the Confucian case. In the closing encounter (sec. 59), the Legalist officials taunt the Confucians with
the political failure that marked the career of their master, and
demand to know why, in the face of opposition and indifference,
Confucius yet persisted in preaching his doctrines. The literati,
in a passage that strikingly foreshadows Buddhist descriptions of
the compassionate bodhisattvas, reply by depicting their master
as driven onward, in spite of repeated disappointment, by his
overwhelming pity for mankind: "He suffered and grieved for
the ills of the world, like a loving mother bending over her dead
child; though she knows there is nothing she can do, how can she
stop herself?"

The *Lun heng* or *Critical Essays*

Many other works of the period no doubt deserve to be mentioned here. Among these are the important lexical works: the
Erh ya (included among the Thirteen Classics), a collection of
glosses on words in the Classics, dating probably from late Chou
times; and the *Shuo-wen chieh-tzu* (preface dated A.D. 100) by
Hsü Shen, the first real dictionary of the Chinese language. The
Han writers also produced a number of collections of anecdotes
or biographies culled from earlier authors, or short philosophical
works, most of them basically Confucian in outlook and of interest mainly to specialists. One work, however, stands out for its
novelty, wit, and breadth of information, and therefore deserves
special attention. It is the *Lun heng* or *Critical Essays*.

The *Critical Essays,* in eighty-five sections, is by a scholar of
the Latter Han named Wang Ch'ung (A.D. 27–97?). The purpose

of the work, as the author himself states, is to combat "fictions and falsehoods." Han Confucianism had absorbed many ideas from other schools of thought, along with a large amount of popular superstition and legend, and Wang Ch'ung's particular target is this mass of inane and pseudoscholarly lore expounded by so many of the second-rate Confucian pedants of his day. Applying the same critical spirit we have seen at work in the selection from the *Lü shih ch'un-ch'iu,* combined with a rather crude system of empirical observation and plain common sense, he proceeds to examine each bizarre assertion of the scholars and show it up as the absurdity it is. He even extends his attacks to the Confucian Classics themselves, though here, with the literal-mindedness that is one of his failings, he often calls them to account for what is patently only metaphor or poetic license.

Wang is keenly conscious of style; he frequently condemns other writers on stylistic grounds and is at pains to defend his own work from the charges of verbosity and lack of elegance which he believes will be leveled at it. He employs what would appear to be the ordinary colloquial language of his day, in contrast to the archaisms of a writer like Yang Hsiung, and his work is marked by an easy, chatty flavor. Because of his skepticism and attacks on superstition, he has in recent years been hailed in communist China as an early exponent of materialism. In the past, however, his book was more often read not for the philosophy implied in it but for the wealth of engaging information and opinion which it contains and its incisive, witty style. As an example I quote a passage in which he debunks an old Confucian tale about a miraculous plant that was said to have grown at the courts of the ancient sages.

Again the Confucians assert that in ancient times the auspicious *ming* pods grew on either side of the palace steps. On the first day of the month the plant grew one pod, and it continued to put out a new one each day until the fifteenth. On the sixteenth, one pod fell off, and this continued each day until the end of the month, by which time all the pods had fallen. With the new month the process began again. The king, facing south from his throne, could thus look at the number of pods growing on the plant and tell what day of the month it was without troubling to consult the calendar.

Now if Heaven is capable of producing pods like these to indicate the day of the month, why couldn't it make pods that had the name of the day written on them so that the king, by looking at the inscription, would know what day of the sixty-day cycle it was? As it is, if he only knows the number of the day and not its name, then he still has to consult the calendar to get the full information. If, after looking to see the number of the day, he still must go to this bother, I fail to see how the appearance of the *ming* pods can be considered such a blessing.

These pods or fruits which grow on the *ming* plant are like the pods on a bean stalk. In spring and summer the plant is not fully developed, so that we must assume that the pods appear only toward the end of autumn. In the winter months, when the cold becomes severe and frost, snow, and hail come down, all plants wither away. Would the Confucians dare to contend that the *ming* pods alone do not die in winter? Assuming that the plant lives and dies in the same way as everything else, its pods must sprout in the late autumn. It would therefore be possible to examine them and determine the day during the last month of autumn, but they would be no help at all during the other three seasons of the year.

Moreover, as we have seen, one pod grows each day for fifteen days, and then on the sixteenth the pods begin to fall. Hence by the twenty-first, six pods will have fallen. The fallen pods become scattered and lost, so it would be impossible to count them. Therefore in order to know the number of the day one must count the remaining pods and then determine the day by mathematical calculation, which is a trouble and a burden and no kind of blessing at all.

If the pods grew inside the hall, then the ruler of men, seated on his throne between the door and the back window, could look at the pods and determine the day of the month, though this would be no great joy, as we have seen. Now, however, they tell us that the pods grow by the steps, which means they are outside the hall. Concerning the hall of the ruler, Mo Tzu asserts that that of the sages Yao and Shun was raised three feet off the ground. The Confucian scholars maintain that this is too mean a dimension, but let us assume for the moment that it is correct. If the hall is three feet off the ground and the *ming* pods are growing at the foot of the steps, then the ruler, wishing to examine the pods, cannot possibly do so from his seat between the door and the window. He must walk to the edge of the hall and look down before he can count the pods. Now if he has to get up and go look outside, wouldn't it be better just to hang a calendar on the screen by his seat where he could glance at it whenever he wished merely by turning his head?

Heaven, it is said, produces such auspicious plants in order to delight the ruler. But if he has to get up from his seat and go look outside in order to find out the day of the month, then it has in fact produced nothing more than a nuisance to add to his burdens! (*Lun heng,* ch. 17, *Shih ying.*)

SUGGESTED READINGS

GENERAL WORKS

William Theodore de Bary, *et al. Sources of Chinese Tradition.* 1960.

Fung Yu-lan. *A History of Chinese Philosophy.* Vol. I, *The Period of the Philosophers.* 1937.

Arthur Waley. *Three Ways of Thought in Ancient China.* 1939.

TRANSLATIONS

The Confucian Writings

James Legge. *Confucian Analects.* (Vol. 1 in *The Chinese Classics.*) 1893.

Arthur Waley. *The Analects of Confucius.* 1938.

James Legge. *The Works of Mencius.* (Vol. 2 in *The Chinese Classics.*) 1895.

Homer H. Dubs. *The Works of Hsün Tzu.* 1928.

James Legge. *Li Ki* (*Li chi*). (Vols. 27–28 in *Sacred Books of the East.*) 1885.

John Steele. *The I-Li, or Book of Etiquette and Ceremonial.* 2 vols. 1917.

James Legge. *The Hsiao King or Classic of Filial Piety.* (Vol. 8 in *Sacred Books of the East.*) 1899.

James Legge. *The Yi King* (*I ching*). (Vol. 16 in *Sacred Books of the East.*) 1882.

Richard Wilhelm. *The I Ching, or Book of Changes.* 2 vols. 1950.

The Mohist Writings

Y. P. Mei. *The Ethical and Political Works of Motse* (selections). 1930.

The Taoist Writings

Arthur Waley. *The Way and Its Power.* 1935.

J. J. L. Duyvendak. *Tao te ching, the Book of the Way and Its Virtue.* 1954.

Herbert A. Giles, *Chuang Tzu.* 1889. 2d ed. rev., 1926.

Lionel Giles. *Taoist Teachings from the Book of Lieh Tzu* (selections). 1912.

Anton Forke. *Yang Chu's Garden of Pleasure* (*Lieh Tzu*, ch. 7). 1912.

A. C. Graham. *The Book of Lieh-tzu.* 1960.

The Legalist Writings

J. J. L. Duyvendak. *The Book of Lord Shang.* 1928.

W. K. Liao. *The Complete Works of Han Fei Tzu.* 2 vols. 1939, 1960.

The Eclectic Writings

Lewis Maverich. *The Kuan-Tzu: Economic Dialogues in Ancient China* (selections). 1954.

Evan Morgan. *Tao the Great Luminant, Essays from Huai-nan Tzu* (selections). 1935.

E. M. Gale. *Discourses on Salt and Iron*, Chapters I–XIX. 1931. Chapters XX–XXVIII, *Journal of the North China Branch of the Royal Asiatic Society*, LXV (1934).

Alfred Forke. *Lun Heng.* 2 vols. 1907, 1911.

POETRY

POETRY, which occupies such an important place in later Chinese literature, is represented among the earliest extant works of the language. The *Book of Odes,* one of the Five Classics, contains poems that are probably almost as old as the oldest examples of Chinese prose. In spite of this fact, the amount of ancient Chinese poetry that has been preserved is rather small, and its place in the early literary tradition relatively minor, particularly when compared, for example, with the place of poetry in the literature of ancient Greece or India. The *Book of Odes* contains only about three hundred poems, most of them quite short, and from the century or two following its presumed date of compilation we have almost no examples of poetry at all. The state of Ch'u provides us with a few works of late Chou date, and these are followed in the Han by a scattering of songs and a number of descriptive poems in the *fu* or rhyme-prose style. Perhaps there were periods when little or no poetry was written; perhaps, as is undoubtedly the case in the Han, only a fraction of the output has survived. Whatever the reason, the amount of early Chinese poetry that has been handed down, especially when compared with that of prose, is pathetically small. Stripped of exegetical material, it would hardly fill one volume in modern print.

In spite of its size, however, its intrinsic value is often very great indeed, and its importance, because of its antiquity and the influence which it has exercised upon the later development of poetry in China, considerable. I shall therefore discuss its form and content in some detail, and attempt to illustrate its main characteristics through translations. I ask the reader to keep in mind, however, that in the case of poetry, even more than in that of prose, much of the beauty and music which give value to the original becomes hopelessly lost in the transition to another language.

The *Shih ching* or *Book of Odes*

The *Book of Odes* is a collection of 305 songs. It was probably compiled around 600 B.C., though many of the songs undoubtedly date from several centuries earlier. The Han historian Ssu-ma Ch'ien tells us that Confucius selected the poems from an earlier compilation of over three thousand, arranged them in their present order, and worked over the musical accompaniments to which they were customarily sung (*Shih chi* 47). We have no way to determine the validity of this statement, though we do know from the *Analects* that Confucius valued the songs highly, urged his students to study them, and frequently made use of them in his teaching.

A second tradition, dating at least as early as the Han dynasty, claims that the songs were collected by officials sent out among the people for that specific purpose. The songs were then presented to the Chou ruler, who thereby judged the mores and temper of his subjects. There may well be some truth to this assertion, since many of the poems express the kind of complaints against bad government, corrupt officials, and unduly heavy military service which it would profit a ruler to hear, and some of them quite obviously were specifically written for the king's ears. The *Kuo yü*, it should be noted, clearly states that the Chou ruler "caused men from the highest official rank down to the lower aristocracy to present poems," presumably of an admonitory

nature (*Kuo yü, Chou yü* 1). Though many of the songs in the
Odes are said to come from different localities, they have apparently been revised at some period to make the rhymes conform
to a standard dialect, and this may well have been done by the
officials who compiled them for the Chou court. The musical
settings to the songs were already lost by Han times and nothing
definite is known of them. It should be borne in mind, however,
that most, if not all, of the poems were intended to be sung, not
read.

Though the *Book of Odes* was one of the works condemned to
destruction by the Ch'in's "burning of the books," it managed to
survive, either in hidden manuscripts or in the memories of
scholars, and three versions of the text received official recognition
in the early Han. These were later replaced in favor by a fourth
version, the so-called Mao text, and survive only in fragments.
We know from fragments of one version that the order of the
poems differed slightly from that of the Mao text, the present
standard text; but how else the versions may have differed we
cannot say.

The anthology is divided into four sections called *feng, hsiao
ya, ta ya,* and *sung.* According to some commentators, these
names are technical terms referring to the types of music used to
accompany the songs, but they have customarily been interpreted
as descriptive of the songs themselves. The titles of the individual
songs are in most cases taken from the opening words of the
song.

The title of the first section, *feng,* literally "wind," has been
variously interpreted to mean "mores" or "folkways," or, by
those who stress the political significance of the poems, "criticisms." I shall evade the question by calling them "airs." The
section contains 160 songs ascribed to fifteen states of northern
China, of which four were within the immediate domain of the

Chou ruler. For this reason they are often called *kuo feng* or
"airs of the states." By no means all of the states that existed
within the hegemony of Chou culture are represented, and no
one has succeeded in explaining why no folk songs from such
important states as Lu or Sung are included.

The poems in this section are clearly folk songs, though they
may have received some literary polish from the hands of the
men who first wrote them down or the compilers of the anthology. For the most part they deal with the lives of the common
people, their daily occupations, their festivals and outings, their
joys and hardships. We have songs of courtship and marriage,
work songs, songs about hunts, and songs to accompany games
and dances. We read of jilted sweethearts and neglected wives,
harsh officials, fickle friends, families sorrowing for their absent
sons, and soldiers grumbling of the weariness of war. These are
the heart of the *Odes,* the songs that hold the greatest appeal for
the modern reader. In their sharply etched descriptions and
declarations of feeling, the world of ancient China comes vividly
alive and we see, more clearly than through any other text, into
the minds and hearts of its people.

Most of the songs are quite short, often only two or three
stanzas. As is customary in folk songs, a single refrain is frequently repeated throughout the whole poem. The basic line is
a four-character one, with occasional variations. At times, for
example, it is filled out by exclamatory particles in the first or
fourth place, like the *la*'s or *o*'s of English ballads, so that the
line becomes essentially a three-character one. Foot rhymes are
used throughout, in the even-numbered lines, and sometimes in
the odd-numbered ones also, as well as head rhymes, internal
rhymes, and alliteration. These, incidentally, represent what is
probably the earliest known use of rhyme in the poetry of any
culture. In spite of the fact that, due to sound changes, some of

the rhymes have drifted apart over the centuries, the poems, when read in standard modern Chinese pronunciation, still retain a wonderfully musical sound, with lively and complex rhythmical patterns.

Many of the poems make use of metaphor, usually implied by juxtaposition rather than specifically stated, as will be clear from the examples quoted later on. The metaphors are mostly drawn from nature—flowers, insects, birds, the state of the weather—and are symbolic of the actions and emotions of the person described in the song. Sometimes, however, they are employed for contrast, the joy, serenity, or freedom of the natural world and its creatures being set in poignant antithesis to the anguish and turmoil within the singer's heart.

The language of the *Odes* is difficult because of its antiquity, because we have so few other sources on the life and customs of the period, and because poetry, particularly when it employs such a brief line, is bound to be highly elliptical and impressionistic. Moreover, unless one correctly understands the metaphor with which so many of the songs begin, he may completely mistake the emotional tenor of the poem, and it is not always easy to guess what symbolism the Chinese of ancient times attached to the various trees, animals, natural phenomena, etc., that appear in the metaphorical sections. To take a striking example, the rainbow, which has such auspicious connotations in Western literature, seems in one poem (# 51 of the Mao text), to be an omen of ill fortune or sexual misconduct. As a result of these difficulties, interpretations of individual songs may vary considerably, as the reader will soon discover if he compares the various translations of them available in European languages.

A word should also be said about the binomial descriptive terms which play such a large part in the *Odes* and later Chinese poetry. They figure prominently in prose as well—in the tenth chapter

206   POETRY

of the *Analects*, for example, Confucius' behavior is described almost entirely in such binomial terms—but it has seemed best to discuss them in connection with poetry, a medium in which sound is often as important as meaning. These terms function usually as adjectives or adverbs, though sometimes they may stand alone as verbs. There are three types. The first consists of a simple repetition of a single character. For example, the epithalamium quoted later on, # 6, begins:

> *T'ao chih yao-yao*   *Yao-yao* is the peach tree,
> *Cho-cho ch'i hua*   *Cho-cho* are its blossoms.

Here the doublet *yao-yao*, defined by commentators as descriptive of youthful beauty, depicts the appearance of the peach tree, while *cho-cho*, defined as bright and full, describes its blossoms.

The other two types are known by the technical terms *shuang-sheng* ("double initial"), and *tieh-yün* ("repeated final"). A *shuang-sheng* consists of two words that begin with the same initial sound, in other words, an alliteration; a *tieh-yün* consists of two words with the same final sound, or rhyme. To give examples, in the very first song in the *Odes* we find the phrase: *yao-t'iao shu nü* (a good girl who is *yao-t'iao*). *Yao-t'iao*, whose components rhyme, is a *tieh-yün* and is defined as "modest and retiring." A few lines farther on we find: *ts'en-tz'u hsing ts'ai* (the water mallows are *ts'en-tz'u*). *Ts'en-tz'u* is a *shuang-sheng* or alliteration, *ts'* and *tz'* representing the same initial sound, and describes the uneven lengths of the water mallows.

Such binomial terms, which not only carry forward the meaning of the song but also provide interesting repetitions of sounds, obviously add greatly to the musical effect. They also constitute a real problem for the translator. Some are descriptive of sounds and hence may be rendered by onomatopes, which are fortunately plentiful in English. But many others refer to form, action, mood,

or moral quality, and here almost no equivalents are available—
with pell-mell, hodgepodge, dillydally, and a few others, one
exhausts the supply of acceptable English words that convey anything approximating the musical value of the terms in Chinese.
The translator is obliged, therefore, to abandon any hope of
getting over the sound of the original and to concentrate on the
meaning. But here again he is faced with a dilemma. In the
case of simple repetitions he may repeat the adjective in translation. But what about the alliterative and rhyming terms? Shall
he translate them by two words, giving an effect which is heavier
and more disjointed than the original, or by one, giving an effect
that is too light? Probably he will end up by adopting first one
alternative and then the other, thereby obscuring the balance that
is so important a part of the original. Fortunately the songs in
the *Odes* are usually sturdy enough in themselves to survive such
buffeting. But in the long descriptive poems of the Han, where
the sheer music and swing of the language play such a vital part
in the total effect—where one encounters as many as eight con-
secutive binomial terms descriptive of lofty mountains or four-
teen terms descriptive of rushing water—one wonders if translation should even be attempted.

But to return from such disturbing thoughts to the subject of
the *Odes*. The earliest systematic commentary on the poems is
that found in the Mao text, consisting of brief introductions to
each poem explaining its general meaning and usually assigning
it to some period of early Chou history, as well as glosses on
individual words. Presumably these comments represent the views
of a scholar named Mao (or, according to another version, two
scholars of that name), who served at the court of Liu Te, a son
of Emperor Ching of the Former Han who was enfeoffed as
king of the region of Ho-chien in 155 B.C. Mao is at best a shadowy figure, but these comments attributed to him, along with

a general preface to the *Odes* (now generally believed to have been written by a scholar of the first century A.D. named Wei Hung who may also be the author of the introductions to the individual poems), have had an enormous influence upon later interpretations of the *Odes*.[1]

These comments in the Mao text are designed, in almost all cases, to give the songs a political significance and, wherever possible, to relate them to some specific historical person or event. If the song expresses joy or contentment or reflects a state of social order, for example, Mao (or whoever is responsible for the comments) assigns it to the reign or domain of a "good" ruler, since, according to Confucian doctrine, these are the conditions that prevail among the people when a truly wise sovereign is present to lead them in the path of virtue. If the song grumbles or complains of some ill (no matter how private), Mao attributes it to the time of an "evil" ruler and interprets it as political satire or reprimand. In cases where the grievance seems to be too personal in nature to admit such a view, he resolves the difficulty by interpreting the whole poem metaphorically—for example a jilted lover or an abandoned wife becomes a metaphor for an abused and misunderstood official complaining to his lord. Such complaints and censures, which appear in the first three sections of the *Odes,* are called in the preface "songs of change," that is, songs of a time of political and moral deterioration, and come after the songs that deal with sunnier and more well-ordered eras. The men of Confucius' time, who were presumably responsible for the present arrangement of the anthology, believed that they were living in an age which had sadly declined from

[1] We know from quotations preserved in other works that the proponents of the other three versions of the *Odes* in the early Han sometimes differed widely from Mao in their interpretations of the meaning, date, and purpose of individual songs. Just how their interpretations of the Classic as a whole differed, however, we cannot say.

the virtue and stability of early Chou, and they chose to point
up this process of decline, and to appeal for its reparation, in the
very order of the poems.

To give some examples of Mao's type of interpretation, the
following song from the "airs of Chou-nan," # 6 in the Mao
text, is clearly an epithalamium. Because it is happy in tone and
because it is said to come from Chou-nan, which was within
the immediate domain of the Chou ruler, Mao regards it as a
wedding song of the consort of the Chou king himself, expressing
the virtues of happy wedlock which the new queen will display
for the edification of her subjects. As far as the content of the
song itself is concerned, however, it could be from any region
of the empire and refer to any type of marriage. Exactly what
connection the peach tree had with marriage in the minds of
the ancient Chinese we cannot say, though obviously here it is
being used as a symbol of the beauty and future fruitfulness of
the bride.

> Lovely the young peach tree,
>   Shimmering its blossoms.
> This girl goes to a new home
>   To order well its chambers.
>
> Lovely the young peach tree,
>   Plentiful its fruit.
> This girl goes to a new home
>   To order well its rooms.
>
> Lovely the young peach tree,
>   Rich its leaves.
> This girl goes to a new home
>   To order well its people.

In the case above, Mao's interpretation does little or no violence
to the spirit of the song itself. The same, however, cannot be
said for the next example, one of the "songs of change." It is from

the "airs of Pei," # 41 in Mao. Though the identity of the speaker is not clear, the poem is quite obviously a love song of some kind. Yet Mao gives it an uncompromisingly political interpretation: the peasants, oppressed by a cruel government (the cold wind of the song), urge each other to flee to another state. The private dilemma of two lovers is transformed into a public crisis; what in the original is a timeless expression of urgent pleading is given a specific temporal and factual context.

> Cold is the north wind,
>> The snow falls thick.
> If you are kind and love me,
>> Take my hand and we will go together.
>> You are modest, you are slow,
>> But oh, we must hurry!
>
> Fierce is the north wind,
>> The snow falls fast.
> If you are kind and love me,
>> Take my hand and we will home together.
>> You are modest, you are slow,
>> But oh, we must hurry!
>
> Nothing so red as the fox,
>> Nothing black as the crow.[2]
> If you are kind and love me,
>> Take my hand and we will go in the same carriage.
>> You are modest, you are slow,
>> But oh, we must hurry!

Though such interpretations as these often appear far-fetched indeed, Mao and the commentators who followed him did not concoct their theory of the political import of the *Odes* out of thin air. We have already noted the tradition that the songs in

---

[2] Commentators usually take these as omens of evil, but Waley (*The Book of Songs*, p. 38) suggests the very plausible meaning: "Nothing so red as the fox, nothing black as the crow, and no one truer than I."

the *Odes* were collected by officials of the king specifically for the purpose of keeping him informed of the sentiments and grievances of the people, and if one accepts this idea he is already obliged to find political significance in at least some of the poems. In the *hsiao ya* and *ta ya* sections which follow the "airs," we actually find poems that are clearly political in nature, sometimes concluding with a statement that the poet composed the poem for the purpose of expressing his discontent and delivering a reprimand. Moreover we know that, during the Spring and Autumn period, statesmen and diplomats were in the habit of quoting the *Odes* as a means of expressing their opinions discreetly and with becoming indirection. The *Tso chuan* is full of descriptions of meetings and diplomatic conferences at which the exchange of ideas is carried on almost exclusively in this medium (and woe to the statesman who failed to recognize an allusion and interpret it correctly!). In the process, lines were often quoted out of context, or whole poems used to express ideas or sentiments quite foreign to the original meaning of the poem. Thus in time the poems, particularly those of the "airs" section, acquired a set of allegorical connotations, usually of a political nature, and it was no doubt these which Mao used as the basis of his interpretations.

In addition it should be noted in Mao's defense that the Chinese have always had a passion for occasional poetry, poetry tied to a particular time and place and expressing the emotions inspired by a particular set of circumstances. It was quite natural for commentators, therefore, especially when faced with a body of poetry said to have been selected and edited by Confucius himself, to search for historical references and attempt to relate the poems to specific historical persons and occasions. In an age when there was no concept of "pure literature" devoid of didactic content they quite understandably assumed that if Confucius had gone to the trouble of selecting and handing down what appeared to be only simple folk songs, it was not because of any deep interest in the art of balladry for its own sake, but because he believed they embodied some kind of political and moral wisdom. Moreover, such a view made it conveniently possible for generations of serious-minded scholars to study and enjoy the ancient folk songs of their culture while at the same time assuring themselves that they were dealing with works of profound depth and import.

Mao's text of the *Odes* and his commentary won wide recognition among scholars of the Latter Han, one of the most distinguished of whom, Cheng Hsüan (127–200), wrote a sub-commentary on it; and his strongly political and moralistic interpretations of the songs were accepted with little opposition until Sung times. Considering the absurdity of some of Mao's interpretations, this seems almost incredible. Consider, for example, this poem, # 91, from the "airs of Cheng":

> Blue, blue your collar,
>   Sad, sad my heart.
> Though I do not go to you,
>   Why don't you send word?
>
> Blue, blue your belt-stone,
>   Sad, sad my thoughts.
> Though I do not go to you,
>   Why don't you come?
>
> Restless, heedless,
>   I walk the gate tower.
> One day not seeing you
>   Is three months long.

Granted that students in ancient China may, as Mao asserts, have worn uniforms with blue collars, can one seriously believe that this is a complaint against students who do not go to school but spend their time idly walking the gate towers of the city?

This is what Mao says it is, and scholars of later generations who wished to pass the government examination in the Confucian Classics were no doubt obliged to give sequacious assent, since his was the officially approved interpretation. But privately there must have been many with grave misgivings.

It remained for the great Sung scholar Chu Hsi (1130–1200) to clear away the worst of this nonsense. He did not for a moment reject the notion that the *Odes* were on the whole didactic, and often political, in nature. But he allowed that among the "airs" there were some that were purely romantic, such as this one— lascivious and abandoned songs, as he called them, since pre-marital romance was in itself to be condemned—and from his time on the silliest of Mao's distortions were discarded. Ch'ing scholars did a prodigious amount of philological research on the *Odes,* and more recently Chinese, Japanese, and Western scholars, employing the techniques of comparative literature and an-thropology, have been able to elucidate many of the folk customs and beliefs that underlie the poems. Gradually we are coming to have a clearer view of what the songs originally meant, though this does not excuse us from the obligation of learning also what they meant to the generations of traditional Chinese scholars who followed the views of Mao and his school. And, when one has finished scoffing at the idiocies of Mao's interpretations, it does no harm to consider that he and his contemporaries two thousand years ago had neither the techniques of philology nor those of comparative anthropology to aid them, and were forced to con-struct their interpretations solely on the basis of what they knew, or thought they knew, of early Chou history and society. The more conscientious of the Han scholars of the *Odes,* we are told, "left in doubt the points they were doubtful about" (*Shih chi* 121). But once Confucianism had become the orthodox creed of the state, this approach was hardly feasible. The *Odes* was one of the Five Classics, and for a scholar to admit that he could not understand the nature and intent of the poems in it would have been an affront to the Sage who compiled it and a disservice to the state which espoused it as a wellspring of wisdom.

The popularity of Mao's commentary becomes more understandable if we consider also that many of the songs actually cry out for some kind of context or explanation that will give them more meaning than they possess in themselves. Take, for example, the following, # 61, from the "airs of Wei":

> Who says the River is wide?
>   On a reed one can cross it.
> Who says Sung is far?
>   On tiptoe one can see it.
>
> Who says the River is wide?
>   It won't hold a sliver of a boat.
> Who says Sung is far?
>   One can get there before the morning is out.

The state of Wei, to which this song is assigned, was situated north of the Yellow River, that of Sung immediately south of it. Perhaps we have here the reproach of a young girl whose lover has failed to appear at a rendezvous and is making excuses about the difficulty of crossing the river, though this is by no means certain. Mao says it was written by the mother of Duke Hsiang of Sung, a lady of Wei who, having separated from her husband, the former duke of Sung, and returned to Wei, now longs to visit her son but is prevented from doing so not by distance (as she points out), but by the dictates of propriety. Regrettably such an explanation most likely has no basis in fact, but if it did it would supply us with a speaker for the piece and an idea of what emotion prompted her to write. It is obvious that readers would welcome some such information as an enhancement to their understanding of the poem.

In the following example, # 81, from the "airs of Cheng," the emotional content of the poem is vivid and immediately apparent. But again we have no inkling of who the speaker is— a spurned lover, a deserted friend, a cast-off wife?—and this prevents us from picturing the situation. Mao's explanation that it is a courtier who has been forced to abandon his lord because of the latter's evil ways but still thinks longingly of him, seems impossibly contrived.

> Walking the great road
>   I catch hold of your sleeve.
> Do not hate me,
>   So quickly forgetting old times! [3]
>
> Walking the great road
>   I catch hold of your hand.
> Do not despise me,
>   So quickly forgetting the good times!

As may be seen from this example, the songs of the *Odes* are often pure vignettes of feeling. Sometimes they describe a scene, sometimes they tell a story, but more often the scene and the story are outside the poem, or merely hinted at within it, the body of the poem being given up to an expression of the emotions they arouse. For this reason it is often possible to say with assurance that such and such a poem is about love or anguish or desertion, but not exactly what kind of love or anguish, whose, or why. Hence the poems lend themselves readily to metaphorical interpretation. Take the following, # 85, from the "airs of Cheng":

> Dry leaves, dry leaves,
>   The wind tosses you about.
> Brothers, oh brothers,
>   As you sing so must I follow.

[3] Or perhaps the meaning is "I cannot so quickly forget old times."

> Dry leaves, dry leaves,
>   The wind blows you along.
> Brothers, oh brothers,
>   As you sing so must I too.

Here someone is being made to do something against his or her will by "brothers," like dry leaves that have no choice but to be blown here and there by the wind. The emotion of the poem is clear, the symbolism indescribably lovely. Presumably it is the song of a young girl who is being forced by her family to marry against her wishes. Mao, however, says that it refers to a ruler who is overborne by his ministers and must "follow their tune." Here his assertion, I think, may be taken to mean that the poem, because of its lack of context, could as well be interpreted to refer to a helpless ruler, and may actually have been used in that sense in the allusive language of the diplomats. The two interpretations do not conflict, but actually complement each other and give an added depth to our reading of the poem.

A few of the poems do refer to actual historical persons or events. In the following example, # 16, from the "airs of Shaonan," we have a mention of a Lord Shao. This has been taken to mean Chi Shih, the duke of Shao, mentioned in the *Book of Documents* (see above, p. 35). Though this may not be correct, we obviously have a reference to some historical figure beloved by the people.

> The spreading sweet pear
>   Hew not, hack not.
>   Lord Shao camped there.

> The spreading sweet pear
>   Hew not, chop not.
>   Lord Shao stopped there.

> The spreading sweet pear
>   Hew not, pluck not.
>   Lord Shao rested there.

Again we find some poems that we recognize, without Mao's nudging, as obvious political satires. In the following poem, # 113, there is no need to strain the bounds of credibility to perceive that it is a complaint of the farmers against rapacious tax officials.

> Big rat, big rat,
>   Don't eat my millet!
> Three years I've served you
>   But you will not care for me.
> I am going to leave you
>   And go to that happy land.
>   Happy land, happy land,
>   Where I'll find my place.
>
>   .   .   .
>
> Big rat, big rat,
>   Don't eat my sprouts!
> Three years I've served you
>   But you give me no comfort.
> I am going to leave you
>   And go to those happy fields.
>   Happy fields, happy fields,
>   Who there will moan for long?

I would like to give one more example from the "airs" section to illustrate the delightful rhythms in which these songs abound. The content of the poem, # 46, from the "airs of Yung," has to do with some scandal that took place in the women's chambers of someone's household. As one must not strip away the vine and leave the wall bare and unprotected, so one must not strip off the cover of secrecy from the shady doings that take place in the bedchamber, or in this particular bedchamber, at least. Mao as usual refers it to a specific scandal, an adulterous affair between a prince of Wei and the Wei ruler's mother.

Thorn vine on the wall,
  Must not be stripped.
Words in the chamber,
  Must not be told.
  What could be told
  Would be the ugliest tale.

Thorn vine on the wall
  Must not be pulled down.
Words in the chamber
  Must not be recited.
  What could be recited
  Would be the longest tale.

Thorn vine on the wall
  Must not be bundled off.
Words in the chamber
  Must not be rehearsed.
  What could be rehearsed
  Would be the most shameful tale.

The poem begins with a three-character line, *Ch'iang yu tz'u,* followed by four-character lines. The latter, however, all either end in a light exclamatory particle, *yeh,* or contain the possessive particle *chih,* also light, so that rhythmically they contain only three strong beats. The stanzas contain six lines; the second, fourth, fifth, and sixth lines rhyme, the rhyme falling in the third place, the last of the strong beats. One rhyme in the first stanza has drifted slightly off in modern pronunciation. The following transcription will, I hope, give some impression of the engaging music and rhythm of the original.

Ch'iang yu tz'u
  Pu k'o sao yeh
Chung kou chih yen
  Pu k'o tao yeh
  So k'o tao yeh
  Yen chih ch'ou yeh

Ch'iang yu tz'u
  Pu k'o hsiang yeh
Chung kou chih yen
  Pu k'o hsiang yeh
  So k'o hsiang yeh
  Yen chih ch'ang yeh

Ch'iang yu tz'u
  Pu k'o shu yeh
Chung kou chih yen
  Pu k'o tu yeh
  So k'o tu yeh
  Yen chih ju yeh

The second section of the *Odes,* known as *hsiao ya,* consists of 74 poems arranged in "decades" or groups of ten, which take their titles from the first poem in the group. (In addition it lists six titles for which the texts have been lost or for which musical compositions, but not texts, existed.) *Ya* means "elegant" or "refined"; here it is probably intended to emphasize the fact that most or all of these songs are by courtiers or members of the aristocracy rather than by the common people, and were from the first written in the language of the Chou capital. *Hsiao* or "lesser" is used to distinguish this group from the next one, known as *ta ya* or "greater *ya.*"

The poems in this group, which I shall call "lesser odes," are generally longer than the "airs" and are concerned mainly with the lives of the nobility and the court. Some of them, it is true, particularly in the latter part of the section, seem to be folk songs very much in the manner of the "airs" and usually dealing with romantic love. These poems are invariably given a political interpretation by Mao, and if this interpretation dates from Chou times, it may explain why they are included here rather than among the "airs." On the other hand, one should not dismiss the possibility that the poems are actually political satires dressed in a folk song disguise.

Lest the reader think that I too have uncritically accepted Mao's doctrine, let me explain this statement. Many of the songs of the "lesser odes" are joyous affairs dealing with feasts, sacrifices, hunts, and other more or less public occasions in the lives of the gentry. But many of them are bitter laments on the hardships of war, and many others are outspoken and unmistakable complaints against misrule, slanderous officials, luxurious living in high places, and similar political ills. In the case of such songs, there is no doubt that they were written deliberately for the purpose of remonstrating with the rulers of the time and opening their eyes to the evils about them. Such songs of censure often employ metaphors similar to those used in the folk songs of the "airs," and it seems quite possible that by the time these songs were composed— probably the Spring and Autumn period shortly before the time of Confucius—the folk song style had become a conventional literary device for expressing political dissatisfaction, perhaps because it provided a cloak of anonymity to protect the poet. Therefore, though I do not for a moment question the genuine folk song nature of the "airs," I would urge caution in assuming that what appear to be similar folk songs among the "lesser odes" are in fact the same thing.

The festive and hunting songs are of relatively minor interest. They have a hale and comradely air, an appropriate spirit of community well-being. They abound in the loving descriptions of foods and household furnishings, of the dress, armor, and equipage of the nobility so typical of the literature of a feudal age— descriptions which are a mine of information for scholars of material culture but a burden to the average reader, who cannot appreciate the pageantry for the jumble of difficult and obscure terms that confront him.

Much more interesting and moving, because of their passionate feeling, are the laments and censures. Such lines as the following on the hardships of battle, for instance, the last stanza of # 167, cannot fail to touch the reader, whether or not he knows anything about the material culture of ancient Chou:

> Long ago we set out
>   When willows were rich and green.
> Now we come back
>   Through thickly falling snow.
> Slow, slow our march;
>   We are thirsty, we are hungry.
> Our hearts worn with sorrow,
>   No one knows our woe.

Again, in contrast to the "airs" the poems in this section contain many references to specific historical persons and events. Moreover, some of the poems are "signed"; that is, in the last line the poet explains why he wrote the poem and sometimes even records his name. In other words, these are the works of individual poets and were written in response to some particular situation. This is especially true of the political complaints, where the poet pictures himself as the victim of slanderous officials who have turned the ruler against him—the theme so common in later Chinese poetry. It is understandable that Mao should have spied political criticism everywhere in the *Odes,* when so many poems are so clearly devoted to that theme. These poems tend to be quite long and occasionally rather repetitious in their disgruntlement. The following stanza from # 195 will give an idea of their tone:

> Our tortoises[4] are disgusted,
>   They give us no more counsels.
> Many are the planners

[4] Used for divination.

> And nothing is achieved.
> Their speeches fill the court,
>> But who dares take the blame?
> Like travelers forever asking the way,
>> They never reach the journey's end.

The view of the *Odes* as a collection of bitter complaints was certainly overdone by the Han scholars, as when the historian Ssu-ma Ch'ien propounds the sweeping generalization that "most of the three hundred poems of the *Book of Odes* were written when the sages poured forth their anger and dissatisfaction" (*Shih chi* 130). Such a statement all but ignores the numerous hymns of praise, the joyous folk songs and festive ballads that occupy so much space in its pages. But there is no denying that many of the poems in the *hsiao ya* and *ta ya* sections do fit this description (and these were probably the poems that interested Ssu-ma Ch'ien and his contemporaries most, because they fitted so well with the Han concept of what a poem should be and do). Even what seems at first glance to be a kindly description of a banquet may end on a sour note of censure. The following poem, # 220, begins with an account of the happy, orderly feasting at a gathering of the gentry, the wine and food served, the musical entertainment. But this is how it ends. (The poem employs a number of binomial terms to describe the behavior of the guests, which add greatly to the metrical fun, though their exact meaning is not always certain. I have tried to suggest their effect by doubling the adjectives.)

> When guests first take their seats,
>> Mild, mild is their courtesy.
> Before they have drunk,
>> Fine, fine is their deportment.
> But after they have gotten drunk
>> Their deportment is frightful, frightful.

They leave their seats and move about,
    Insist on dancing round and round.
Before they have gotten drunk,
    Sedate, sedate is their deportment.
But after they have gotten drunk,
    It is scandalous, scandalous.
Once they have gotten drunk
    They lose all sense of order.

The guests have gotten drunk,
    Shouting, bawling;
They upset our baskets and dishes
    And insist on dancing—stagger, stagger.
Once they have gotten drunk
    They do not know their blunders.
With crooked caps sliding off
    They insist on dancing, on and on.
If those who are drunk would only go,
    They'd have their blessing along with the rest.
But as long as they refuse to leave
    They spoil the power of the feast.
Drinking wine is a great delight,
    But only if done with a sense of deportment.

The 31 poems of the next section, the *ta ya* or "greater odes," are in many instances identical in nature with those of the "lesser odes" section, and it is often impossible to guess why a given poem appears in one section rather than the other. Nevertheless the over-all tone of the *ta ya* is rather different. The section contains many poems, some of considerable length, on the founders of the house of Chou, how they gathered a loyal band of subjects about them through their virtuous ways, how they gradually rose to power, overthrew the last emperor of the Yin dynasty, and set up a new rule—accounts which parallel those found in the *Book of Documents*. We have the legends of the first Chou ancestor, the hero Hou Chi, descriptions of the royal capital, hymns of praise on the joyous times of early Chou, and records of battles and enfeoffments. In other words, these poems are more "public" and national in character, more concerned with the affairs of the ruling house, than those of either of the preceding sections. The following stanzas from # 235, an important expression of the concept of the mandate of Heaven, will illustrate the solemn, patriotic, and "historical" character of such pieces.

> King Wen is on high,
> He shines in Heaven.
> Chou is an old people
> But its charge is new.
> The leaders of Chou became illustrious.
> Was not God's charge timely given?
> King Wen ascends and descends
> On the left and right of God.
>
> August was King Wen,
> Continuously bright and reverent.
> Great was the appointment of Heaven.
> There were Shang's grandsons and sons,
> Shang's grandsons and sons,
> Were they not numberless?
> But the Lord on High gave his command
> And they bowed down to Chou.
>
> The charge is not easy to keep;
> May it not end in your persons.
> Display and make bright your good fame
> And consider what Heaven did to Yin.
> The doings of high Heaven
> Have no sound, no smell.
> Make King Wen your pattern
> And all the states will trust in you.

The following, the first three stanzas of an eight stanza poem on the hero Hou Chi (# 245), illustrates the narrative type of poem in which this section abounds. Though it begins in true epic style with a description of the miraculous birth of Hou Chi or Lord Millet, the ancestor of "the people" (the Chou tribe), it comes to an end long before reaching epic proportions.

She who first bore our people
Was Lady Yüan of Chiang.
How did she bear them?
She knew how to make *yin* and *ssu* sacrifices,
That she might not be childless.
She trod in the footprint of God's big toe and was quickened;
She was magnified, she was blessed;
She was stirred to pregnancy; quickly it came.
She bore him, she nurtured him:
This was Hou Chi

She fulfilled her months
And her first-born came forth.
There was no rending, no tearing,
No injury, no harm,
Showing that it was divine.
Did the Lord on High not give her ease?
Did he not receive her sacrifices?
Effortlessly she bore her child.

They laid him in the narrow lane,
But the oxen and sheep stood about to shelter him.
They laid him in the forest of the plain,
But he was found by the woodcutters of the forest.
They laid him on the cold ice,
But the birds covered him with their wings.
When the birds had departed,
Hou Chi began to wail.

But in this section, too, as in the "airs" and "lesser odes" sections, the sound of praise is not unending. As we read on we soon come to the odes of "change," bitter, impassioned outcries against rulers who have discarded the virtuous ways of their predecessors and brought grief to the realm. Here, for example, is one stanza from # 264, a lament on the times which points out an evil that was to beset so many later dynasties: women meddlers in politics.

> Clever men build cities,
>   Clever women topple them.
> Beautiful, these clever women,
>   But they are owls, they are kites.
> Women have long tongues,
>   Stairways to ruin.
> Disorder is not sent down from Heaven
>   But bred by these women.
> Impossible to teach, impossible to instruct,
>   Such are women and eunuchs.

Mao, needless to say, pegs each of these complaints to a particular period and identifies the villains (in the case of the poem above, Pao-ssu, the notoriously evil consort of King Yu [eighth century B.C.]). As in the case of all Mao's assertions, there is little profit in inquiring whether the piece is actually by a poet at the court of King Yu, or by one who lived in a later but similarly chaotic age. The only thing certain about the poem is the incontestable sincerity of the writer's rage.

As in most ancient societies, periods of misrule in early China seem invariably to have been accompanied by natural disasters. These were regarded by the Chinese not only as cosmic reflections of the human condition, but were believed to be called forth by the bungling of an evil or incompetent ruler. In # 258 we have a description of a fearful drought, two stanzas of which I quote below. There is no reason to doubt that the poet is referring to an actual drought that tormented the realm, and his tone is more one of bafflement and despair than of bitterness. Yet in crying out to the spirits, he is also crying out against the rulers of the time, since any complaint against Heaven is inevitably a complaint against its representative on earth, the Son of Heaven. As Arthur Waley has pointed out (*Book of Songs,* p. 304), in many of these complaints and lamentations the words Heaven or Lord on High are no more than "ironical cover-names" for the actual target, the ruler and his court. Though the drought poem may in some ways be an exception, most of the lamentations which cry out to Heaven are thus clearly political censures.

> The drought is too great,
>   It cannot be stopped.
> It flames, it burns.
>   We have no refuge.
> The great fate draws near,
>   No one to look up to, no one to look round for.
> The company of lords, the ancient governors
>   Give us no aid.
> Father, mother, ancient ancestors,
>   How can you bear to treat us like this?
>
> The drought is too great,
>   It parches the hills and rivers.
> The drought demon is cruel,
>   Flaming, scorching.
> Our hearts cower before the heat,
>   Our grieving hearts are seared.
> The company of lords, the ancient governors,
>   Pay us no heed.
> Bright Heaven, Lord on High,
>   Why do you make us cringe?

The last section of the *Odes,* consisting of 40 poems, is known as *sung* or "hymns." These are divided into three groups, 31 poems attributed to the Chou court and four to the court of the duchy of Lu, and five designated as hymns of Shang. These last, it is generally agreed, do not actually date from the Shang dynasty, the predecessor of the Chou, but belong to the state of Sung, which was held in fief by the descendants of the Shang rulers. It is possible, however, that they incorporate genuine Shang period legends.

The poems in this section, as the title implies, are hymns of praise, ceremonial pieces depicting sacrifices, feasts, and musical performances or celebrating the glory of the dynasty and its military achievements. Though the Chou hymns contain a few pieces in which rulers express fear that they may not be able to fulfill their duties and implore their ancestors for aid, there are no lamentations, complaints, or hints of disorder or misrule. All is joy, reverence, happy harvests, and stunning victories. Unlike the poems of the other sections, these are, to use a word now in disfavor, propaganda pieces designed to show how prosperous and orderly was the domain of the Chou rulers. The rhymes are much freer than those of the poems of the earlier sections, and some poems employ no rhymes at all, perhaps indicating that they were intended to be chanted rather than sung, or sung at a slower tempo. The following brief song, # 279, will illustrate the exultant and ceremonial tone of the hymns:

> Rich is the year with much millet and rice,
> And we have tal granaries
> With hundreds and thousands and millions of sheaves.
> We make wine and sweet spirits
> To offer to ancestor and ancestress,
> Thus to fulfill all the rites
> And bring down blessings in full.

The inclusion of the hymns of Lu and Shang (Sung) may have been due to Confucius, who was born in Lu of a family that had emigrated from Sung. The hymns of Lu tend to give a very exaggerated picture of the military might of that rather small state, while those of Sung are mainly praises of the ancestors of the Shang state and recitals of the legends connected with their names.

Such, then, is the *Book of Odes,* the first anthology of Chinese poetry. Outside of a few poems recovered from inscriptions, it represents all we know of early Chinese poetry. Because of its venerable age (in a culture where the oldest is most often thought to be the best) and its association with the name of Confucius, it has been studied and revered throughout the centuries, though an excess of reverence has often blinded scholars to the true nature of some of the poems it contains. Even without the aura of sanctity that attaches to it as one of the Five Classics, its catchy rhythms, its archaic turns of phrase and, above all, its variety and depth of feeling would assure it a place of unique importance in the history of Chinese poetic literature.

The four-character meter of the *Odes* does not seem to have had a very great influence on later poetry. Poets such as T'ao Yüanming (365–427) occasionally composed in it, but for all practical purposes it died with the Chou, perhaps because the music that accompanied it also died at that time and was replaced by new varieties of music calling for new meters. But the metaphorical element of the songs—the particular metaphors, as well as the device itself of establishing a delicate and poignant tension between an image from the natural world and a condition of the heart—dominates later poetry, giving to the best of it its characteristic combination of clear, incisive descriptive power and emotional depth. Finally the idea, implicit in the *Odes,* that poetry, as the expression of emotion, is the most appropriate vehicle for social and political criticism, though sometimes challenged by later critics, became a basic concept of Confucian literary theory. Western readers are sometimes startled when reading the works of T'ang poets such as Tu Fu (712–770) to find them complaining of heavy taxes, military conscription, or the price of rice, since we tend, for some reason, to think of "social consciousness" in poetry as a modern invention. Far from being modern, however, the T'ang poets in their censures are actually carrying on a tradition that began with the *Book of Odes*.

Not all of the 305 songs of the Odes are breath-taking masterpieces. Some are hardly more than ejaculatory doggerel, others enigmatic pieces whose real meaning we may never discover. The hymns are tiresomely institutional, the lamentations often maudlin with self-pity. The beliefs and folkways that underlie the songs are still imperfectly understood; the original pronunciation of the songs can be only tentatively reconstructed and the music that accompanied them is lost forever.

Nevertheless, when all this has been said, there is still enough beauty and interest in the *Odes* to repay years of study. Moreover, it is a simple, unaffected beauty, an exuberance and genuineness of feeling that, as Chinese literature grows more sophisticated and self-conscious in the centuries that follow the time of the *Odes,* is all too often lost.

The Chinese poetic tradition, unlike many others, does not start off with a great epic or epic cycle; indeed it never seriously takes up the epic form at all. In this sense it does not (fortunately or unfortunately), begin with such a flourish as that, say, of Greece. But in the *Book of Odes* it possesses what must, along with the *Manyōshū* of the Japanese, be one of the loveliest collections of lyrics produced by any ancient society.

The *Ch'u Tz'u* or *Elegies of Ch'u*

Chinese poetry, one might say, started twice. The three hundred or so poems of the *Book of Odes* represent, we may suppose, some of the finest products of a great poetic tradition that flourished among the people of northern China during the early and middle years of the Chou dynasty. But so far as we can judge, none of them date from any later than about 600 B.C. Whether people suddenly tired of the medium, or were too distracted by the social and political turmoil of the times to put their minds to poetry writing, or whether, as tradition has it, with the decline of the power of the Chou court, the officials no longer made it their business to collect and preserve what poetry was still composed, we cannot say. All we know is that, if one is to judge from the literary remains of the age, the voices that had sung so melodiously for centuries suddenly fell silent. When poetry reappears, it is from an entirely different quarter, new songs in a new meter from the land of Ch'u, far to the south in the Yangtze valley.

The *Ch'u Tz'u,* often referred to in English as the *Elegies of Ch'u,* is an anthology of poems attributed to Ch'ü Yüan, a statesman of Ch'u in late Chou times, along with a number of works by his disciples or later imitators. It contains seventeen titles, though many of these are actually groups or cycles of poems, so that the total number of individual poems is considerably larger. Our present version of the anthology was put together, with a commentary, by Wang I (d. A.D. 158), a scholar of the Latter Han, who included a group of his own poems, though he states that the collection was originally compiled a century and a half earlier by Liu Hsiang (77–6 B.C.).

There has been much controversy among scholars concerning the attributions of the poems, particularly over the question as to

which, if any, of the poems attributed to Ch'ü Yüan are actually
from his hand. The story of Ch'ü Yüan, the loyal minister to King
Huai of Ch'u (329–299 B.C.), was already well known to men of
the early Han. A commentary, now lost, on Ch'ü Yüan's most
famous poem, the *Li sao,* was compiled by Liu An, the king of
Huai-nan (d. 122 B.C.). Shortly afterwards the historian Ssu-ma
Ch'ien, apparently utilizing Liu An's work, wrote a biography of
Ch'ü Yüan (*Shih chi* 84). According to his account, Ch'ü Yüan
was a nobleman of Ch'u who at first enjoyed great favor under
King Huai but later, due to the slanders of a court rival, became
estranged from the king. He remained out of favor, and was
finally banished to the south by King Huai's son and successor,
King Ch'ing-hsiang (298–265 B.C.). There he committed suicide
by throwing himself into the Mi-lo River, a tributary of the
Yangtze. His poems, outbursts of grief and anger at the injustice
of his fate, were believed to have been written during the time of
his estrangement and banishment. The poems were deeply admired and often imitated by Han scholars, and their reputed
author came to symbolize the loyal minister who, because of the
calumny of rivals and the blindness of the ruler, is rejected by his
sovereign.

It is impossible at this date to say just what historical basis there
is for this account or what connection Ch'ü Yüan actually had
with the poems that bear his name. It seems best, therefore, to
leave aside the question of authorship and proceed to an examination of the poems themselves.

The first poem in the *Ch'u T'zu,* attributed to Ch'ü Yüan,
is entitled *Li sao* or *Encountering Sorrow.* It is a narrative in
374 lines, the longest poem in pre-Han literature, and is written
in a meter quite different from that of the *Book of Odes.* The
meter, called "sao" meter after the poem itself, is based upon a
line which David Hawkes, who has produced the first complete

English translation of the *Ch'u Tz'u,* has represented as *tum
tum tum te tum tum,* the *tum*'s representing "full words" or
words that are stressed in speech and whose meaning is vital to
the sense of the line, the *te*'s representing light, unstressed particles which help out the sense but could be omitted without any
great loss. There are frequent variations of this rhythm, such as
tum tum te tum tum or *tum tum tum te tum tum tum.* A
breathing particle or carrier sound, represented by a character
pronounced *hsi* in modern Chinese, occurs at the end of the odd-
numbered lines, and the rhyme at the end of the even-numbered
ones.

The text of the poem as we have it appears in places to be confused or damaged, and interpretation is made doubly difficult by
the murky allegory that pervades many passages. In the following
description of the content of the poem, as in all my remarks on
the *Ch'u Tz'u,* I am greatly indebted to the translation of David
Hawkes in his *Ch'u Tz'u: The Songs of the South.*

The poet begins by introducing himself and tracing his ancestry,
as was the custom among Chinese nobles, back to one of the
mythological rulers of antiquity. He then proceeds immediately
to the theme of his poem: his own sincerity, integrity, and
abundant worth, and his desire to guide and assist his erring
lord, who appears here under the sobriquet "Fair One." Here
also he introduces one of the characteristic allegorical devices of
the poem, the use of fragrant plants and flowers to symbolize
virtue and ability.

> I am a descendant of Emperor Kao-yang;
> My father's name was Po-yung.
> When the constellation *She-t'i* pointed to the first month
> > of the year,
> On the day *keng-yin* I was born.
> My father, observing the aspect of my birth,

Divined and chose for me auspicious names.
The personal name he gave me was Upright Model;
The formal name he gave me was Divine Balance.
Having from the first this inborn beauty,
I added to it fine adornments,
Picking selinea and angelica to wear
And twisting autumn orchids for a belt.
I hurried on, as though I could never catch up,
Afraid that the years would leave me behind.
In the morning I plucked mountain magnolias;
At evening I gathered sedges on the islets.
Days and months sped by, never stopping;
Springs and autumns gave way to each other.
I thought how the flowers were falling, the trees
                                     growing bare,
And feared my Fair One too would grow old.
Hold fast to youth and cast away the foul!
Why will you not change your ways?
Mount brave steeds and gallop forth!
Come, I will go before and show you the way.

The poet next introduces another theme beloved by Chinese writers, the "lessons of history," referring to the sage rulers of antiquity who honored "pepper and cinnamon" (worthy men), and the tyrants who brought about their own downfall. He then continues with an attack on the evil men of his own day, who have led astray the ruler, here referred to as the "Fragrant One."

The conspirators steal their heedless pleasures;
Their road is dark and leads to danger.
What do I care of the peril to myself?
I fear only the wreck of my lord's carriage.
I hastened to his side in attendance
To lead him in the steps of the ancient kings,
But the Fragrant One would not look into my heart;
Instead, heeding slander, he turned on me in rage.

The poet expands on his sorrow, calling upon Heaven to witness his loyal intentions, railing at the men of the time, and bewailing his fate. Once more he describes the many flowers and plants which he has grown and with which he adorns himself and, in the course of this, appears to picture himself as a woman spurned by her royal lover, for he says:

> All your women are jealous of my fair face;
> They chatter and gossip and call me wanton.

He continues in this vein, determining finally to set out upon a journey, when someone appears and attempts to reason with him. This person, called Nü Hsü, has traditionally been identified as the poet's sister, who is otherwise unknown, but it seems more likely that the name means simply a servant girl or girls, or a lady in waiting (if the poet is still imagining himself as a woman). Whoever the speaker, he or she begins the admonition with another "lesson from history," the fate of Kun, a minister of ancient times who tried unsuccessfully to bring a flood under control.

> Kun with his steadfastness forgot his own safety
> And in the end perished on the plain of Yü.
> Why be so proud, so fond of beauty?
> Why must you alone have such fine adornments?
> Thorns and weeds fill the palace now;
> Why stand apart and refuse to compromise?
> Can you go from door to door convincing others?
> Will you say to them, "Look into my heart"?
> If others band together and love their cliques,
> Why must you stand alone, ignoring advice?

The poet, however, refuses to be swayed, but journeys south to the grave of the sage Shun, where he continues his plaint, delivering volleys of historical allusions to prove that the virtuous prosper and the wicked fail, and swearing that he will never compromise with the evil of his age. He then sets off on a fantastic journey to mythical realms.

> Yoking four jade dragons to a phoenix carriage,
> I rose on the wind and journeyed abroad.
> In the morning I set out from Ts'ang-wu;
> By evening I reached the Hanging Gardens.
> I wanted to rest a while by its spirit gates,
> But the sun hurried on to its setting.
> I ordered Hsi-ho[5] to slacken his pace,
> To linger by Yen-tzu and not press on.
> Long, long the road, far the journey,
> But I must go searching high and low.
>
> .   .   .
>
> I ordered my phoenixes to fly aloft
> And continue onward day and night.
> Whirlwinds gathered together to meet me;
> Leading clouds and rainbows, they came in greeting,
> Joining and parting in wild confusion,
> Rising and falling in jumbled array.
> I commanded Heaven's porter to open for me,
> But he leaned on the gate and eyed me with scorn.

Unable for some reason to gain access to Heaven, he continues on his way. He longs for a mate, and begins paying suit to a variety of legendary beauties. All his efforts fail, however, due to the disdain of the ladies or the bungling of inept go-betweens. At the end of the passage he returns abruptly from the courtship allegory (if allegory it is), to the image of the ruler, sunk in delusion like one in deep sleep:

> Deep within his palace chambers
> The wise king slumbers and will not wake.
> I must hold back my thoughts and not speak them,
> Yet how can I go on like this forever?

[5] The charioteer of the sun. Yen-tzu is the mountain where the sun disappears beneath the earth.

This would seem to suggest that the various women the poet
has been unsuccessfully wooing are intended to be symbols of the
slumbering and unapproachable king. He then consults a diviner
and is advised to search farther afield for a bride. He hesitates,
however, and complains further on the state of the world. In
the course of this diatribe, he singles out several fragrant plants
for special condemnation:

> I thought that orchid could be trusted,
> But he is faithless and a braggart.
> He turns from beauty to follow the vulgar,
> Yet expects to be ranked among the fragrant flowers.
> Pepper is all flattery and insolence . . .

Here the plant names appear to refer to the poet's particular
enemies; commentators identify them with certain ministers at
the court of King Ch'ing-hsiang. The poet then sets off once
more in his dragon-drawn chariot and journeys to the fabulous
K'un-lun Mountains of the west, the description being much like
that of his earlier flights. The passage ends:

> I curbed my will and slackened my pace,
> My spirit soaring high in the distant regions.
> I played the Nine Songs and danced the Shao music,
> Stealing a little time for pleasure.
> But as I ascended the brightness of heaven,
> Suddenly I looked down and saw my old home.
> My groom was filled with sadness, and the horses in their
> > longing
> Pulled about in the reins and refused to go on.

The poem concludes with a brief section called a *luan,* an
envoi or reprise which sums up the meaning of the poem:

> It is over! There is no one in the kingdom who knows me!
> Why long for my old city?
> Since there is no one worthy to join me in just rule,
> I will go to P'eng Hsien in the place where he dwells.

Our understanding of the final passage, and hence of the poem as a whole, is greatly impeded by the fact that we do not know for certain who P'eng Hsien is. Commentators identify him as a worthy minister of the Shang dynasty who, when his advice was unheeded, drowned himself in a river. They thus take the last line as an expression of the poet's determination to do likewise, linking the poem to the tale of Ch'ü Yüan's suicide. On the other hand, P'eng Hsien may be the patron deity of some mystic cult whose practices the poet has decided to follow.

The culture of Ch'u, though influenced by that of the northern states which clustered about the Chou court, seems to have been very different in many ways from that of the north, and it is only natural that these differences should be reflected in the poetry of the two regions. The *Li sao,* as I have said, is much longer than and in a different meter from the songs of the *Odes.* Furthermore, though it takes up a theme that is represented in the *Odes*—the loyal minister rejected by a wayward ruler—its treatment is wholly different from anything attributed to the poetic tradition of the north. Nowhere in the *Odes* do we find anything to match the fantastic flights and journeyings, the air of mystery and magic which pervades the *Li sao.* With this poem we enter a wholly different world, and Chinese critics have been quite justified in regarding it and its imitations as works of an entirely new poetic genre.

Naturally enough, they have read the poem in the light of the Ch'ü Yüan legend, interpreting its erotic imagery, its symbolism of fragrant plants and long, unsuccessful searching, as political allegory, since they believed they knew who the author was and what the circumstances were that prompted him to write. If we reject the legend, as some scholars have felt obliged to do, we are left with a literary riddle, a curious hodgepodge of highly personal outcry and obscure fantasy, the import of which it is impossible to divine. It seems best, therefore, to retain the traditional attribution and the essentials of the Ch'ü Yüan story, while admitting that the meaning of individual passages in the poem is still uncertain. Thus we may enjoy the rich and impassioned language of the poem—for this is its chief beauty—and at the same time feel that we have at least the gist of its message.

The *Li sao* is the longest poem in the *Ch'u Tz'u* and one of the earliest. Its powerful rhythm, eloquent and exotic imagery, and indubitable sincerity of purpose qualify it as a masterpiece of early Chinese poetry, which, in spite of the difficulties of interpretation, deserves the high position it has been accorded by native critics. Nevertheless, there are several aspects of the poem which I have always felt hindered my own appreciation of it.

One of these is the rather unseemly vanity of the poet. No one could possibly doubt his sincerity, and we are in no position to determine whether his enormous self-confidence was justified or not. Yet his repeated emphasis upon his own golden qualities, in contrast to the universal corruption of the rest of society, cannot help but grate at times on our nerves. He might, one feels, have protested a little less.

This aspect of the poem has troubled Chinese critics as well. So far as I know, the historian Pan Ku, in a preface to the *Li sao,* was the first to voice a complaint, objecting that Ch'ü Yüan was "parading his talent and advertising himself" in the *Li sao*. Since Confucianism traditionally abhors any display of competitive spirit, Pan Ku's charge carried considerable weight, and a great deal of critical ink was expended over the centuries in the controversy which ensued. Inevitably, since legend says that Ch'ü Yüan drowned himself in despair, Chinese critics have also become involved in lengthy debates over the problem of if and when suicide is justifiable for a statesman, and whether Ch'ü Yüan's death served any useful political purpose. This last question, fortunately, need not exercise Western readers who are interested in the poem alone, nor need another question much debated by Chinese critics: whether Ch'ü Yüan and the other poets of the *Ch'u Tz'u* were justified in utilizing in their works myths and legends not found in the Confucian Classics.

A second difficulty is posed by the allegory of the fragrant plants. Judging from other works of the *Ch'u Tz'u* or the poems of the *Odes,* such allegory came quite naturally to the Chinese of this period, particularly to the people of the state of Ch'u. It is unfortunate that plants such as orchid, pepper, or angelica carry no correspondingly symbolic overtones for Western readers. There is a gap here which must be bridged by study and consideration of the original poem in its own cultural framework. Nevertheless, no matter how much one endeavors to grasp the mood the poet is trying to convey, he will almost certainly be bothered by sly twitchings of mirth at the thought of a Chinese gentleman laden with such a burden of posies. At one point in particular, after the poet has been refused admittance to Heaven by the surly porter and tells us that "Knotting orchids, I stood in indecision," there seems a real danger that inadvertent humor may intrude its fatal presence.

There is a third difficulty, for which, like the second, the poet himself can hardly be held accountable. This is the unrelieved mood of frustration and despair which dominates the poem. The reader keeps expecting that the poet, having fully explained his predicament, may then go on to suggest some way out; that with each embarkation upon a new journey, the poem may take a brighter turn. By the time he comes to the end, he realizes that such hopes are vain. As I say, we can hardly criticize the poet for not offering a solution if he saw none. Perhaps the poem is in fact more powerful and moving because of this utter pessimism. It is undoubtedly the flight metaphor which misleads us, suggesting that with the escape to supernatural realms, and the magical powers which the poet so patently possesses in being able to make such journeys, there will somehow come a corresponding escape from the dilemma. When we find him at the end of the poem looking down from the heavens at his old home and concluding with a cry of despair, we may be reminded that Chaucer's Troilus from a similar vantage point looked down and laughed. The comparison is perhaps farfetched and unfair, but the English reader may nonetheless find himself tempted to make it.

The next work in the *Ch'u Tz'u* is a group of poems entitled "The Nine Songs." Actually it comprises eleven pieces, nine shamanistic songs, plus a hymn to soldiers fallen in battle and a fragment of some kind of ceremonal hymn. Wang I states that the songs were composed by Ch'ü Yüan during his banishment in the south, where he became familiar with the religious songs of the common people and, using them as a basis, composed his own songs to express his sorrow and longing for his sovereign. Fortunately in this case the question of the Ch'ü Yüan legend need not concern us. Apparently the songs were collected from among the people—most likely, judging from the names of the deities invoked, from a number of regions—and put into a uniform and polished form. The songs, or at least the originals upon which they were based, probably antedate the *Li sao,* and the redactor may indeed have been Ch'ü Yüan, though Hawkes believes that it was someone who lived shortly after him and was familiar with his work. It is not difficult to view them as expressions of Ch'ü Yüan's particular plight, as has traditionally been done. But such an interpretation is in no way necessary to make sense of them. Their general meaning is quite clear without it.

The meter of the "Nine Songs" is closer to that of the *Book of Odes.* The basic line is a four-word one, broken in the middle by the breathing particle *hsi.* This rhythm is varied occasionally by lines with more than two words before or after the caesura.

The songs are in the form of invocations by shamans or shamanesses to various deities. Sometimes the speaker seems to be the worshiper or worshipers, sometimes the deity; descriptive passages portray the beautiful dress of the shaman or the appearance of the god. The songs are apparently designed to accompany the actions of a ritual of invocation, perhaps a religious dance or pantomime. Such pantomimes may, as Hawkes has suggested, have been adapted and presented at the Ch'u court as masques for the entertainment of the nobility. No doubt if we could view the actions which accompanied the words, we would have no trouble in understanding the texts. But from the texts alone it is often difficult to decide just who is speaking—the worshiper, the deity, or a third party commenting on the scene. For this reason interpretations, and hence translations, of the songs are apt to vary widely.

The imagery of the songs is frankly erotic. The worshiper, adorning himself or herself in beautiful attire, invites the deity to a rendezvous. If the deity appears, the worshiper is in ecstasy, but more often the deity seems to hesitate, or to depart too soon, and the worshiper is left vainly searching for him in grief and longing. It is this last theme of frustrated searching that has made the songs so amenable to allegorical interpretation as expressions of Ch'ü Yüan's plight.

If we knew more about these deities and their cults, we would doubtless be able to understand the songs far better. But the old religion of the shamans, whatever its original prevalence, in time, as Hawkes has noted, came to be "superseded, discouraged, persecuted and mocked" [6] (though fragments of its mythology survived, particularly in popular Taoism). When the old state

[6] David Hawkes, "The Supernatural in Chinese Poetry," *The Far East: China and Japan* (Univ. of Toronto Quarterly Supplements, 1961), p. 316.

of Ch'u was destroyed and the empire united under the Ch'in, and later the Han, Confucian-minded scholars, though they may well have been familiar with such cults, seldom deigned to mention them in their writings. They were willing to countenance the "Nine Songs" themselves, because they believed that, though cast in the form of shamanistic hymns, they were actually the pleas of a loyal and unjustly maligned statesman. But the world of erotic imagery and superstitious beliefs from which such shamanistic hymns sprang only filled them with repugnance, and they allowed it to pass out of existence or to subsist in corrupted form among the illiterate masses, without bothering to describe it. Lacking their aid, therefore, we must be content to appreciate the songs as best we can. Their exquisite poetry—the finest perhaps in the entire anthology—and their mood of ecstatic longing come through in spite of the limitations in our understanding, and it is these qualities for which the "Nine Songs" will always be most highly prized.

The following are translations of the second and eighth songs. The former is addressed to a male deity known as Yün-chung Chün or "The Lord Among the Clouds." As in all these songs, it is possible that a group of worshipers, rather than a single shaman or shamaness, is addressing the god.

> I bathe in orchid water,
>   Wash my hair with scents,
> Put on colored robes,
>   Flower-figured.
> The spirit, twisting and turning,
>   Poised now above,
> Radiant and shining
>   In endless glory,
> Comes to take his ease
>   In the Temple of Long Life,
> And with the sun and moon

To pair his brilliance.
Riding his dragon chariot,
 Drawn like a god,
He hovers and soars,
 Roaming the vastness:
Spirit majestic,
 But now descended,
Swiftly rising
 Far off to the clouds.
He looks down on Chi-chou,
 The regions beyond;
Crosses to the four seas;
 What land does he not visit?
I think of you, Lord,
 Sighing.
You afflict my heart,
 Sorely, sorely.

The latter is addressed to Ho-po, "Lord of the River," the spirit of the Yellow River. The Yellow River, rising in the fabled K'un-lun Mountains, flowed into the sea in nine channels known as the Nine Rivers.

I sport with you
 By the Nine Rivers.
Fierce winds rise,
 Dashing waves.
I ride a water chariot
 With lotus canopy,
Drawn by two dragons
 Between a pair of river serpents.
I climb K'un-lun
 And gaze at the four quarters,
My heart bounding upward,
 Restless and astir.
Though the sun is setting,
 In my grief I forget to go.

Thinking of that distant shore,
   I lie awake longing.
Of fish scales is his house,
   With dragon halls,
Gates of purple cowrie,
   Palaces of pearl.
What does the Spirit do,
   Down in the water?
He rides a white turtle,
   By speckled fish attended.
I sport with you
   Among the river isles.
Wild are the waters
   That come rushing down.
You take my hand
   And journey east,
Escorting your fair one
   To the southern shore.
Waves, surge on surge,
   Come to greet us;
Fishes, shoal on shoal,
   To be my bridesmaids.[7]

The "Nine Songs" are followed by a mysterious poem known as *T'ien wen* or *Heavenly Questions*. Wang I states that it was composed by Ch'ü Yüan when he viewed the pictures of the various deities, ancient sages, and fabulous creatures painted on the walls of the Ch'u ancestral temples and shrines. As in the case of the "Nine Songs," the question of Ch'ü Yüan's authorship need not trouble us here. What *is* troubling is the problem of the nature and purpose of the poem itself.

It consists of a long series of questions on the origin of the universe, the nature and movement of heavenly bodies, and the

[7] As Hawkes suggests, this last section of the poem may refer to the old custom of sacrificing a young girl each year as a "bride" for the Lord of the River. She was placed on a couch and left to float down the river until the couch overturned and she drowned.

legends of the past. Some critics have attempted to see it as an expression of skepticism, a challenging, in the form of questions, of traditional beliefs and myths. This seems hardly likely, however, when we note that the poet himself often appears to accept these beliefs and to base the wording of his questions on them. Another suggestion is that it is a kind of ritual catechism designed to test the knowledge of an initiate. But this theory likewise seems unacceptable since, as Hawkes has shown, an examination of the wording of the questions reveals that the poet is not seriously seeking information, but rather posing a number of riddles or conundrums based on the body of myth and legend accepted by the men of his time.

If I may add still another hypothesis, I should like to suggest that the questions are in fact a series of storytellers' topics. We know that the legends of China must have been handed down orally for many centuries before they, or some of them, found their way into the pseudo-historical and philosophical works of Chou and Han times. It seems quite possible, therefore, that there were storytellers or "scholars" in the state of Ch'u, perhaps professionals, who possessed a whole cycle of tales to explain the topics suggested in the "Questions." Thus, for example, if the storyteller began by quoting the passage from the "Heavenly Questions" that reads: "When Chien Ti was in the tower, how did K'u favor her?", his listeners would know that they were about to hear the tale of the ancestress of the Shang dynasty who, shut up in a tower, became pregnant by swallowing a bird's egg sent her by the hero K'u. Or again, if the storyteller announced: "Lord Millet was the first-born. How did God favor him?", they would settle back to listen to the saga of Hou Chi or Lord Millet, the heroic ancestor of the royal family of Chou. If this hypothesis is correct, the "questions" would in fact be no different from the headings in the *Just So Stories*, except that the storyteller, instead of announcing his subject as "How the elephant got his trunk," would ask, "How did the elephant get his trunk?" His listeners probably knew as well as you or I do how the elephant got his trunk. The "question" simply cued them in on what particular story they were about to hear.

How the storytellers' "table of topics" came to be compiled in verse form, I do not know, though it seems quite plausible that somewhere along the line an enterprising professional would have delighted in summing up the vast scope of his lore in elegant literary form.

It may be noted that one large section of the *Han Fei Tzu,* the *Chu-shuo* or "Collected Stories," contains what in some ways seems to be a parallel to the *Heavenly Questions.* It consists of brief passages, called *ching* or "classics," that state general principles and allude in a cryptic way to various historical and legendary figures which illustrate them. These are followed by passages called *chuan* or "commentaries" which relate in full the anecdotes referred to in the *ching.* In other words, the *ching* set forth the topics and morals of the stories, while the *chuan* recount the stories themselves. If the *ching* were cast in question form and the *chuan* omitted, we would have something very much like the *Heavenly Questions.* We may surmise, then, that this was a common literary form of late Chou times—a series of brief and deliberately laconic sayings or allusions, which would be followed by the explanations of a teacher or storyteller. In the case of the *Heavenly Questions,* unfortunately, only the former ever got written down.

Because many of the legends referred to in the *Heavenly Questions* are lost or imperfectly known, and because the text has become rather confused, interpretation of the poem is extremely difficult in places. As poetry its interest is slight, but it provides an intriguing glimpse into the legends and mythology of early China, and we can only hope that further research and archeological excavation may in time increase our understanding of the body of lore upon which it is based.

The *Heavenly Questions* is followed by a group of poems known as the "Nine Declarations." Though traditionally attributed to Ch'ü Yüan, it is probable that they were composed later, partly in imitation of the *Li sao*, and may not have been put together as a group until quite far along in Han times. Except for the brief and beautiful "Praise for the Orange Tree," all are laments based upon the Ch'ü Yüan legend and dealing with the themes of rejected loyalty, exile, and suicide which characterize it.

But, though they adopt so much of the *Li sao*'s subject and imagery, they contain almost none of the magical element, the fantastic flights and meetings with deities that lie at the heart of the *Li sao* and the "Nine Songs." They reflect rather the sober, political-minded aspects of the Ch'ü Yüan legend, the aspects which would appeal to scholars of Ch'in and Han times who were not imbued with the old, magic-laden spirit of the culture of Ch'u. Though the poems contain passages of great beauty, the grief motif is often elaborated to tiresome lengths, as if the poets were constantly striving for new hyperboles to express Ch'ü Yüan's sorrow.

One of the poems, the *Huai sha* or *Embracing the Sands*, is quoted by Ssu-ma Ch'ien in his biography of Ch'ü Yüan (*Shih chi* 84), and hence dates at least from early Han times. It recounts the last days of the poet-statesman, when he had been exiled to the region of the Yangtze and its tributaries, the Yüan, Hsiang, and Mi-lo, the last of which was the scene of his suicide. In imagery and mood it borrows heavily from the *Li sao*, though in thought it. is far clearer and more unified than the *Li sao*

ever is. The text followed here is that found in the *Ch'u Tz'u,*
which differs slightly at one point from that in the *Shih chi.*

Warm, bright days of early summer,
When shrubs and trees grow rich with green,
And I, in anguish and endless sorrow,
Hasten on my way to a southern land.
My eyes are dazed by darkness,
Deep stillness lies all around me;
Bound by injustice, grieved by wrong,
I bear the long torment of this pain.
I still my heart and follow my will;
Bowing before injustice, I humble myself.
They would round the corners of my squareness,
But I will not change my constant form.
To abandon the course he has set out upon:
This is a disgrace to a worthy man.
As a builder with his line, I have laid out my plan;
I will not alter my former course.
To be forthright in nature and of loyal heart:
This is the pride of a great man.
If the skilled carpenter never carves,
Who can tell how true he cuts?
Dark patterns in a hidden place
The ill of sight call a formless nothing;
The subtle glance of the keen-eyed Li Lou
The ignorant mistake for blindness.
They have changed white into black,
Toppled "up" and made it "down."
Phoenixes they pen in cages,
While common fowl soar aloft;
Jewels and stones they mix together,
And weigh them in the same balance.
The men in power, with their petty envies,
Cannot recognize my worth.
I could bear high office and bring glory to the world,
Yet I am plunged to the depths and deprived of success.

So I must embrace this jewel of virtue
And to the end share it with no one.
As the packs of village dogs bark,
So they bark at what is strange;
To censure greatness and doubt the unusual,
Such is the nature of the herd.
Though ability and refinement combine in me,
The world does not know my excellence.
Though I have abundance of talent,
No one acknowledges my possessions.
I have honored benevolence and upheld duty,
Been diligent and faithful in full degree;
Yet, since I cannot meet Emperor Shun of old,
Who is there to appreciate my actions?
Many men have been born in an ill age,
But I cannot tell the reason.
The sages T'ang and Yü have long departed;
Though I yearn for them, they are far away.
I will calm my wrath and mend my anger,
Still my heart and be strong.
Though I meet darkness, I will not falter;
Let my determination serve as a model to men!
I walk the road to my lodge in the north;[8]
The day grows dark; night is falling.
I will pour out sorrow and delight in woe,
For all will have an end in the Great Affair of death.

Reprise:

Broad flow the waters of the Yüan and the Hsiang;
Their two streams roar on to the Yangtze.
Long is the road and hidden in shadow;
The way I go is vast and far.
I sing to myself of my constant sorrow,
Lost in lamentation.
In the world no one knows me;
There is none to tell my heart to.

---

[8] North is the direction of winter and death.

I must embrace my thoughts, hold fast my worth;
I am alone and without a mate.
Po-lo, judge of fine steeds, has long passed away;
Who now can tell the worth of a thoroughbred?
Man at his birth receives his fate,
And by it each life must be disposed.
I will calm my heart and pluck up my will;
What more have I to fear?
In the past I have suffered grief;
Long have I sighed.
The world is muddy, no one knows me,
Men's hearts cannot be told.
I know that death cannot be refused;
May I love life no longer!
This I proclaim to all worthy men:
I will be an example for you!

The remainder of the *Ch'u Tz'u* is made up of short pieces or groups of poems. Some of them, such as the narratives *Divination* and *The Fisherman* or the poem *Summons to the Soul*, date probably from late Chou times, while others are Han works, often by known authors. Most of them deal with aspects of the Ch'ü Yüan legend and borrow heavily from the *Li sao* or other earlier pieces.

Of these latter pieces, only a few, I believe, merit discussion here. One such is the *Chiu pien* or "Nine Arguments," a series of poems attributed to Sung Yü. Sung Yü was said to have been a disciple of Ch'ü Yüan and an official at the court of King Ch'ing-hsiang of Ch'u. Too little is known of him and his connection with this group of poems, however, to make a discussion of authorship worthwhile.

The poems themselves, apparently composed as a cycle, deal with many of the *Li sao* themes—slander, unrecognized worth, the deluded ruler—and borrow metaphors and historical allusions from it. But, unlike the other early poems on these themes, they contain no mention of Ch'ü Yüan himself. The themes alone have been extracted from the legend of the exiled statesman and expanded into a universal statement of loneliness, frustration, and despair.

The most beautiful and original parts of the cycle are those which deal with the flight of time, the pressing approach of autumnal decay and winter cold that presage the passing of youth and hope. The cycle opens with a burst of eloquence in which the poet describes the heartless onslaught of autumn and the desolation it brings, so impassioned that it makes much of what follows seem like an anticlimax.

This subject of the passing of time is not entirely unknown in the *Book of Odes*. There, in the "airs of T'ang," we find the earliest Chinese statements on the familiar *carpe diem* theme in the reminders that "The cricket is in the hall,/ The year draws to a close./ If we do not enjoy ourselves/ The days and months will soon pass by!" (# 114), or urgings to feast, play the lute, "And be merry,/ Prolonging day into night,/ Before you grow old and die/ And other men enter your halls!" (# 115).

But for the most part the griefs and ills which the poets of the *Odes* complain of are man-made, the results of human folly and cruelty, and can presumably be corrected by man himself. The universe as a whole is regarded as essentially benign. Though nature or Heaven may at times appear to be indifferent to man, there is seldom any suggestion, except perhaps in the poem quoted earlier on the great drought, that they can be actually inimical, and the early poets, one supposes, would hardly have wasted their breath bemoaning anything so commonplace and irremediable as the passing of time and the onslaught of the seasons.

With the social upheavals that characterized the end of the Chou and the unification of the empire under Ch'in, this sunny view of the universe faded. Fatalism looms large in the philosophical thought of the time and poetry begins to reflect the conviction that it is not only social and political ills alone, but often a kind of cosmic animosity, that frustrate man in his search for achievement and fame. This is the mood underlying the "Nine Arguments" and their passages of mournful complaint. The cold of autumn which blights the world, the heartless winging of time, are not merely symbols of the blighting of the poet's hopes by old age and death, but actual forces attacking and weighing down his spirits.

Yet they are not forces which the poet can conceivably combat. The Chinese never, so far as I know, departed so far from their early optimism as to envision anything like a Manichean "darkness," a universal power of evil surrounding and crushing in upon man, against which man must struggle. Had they done so, they might have found some worthy opponent for their outrage, some surface against which their anger could strike. As it is, the Chinese poet, while burdened by this sense of the passing of time and the rapid approach of death, can only grumble ineffectually. This is the weakness of the theme, and it explains why so much of the poetry that deals with it, while occasionally poignant and sincere, more often lapsed into a tiresome whine. This is particularly true in later Chinese poetry, where the lament on the approach of old age becomes a stock theme and each poet feels obliged to record his indignation and sense of personal affront when he finds that he too is subject to the universal condition of mankind.

Two other poems in the *Ch'u Tz'u* deserve notice, the *Chao hun* or *Summons to the Soul*, and the *Ta chao* or *Great Summons*. As already mentioned in the section on philosophical writings, it was customary in ancient China at the time of a death to perform a ritual that was intended, originally at least, to summon back the soul of the departed. These poems are based upon this custom, and according to tradition were addressed to the wandering soul of Ch'ü Yüan, either by Ch'ü Yüan himself or by one or another of his disciples. Modern scholars regard them as addresses to a king, whose soul is urged to give up its wandering and return to the palace to enjoy a life of extravagant ease. The king in this case, however, was probably not dead, since there seems to be every expectation that he will hear and answer the summons, but only ailing; as Professor Hawkes suggests, the poems may in fact be purely literary pieces written for the entertainment and flattery of an actual monarch. They are noteworthy for their rich and vivid descriptive passages, first of the perils the wandering soul faces in its travels abroad, and later of the gorgeous palaces, lovely waiting women, food, music, games, and other delights that await the soul on its return. In this fondness for description they form a connecting link with the long descriptive poems in the *fu* or rhyme-prose style which are the subject of the next section.

THE HAN FU

The term *fu* or rhyme-prose eventually came to designate a type of poetic composition, usually rather long and descriptive in nature, employing meters much like those of the *sao*-type poems, lush verbiage, and occasional introductions or interludes in prose. (This last characteristic, the ease with which the *fu* passes back and forth from prose to rhymed verse, has prompted scholars to use the term "rhyme-prose.") In early Han times, however, there was no clear distinction made between the *fu* and the *sao* poems from which they in part derived, and the latter were often referred to as *fu* also. As emphasized by Han scholars, the *fu* were designed to be chanted or recited rather than sung in the manner of the *Odes* or the so-called Ch'u songs.

The question of the evolution of the *fu* form is greatly complicated by the fact that what purport to be the earliest specimens of the form cannot in many cases be dated with any assurance. I shall begin the discussion, therefore, with the first example whose date is certain, the *Fu on the Owl* by Chia I (201–169 B.C.), recorded in his biography in *Shih chi* 84.

In many ways it is closer to the poems of the *Ch'u Tz'u* than to the later *fu,* and thus serves as a bridge between the two genres. The statesman Chia I greatly admired Ch'ü Yüan, and his biography records, in addition to *The Owl*, a *fu* entitled *Lament for Ch'ü Yüan*, which he composed and cast into the river where the earlier poet was supposed to have drowned himself. *The Owl*, written when Chia I, after serving at the court of Emperor Wen of the Han, had been sent to the state of Ch'ang-sha in the south to act as tutor to its king, a kind of banishment in disguise, is, like the *Li sao,* highly personal. The poet, deeply troubled by his estrangement from the emperor and the thought of impending death (he was in ill health and died a few years later), attempts to console himself with the Taoist view of life and death as a process of endless and ineluctable change. The meter is more regular than that of the *sao* poems or the later *fu,* consisting of an eight-word line broken in the middle by a caesura, that is, a basic four-word meter. The introduction is not part of the poem itself, but is taken from Ssu-ma Ch'ien's biography of the poet. The date indicated by the poem seems to be 174 B.C., though some scholars would make it 173.

Three years after Chia I became grand tutor to the king of Ch'ang-sha a hoot owl one day flew into his lodge and perched on the corner of his mat. . . . Chia I had been disgraced and sent to live in Ch'ang-sha, a damp, low-lying region, and he believed that he did not have long to live. He was filled with horror and grief at the appearance of the bird and, to console himself, composed a poem in the rhyme-prose style which read:

In the year *tan-o,*
Fourth month, first month of summer,
The day *kuei-tzu,* when the sun was low in the west,
An owl came to my lodge
And perched on the corner of my mat,
Phlegmatic and fearless.
Secretly wondering the reason
The strange thing had come to roost,
I took out a book to divine it
And the oracle told me its secret:
    "Wild bird enters the hall;
      The master will soon depart."
I asked and importuned the owl,
"Where is it I must go?
Do you bring good luck? Then tell me!
Misfortune? Relate what disaster!
Must I depart so swiftly?
Then speak to me of the hour!"
The owl breathed a sigh,
Raised its head and beat its wings.
Its beak could utter no word,
But let me tell you what it sought to say:
All things alter and change;
Never a moment of ceasing.
Revolving, whirling, and rolling away;
Driven far off and returning again;
Form and breath passing onward,
Like the mutations of a cicada.
Profound, subtle, and illimitable,
Who can finish describing it?
Good luck must be followed by bad;
Bad in turn bow to good.
Sorrow and joy throng the gate;
Weal and woe in the same land.
Wu was powerful and great;
Under Fu-ch'a it sank in defeat.
Yüeh was crushed at K'uai-chi,

But Kou-chien made it an overlord.
Li Ssu, who went forth to greatness, at last
Suffered the five mutilations.
Fu Yüeh was sent into bondage,
Yet Wu Ting made him his aide.[9]
Thus fortune and disaster
Entwine like the strands of a rope.
Fate cannot be told of,
For who shall know its ending?
Water, troubled, runs wild;
The arrow, quick-sped, flies far.
All things, whirling and driving,
Compelling and pushing each other, roll on.
The clouds rise up, the rains come down,
In confusion inextricably joined.
The Great Potter fashions all creatures,
Infinite, boundless, limit unknown.
There is no reckoning Heaven,
Nor divining beforehand the Tao.
The span of life is fated;
Man cannot guess its ending.
Heaven and Earth are the furnace,
The workman, the Creator;
His coal is the yin and the yang,
His copper, all things of creation.
Joining, scattering, ebbing and flowing,
Where is there persistence or rule?
A thousand, a myriad mutations,
Lacking an end's beginning.
Suddenly they form a man:
How is this worth taking thought of?
They are transformed again in death:

[9] Wu and Yüch were rival states in the southeast during pre-Ch'in times and Fu-ch'a and Kou-chien the rulers who led them to defeat and glory respectively. Li Ssu, prime minister to the First Emperor of the Ch'in, later fell from favor and was executed. Wu Ting was a king of the Yin dynasty who dreamed of a worthy minister and later discovered the man of his dream in an ex-convict laborer, Fu Yüeh.

Should this perplex you?
The witless takes pride in his being,
Scorning others, a lover of self.
The man of wisdom sees vastly
And knows that all things will do.
The covetous run after riches,
The impassioned pursue a fair name;
The proud die struggling for power,
While the people long only to live.
Each drawn and driven onward,
They hurry east and west.
The great man is without bent;
A million changes are as one to him.
The stupid man chained by custom
Suffers like a prisoner bound.
The sage abandons things
And joins himself to the Tao alone,
While the multitudes in delusion
With desire and hate load their hearts.
Limpid and still, the true man
Finds his peace in the Tao alone.
Transcendent, destroying self,
Vast and empty, swift and wild,
He soars on wings of the Tao.
Borne on the flood he sails forth;
He rests on the river islets.
Freeing his body to Fate,
Unpartaking of self,
His life is a floating,
His death a rest.
In stillness like the stillness of deep springs,
Like an unmoored boat drifting aimlessly,
Valuing not the breath of life,
He embraces and drifts with Nothing.
Comprehending Fate and free of sorrow,
The man of virtue heeds no bonds.
Petty matters, weeds and thorns—
What are they to me?

Much more typical of what the *fu* form was to become in later times is the group of works attributed to Ch'ü Yüan's disciple Sung Yü. In fact these poems appear to be the models and prototypes for many of the works of the famous *fu* writers of the Han. Unfortunately, however, we have no way to determine for sure whether they actually date from the third century B.C., when Sung Yü was supposed to have lived, or indeed are even earlier than Chia I's "Owl."

Among the works attributed to Sung Yü, the most important are the *fu* style poems entitled *Mount Kao-t'ang*, *The Goddess*, and *The Wind*. The first of these, like so many later *fu,* begins with a prose introduction setting the scene. King Ch'ing-hsiang of Ch'u, accompanied by Sung Yü, is visiting the great marsh of Yün-meng. After an exchange of dialogue, the king asks the poet to compose for him a *fu* on the wonders of Mount Kao-t'ang in the region. In a long, rhymed passage, sometimes in lines of six words, sometimes in lines of four or three, the poet proceeds to describe the appearance of the mountain, its rushing streams and the fish and reptiles which inhabit them, its flowering trees, its steep and rugged heights and the strange creatures, flowers, birds, and immortal spirits who dwell there. The king is then pictured setting out upon a hunt, and is finally admonished to "take thought for the myriad directions and care for the ills of the nation,/ Open the way for sages and worthy men and repair the shortcomings of the government." Thus, after enchanting the king (and the reader) with his vivid and exotic descriptions, the poet delivers a little homily on good government.

The Goddess likewise begins with an introduction in which Sung Yü describes to the king a beautiful goddess who appeared to him in a dream. The king requests him to compose a *fu* on the subject, and the poet complies with a long description of the loveliness of the deity and the soft, slow, seductive, shy way she approached. Before the poet may do anything more than stare in rapt attention, however, the goddess departs, leaving him senseless with grief. No moral is drawn, and the purpose of the piece seems to be merely to captivate the reader with a mildly erotic catalogue of feminine charms.

The third of the major *fu, The Wind*, I shall quote in full, since nothing, I realize, is more exasperating than reading descriptions of poems when one cannot refer to the poems themselves. It is one of the finest, and at the same time one of the most puzzling, of the early *fu*. The text is preserved in *chuan* 13 of the *Wen hsüan* or *Anthology of Literature*.

King Hsiang of Ch'u was taking his ease in the Palace of the Orchid Terrace, with his courtiers Sung Yü and Ching Ch'a attending him, when a sudden gust of wind came sweeping in. The king, opening wide the collar of his robe and facing into it, said, "How delightful this wind is! And I and the common people may share it together, may we not?"

But Sung Yü replied, "This wind is for Your Majesty alone. How could the common people have a share in it?"

"The wind," said the king, "is the breath of heaven and earth. Into every corner it unfolds and reaches; without choosing between high or low, exalted or humble, it touches everywhere. What do you mean when you say that this wind is for me alone?"

Sung Yü replied, "I have heard my teacher say that the twisted branches of the lemon tree invite the birds to nest, and hollows and cracks summon the wind. But the breath of the wind differs with the place which it seeks out."

"Tell me," said the king. "Where does the wind come from?"

Sung Yü answered:

"The wind is born from the land
   And springs up in the tips of the green duckweed.
   It insinuates itself into the valleys
   And rages in the canyon mouth,
   Skirts the corners of Mount T'ai

And dances beneath the pines and cedars.
Swiftly it flies, whistling and wailing;
Fiercely it splutters its anger.
It crashes with a voice like thunder,
Whirls and tumbles in confusion,
Shaking rocks, striking trees,
Blasting the tangled forest.
Then, when its force is almost spent,
It wavers and disperses,
Thrusting into crevices and rattling door latches.
Clean and clear,
It scatters and rolls away.
Thus it is that this cool, fresh hero wind,
Leaping and bounding up and down,
Climbs over the high wall
And enters deep into palace halls.
With a puff of breath it shakes the leaves and flowers,
Wanders among the cassia and pepper trees,
Or soars over the swift waters.
It buffets the mallow flower,
Sweeps the angelica, touches the spikenard,
Glides over the sweet lichens and lights on willow shoots,
Rambling over the hills
And their scattered host of fragrant flowers.
After this, it wanders into the courtyard,
Ascends the jade hall in the north,
Clambers over gauze curtains,
Passes through the inner apartments,
And so becomes Your Majesty's wind.
When this wind blows on a man,
At once he feels a chill run through him,
And he sighs at its cool freshness.
Clear and gentle,
It cures sickness, dispels drunkenness,
Sharpens the eyes and ears,
Relaxes the body and brings benefit to men.
This is what is called the hero wind of Your Majesty."

"How well you have described it!" exclaimed the king. "But now may I hear about the wind of the common people?" And Sung Yü replied:

"The wind of the common people
   Comes whirling from the lanes and alleys,
   Poking in the rubbish, stirring up the dust,
   Fretting and worrying its way along.
   It creeps into holes and knocks on doors,
   Scatters sand, blows ashes about,
   Muddles in dirt and tosses up bits of filth.
   It sidles through hovel windows
   And slips into cottage rooms.
   When this wind blows on a man,
   At once he feels confused and downcast.
   Pounded by heat, smothered in dampness,
   His heart grows sick and heavy,
   And he falls ill and breaks out in a fever.
   Where it brushes his lips, sores appear;
   It strikes his eyes with blindness.
   He stammers and cries out,
   Not knowing if he is dead or alive.
   This is what is called the lowly wind of the common people."

The meaning of the poem is perfectly clear. But what, one immediately feels compelled to ask, is its purpose?

Writers of the Latter Han and Six Dynasties period, having in mind, no doubt, the ends to which the *fu* form was put in their time, claimed that the primary function of the *fu* was "to describe." Certainly all of Sung Yü's *fu* we have discussed so far are descriptions of scenes or objects, and the same is true of most of the *fu* by known Han writers; often, in fact, the *fu* comes perilously close to being little more than a catalogue of the names of plants, animals, birds, or what not. If we accept this criterion, therefore, the "Wind" *fu* has fulfilled all the purpose it needs simply by describing to the reader the two kinds of winds. According to our modern concept of pure literature, if the poem does this well and in a way that is pleasurable to the reader, that is all the excuse it needs for existing.

But, as I have stated before, the early Chinese had no concept of "pure literature," or at least they never mention such a concept, and if their left hands happened to write any literature of that type, it was kept a secret from their right hands, which were busy writing polemic and literature of "uplift." Thus we find that such famous *fu* writers of the Han as Yang Hsiung, or the historians Ssu-ma Ch'ien and Pan Ku, when they come to define the *fu,* all insist that its purpose is to instruct or reprimand. This, it will be recalled, was, according to Han theory, the purpose of the songs in the *Book of Odes*; by attributing a similar aim to the *fu,* the scholars were no doubt attempting to invest the new genre with an appropriate air of gravity. That all *fu* did not conform to this definition is obvious; if they had the scholars would hardly, we may suppose, have insisted upon it so emphatically, nor would there have been any reason to change the definition later. The *fu* on *The Goddess* described above, for example, no matter how one interprets it, cannot, so far as I can see, be made to yield up any moral other than that dreams can be fun. And yet this definition of the didactic function of the *fu* cannot be entirely dismissed as an extraneous bit of apologia, since it is obvious that many of the early *fu* were actually written with it in mind.

Let us return now to Sung Yü and his winds. The poem is actually in the form of a debate, a form so often used in the *fu* that some scholars have even attempted to derive the *fu* genre from the florid debates and speeches of the diplomats and rhetoricians of the Warring States period. The king expresses the common-sense, traditional view that the same wind is shared by all men alike, exalted or humble. His pronouncement is in fact a paraphrase of one of the commonest clichés of early Chinese literature, that heaven covers all men and earth bears them up with complete impartiality. Sung Yü, however, comes forward to refute this axiom, propounding instead the startling theory that there are actually two kinds of winds, one for royalty and one for the peasants. If we take the poem at face value, as some critics have done, we must suppose that it is this second view that the poet wishes us to adopt. But can we accept this conclusion so readily?

Sung Yü's assertion is not only completely without precedent in Chinese thought but, as I have said, directly contradicts one of its axioms. The king, on hearing such an argument, would be bound to conclude, I should think, that he was being either grossly flattered or made the butt of a literary jest. Is it possible, then, that the poet's serious opinion is expressed in the words of the king, and that what follows is merely an exercise in fantasy and fine writing? Or is it even possible, returning to the definition of the *fu* as a vehicle for reprimand, that the poet, in his unconventional theory of the two winds, is implying that the king's way of life is so luxurious and so far removed from that of his subjects that the very winds that visit him must be different? That is the way at least one critic seems to have read the poem, the T'ang commentator Lü Hsiang, who states flatly and without elaboration: "King Hsiang was proud and lived a life of luxury. Therefore Sung Yü wrote this *fu* to reprimand him" (*Liu-ch'en-chu Wen hsüan* ch. 13).

I have gone into this point in some detail because it concerns not only our interpretation of the *Wind fu,* but that of many other Han *fu* in the debate form. At first glance one naturally assumes that the last speaker in the debate is supposed to have won the day, particularly as his opponents are often pictured, in terms that border on caricature, as being completely thunderstruck by his arguments and incapable of refuting them. But this note of caricature itself should warn us not to accept too quickly at face value what we read, for the Han writers are capable of great subtlety. And the more we read the piece over, the more uncertain we become as to just which of the opinions expressed is actually that of the poet himself.

Let me cite a few examples. The first concerns not a *fu,* actually, but a prose polemic written by the poet and statesman Ssu-ma Hsiang-ju (179–117 B.C.). Ssu-ma Hsiang-ju had urged Emperor Wu to build a road out of western China in order to open up communication with the barbarian tribes beyond. The project was accordingly undertaken, but proved to be extremely difficult and expensive. When Ssu-ma Hsiang-ju journeyed to Shu, where the work was going on, and heard the complaints of the people there against the project, he wrote a letter in debate form in which the elders of Shu first voice their objections to the project, and then Ssu-ma Hsiang-ju himself, as envoy of the emperor, extols its advantages and explains the emperor's purpose in undertaking it. The piece ends with the elders, apparently completely won over by the envoy's eloquence and logic, departing in embarrassed confusion. Yet Ssu-ma Ch'ien, who records the piece in his biography of Ssu-ma Hsiang-ju (*Shih chi* 117), states that Ssu-ma Hsiang-ju himself had concluded that the project was impractical. Since he had first suggested it, however, he did not dare openly advocate that it be abandoned, but instead "used the words of the elders of Shu to express his own disapproval of the plan in order to criticize the actions of the emperor." In other words, in this case we know for certain that the writer's own opinion, the reprimand which he wishes to make, is embodied in the first view expressed, while the second and opposing view, which appears at first glance to win the argument, is actually only a piece of camouflage added to protect the writer.

The piece referred to above is not a *fu*, it is true, but it should serve to warn us that works written in the debate form are not always as simple as they seem.

Here is another example, a fragment of a rhymed *Remonstrance on Wine* written by the poet Yang Hsiung (53 B.C.- A.D. 18) for Emperor Ch'eng of the Former Han. It was in the form of a debate between a tippler and a strait-laced gentleman. Oddly enough, only the words of the tippler have been preserved (in the biography of Ch'en Tsun, *Han shu* 92).

> You, sir, may be compared to a pitcher.
> Look for a pitcher and one finds it
> Sitting on the edge of a well.
> Perched up high, overlooking the depths,
> When it moves it is constantly on the brink of danger.
> Wine and spirits do not pass its mouth;
> Instead it is loaded with a bellyful of water.
> It cannot move to left or right,
> But is dragged up and down by the well rope.
> Then one morning it is lowered too fast
> And smashes to bits on a brick in the well wall.
> Its body hurtles down to the yellow springs
> And its bones and flesh turn into mud.
> This is the way it looks out for itself,
> No match, indeed, for the leather wine sack!
> The wine sack is a carefree wag,
> With a belly like a great pot.
> All day long he is full of wine;
> You can always draw another draught.
> He is used to being treated like an elder statesman,
> Riding with the ruler in the royal carriage.
> He goes in and out of the Two Palaces,[10]
> And completely runs the affairs of the nation.
> Surely when one can say this much,
> There cannot be anything wrong with wine!

[10] The palace of the emperor and the palace in which the empress dowager and the heir apparent resided.

It should be noted that Yang Hsiung himself was very fond of drinking, and though this would not prevent him from remonstrating with the emperor for overindulgence, one wonders if the second part of the debate, the case against wine, was anything like as spirited as the part above, and whether this may not have something to do with the fact that only the first part has survived.

Many of the debate *fu* raise the same sort of doubt in our minds. A long *fu* by Yang Hsiung, *The Ch'ang-yang Palace* (*Wen hsüan* 9), describes a lavish hunt held there by Emperor Ch'eng for the entertainment of foreign envoys. A scholar then appears and criticizes the hunt for its extravagant wastefulness and the burden it imposes upon the common people, who must abandon their daily labors to collect the beasts used in the hunt. The scholar's host, however, after a long review of Han history, explains that such spectacles are necessary in order to impress the barbarians with the might and glory of the Han and win their allegiance, though he admits that the emperor is concerned "lest later generations mistake what is only a temporary expedient for a regular duty of the state." Here one feels very strongly that Yang Hsiung's own views are expressed in the words of the scholar-critic, and that the so-called rebuttal of them, for all its eloquence, is no more than a rather grudgingly offered sop to the imperial conscience.

I would caution the reader, therefore, that the *fu* often do contain an element of reprimand, and that it is frequently couched in such a way as not to be immediately apparent. I do not wish to press the point further, however, since, as I have said, there are some *fu* which clearly have no moral at all, and others which have a moral tacked so haphazardly on the end that one may regard it perhaps as a pious excuse, but certainly not as the main purpose of the poem.

Such, for example, is the *Seven Incitements* (*Wen hsüan* 34) by one of the early *fu* writers, Mei Sheng (d. 140 B.C.). In this poem an imaginary "prince of Ch'u," who is ill, is visited by a man of Wu, who opines that the prince's ailment comes from too much luxurious living and offers to cure it. He then sets out to rouse the prince from his sickbed by describing to him, in a series of long set pieces, seven types of sensual delights: (1) the beautiful music of the lute; (2) delicious foods and wines; (3) a ride in a wonderful carriage; (4) an outing at a palace, attended by ladies in waiting, musicians, and courtiers who compose lovely descriptive poetry (!); (5) a magnificent hunt; (6) a glorious battle followed by a feast and rejoicing; and (7) a journey to the seashore (including an extended description of the fury and magnificence of the waves). Since the prince is already suffering from overindulgence, it seems odd that his visitor would attempt in this way to stimulate him to further excesses; here the story framework of the poem seems to be no more than a pretext for the poet to display his skill on a series of conventional themes. The prince, however, is not to be roused by such enticements. Though his color begins to improve with the fifth allurement depicted, he protests at the end of each that he is still too feeble to arise and partake. The visitor then proceeds to an eighth enticement, and succeeds in bringing the prince instantly to his feet by (has the reader guessed?) offering to introduce to him sages and philosophers who will plan all his affairs for him. The perfunctoriness of the last section and the alacrity with which the prince responds seem to suggest that at this point the poet was anxious only to make his bow to didactic convention as quickly as possible and be done with the piece. It is significant, however, that he considered such a gesture necessary.

The *fu* were in most cases written by officials or professional scholars at the courts of the emperors or the feudal princes. Often the primary purpose of the writers was simply to give pleasure to their royal patrons through the richness and beauty of their language and the exotic scenes described. Quite rightly the critics evolved two definitions of the purpose of the *fu,* for one could not cover all cases. The real problem with the early *fu* is to decide just what mixture of the two elements, reprimand and pure description, has gone into any particular piece, to determine which aim the poet himself considered fundamental and which merely ancillary. I do not insist on the judgments I have expressed above. Sung Yü's *Wind* may in fact be nothing more than a charming and slyly sycophantic piece of divertisement, or again Mei Sheng's *Seven Incitements* may, as the commentators insist, be intended as a serious reprimand. As in the case of so much of early Chinese literature, it is difficult to determine just at what point interpretation passes over into the realm of fancy.[11]

Ssu-ma Hsiang-ju, mentioned above, is credited with having brought the early descriptive *fu* to its highest level of development. He served for a time at the court of King Hsiao of Liang, where he was a companion of Mei Sheng, the author of the *Seven Incitements.* Later, when Emperor Wu read and admired a poem he had written at that time, Hsiang-ju was summoned to the capital to serve the emperor. This earlier poem was presumably in the form of a debate between two gentlemen of Ch'u and Ch'i respectively, in which they discussed the magnificent hunts of their sovereigns. When Hsiang-ju was presented to the emperor, he asked to be allowed to compose a similar poem on the imperial hunts. What he did, it seems, was to rework his earlier poem, adding a third member to the debate who, after the men of Ch'u and Ch'i have described their hunts, proceeds to

[11] It is interesting to note that Yang Hsiung, one of the most famous *fu* poets, renounced the writing of *fu* in his later years because he felt that their didactic purpose was too often obscured beyond recognition by their characteristic wealth of extravagant language.

overwhelm them with a breath-taking account of the wonders of the imperial hunts and the emperor's way of life. This last part of the poem, often regarded as a separate work, is referred to as the *Fu on the Shang-lin Park*. The entire poem appears in Ssu-ma Hsiang-ju's biography (*Shih chi* 117), but I shall quote only from the last part.

In this section, the narrator proceeds step by step to describe the geography of the imperial park, its rivers, mountains, and wild life, the palaces and lodges it contains and the forests that surround them. He then moves to a description of the hunt itself, and the feasting and entertainments of the court which follow it. Thus far the poem is pure sensuous description. But the moral is not to be forgotten, and in the closing section of the poem the emperor, waking in horror to the wasteful extravagance of such sports, is pictured as dismissing the revelers, renouncing luxury, and throwing open his park to the use of the poor. Instead of preaching to Emperor Wu, the poet simply pictures the emperor as taking, of his own accord, the steps which the poet would like him to take (but which, needless to say, in actual life he never did).

Thus the poem ends with a "message," paradoxically enough, like that of the *Seven Incitements*, a call to the ruler to renounce the very pleasures which the poet has just finished depicting so attractively. Apologists for the poem, such as Ssu-ma Ch'ien, insist that the gravity of the message is sufficient to justify the extravagant language which precedes it, but since the Western reader need not be concerned with "justifications" for good poetry, I will not go into the question further.

What needs some comment here, I believe, is the extraordinary language of the poem. The basic line is a four-word one, like that of Chia I's *Owl*. This is often varied by lines of three or six words and broken by such short phrases as "And then there were," "Next came the," etc., which introduce the sections of the narrative. Much of the narrative, it will be noted, consists simply of lists of birds, animals, precious stones, trees, and so forth. How many of these names were familiar to ordinary Han people and how many were exotic or outlandish, we cannot say. The *Ch'u Tz'u* poems, we have noted, show a marked fondness for exotic landscapes, and this taste carries over into the Han *fu*. Several of the great *fu* writers, among them Ssu-ma Hsiang-ju, were also lexicographers, and it has been suggested that they composed their poems with a brush in one hand and a dictionary in the other. Perhaps the literary men of the day made a kind of game of collecting the names of odd trees, minerals, birds, or what not, which they then worked into their compositions.

These names present a grave difficulty to the translator, since many of them cannot be identified with any certainty today. Commentators, mostly of the T'ang period, can often give nothing more helpful by way of a definition than "a kind of large tree," "a small variety of monkey," which would seem to suggest that the names were already unknown in their time. To evade the problem in translation by simply romanizing the Chinese names does not seem, except in occasional cases, an acceptable solution, since it produces passages like "And then there were *wu* trees, *pao* trees, *ling* trees, and *ts'ai* trees," which convey no picture at all to the reader and are irritating in a different way from the original. In my translation, therefore, I have attempted, on the basis of what hints are supplied by the commentators, to find some sort of English equivalent, though it is quite possible that in my ignorance I have credited to ancient China species of life that never existed there. Since the purpose of the poem obviously is not to convey scientific data, but purely to build up a fabric of rich and exuberant verbiage, such a method seems to me the only acceptable one.

Another problem is posed by the large number of descriptive binomial compounds. Though common enough in other types of poetry and prose, they are particularly numerous in the *fu*, helping to give them their musical, rhapsodic air. Here again commentators are often less then helpful, perhaps because they themselves were at a loss, offering only the vaguest glosses such as "descriptive of high mountains" or "the aspect of rushing water." And again one wonders if such a wealth of epithets would have been easily intelligible to men of the Han; certainly they are hardly so today. Reading a Han *fu* is rather like reading "Jabberwocky." In most cases the characters themselves, with their water, wood, wind, or stone radicals, give the reader enough of a clue to their meaning that he may follow the general contour of the description. But even so, he would, without the aid of commentaries, be hard put at many points to say exactly what is going on. All this dazzling verbiage and ambiguity must, of course, disappear in translation, and the elusive, musical binomes must be reduced to explicit adjectives and adverbs.

Ssu-ma Hsiang-ju lived at a time when the Han dynasty, already firmly established as the ruler of a broad and prosperous China, was spreading its influence, through warfare and diplomatic missions, abroad in all directions. New provinces were added to the empire, new lands opened up, and a stream of foreign envoys began pouring into the Han court, bringing gifts of exotic plants and animals and strange tales of their distant homelands. This newly roused interest in the exotic, the pomp and luxury of the court, and the buoyant self-confidence of the age are well reflected in the works of Emperor Wu's court poet, Ssu-ma Hsiang-ju. Arthur Waley, emphasizing the close relationship between these great descriptive *fu* and the spells and incantations of the "Nine Songs" of the *Ch'u Tz'u*, states that the *fu* achieves its effect "not by argument nor even by rhetoric, but by a purely sensuous intoxication of rhythm and language" (*The Temple and Other Poems*, p. 17). I can think of no better description of the magic of Ssu-ma Hsiang-ju's work.

This, then, is the descriptive section of the *Shang-lin Fu,* in which the representative of the emperor's court, after listening to the speeches of the representatives of Ch'u and Ch'i, recounts the splendors of the imperial park. I have omitted the closing section, a mixture of prose and poetry, in which the emperor solemnly renounces such delights. The text is that found in the *Shih chi* biography of Ssu-ma Hsiang-ju.

"Moreover, what do the states of Ch'i and Ch'u possess, that they are worth speaking about? You gentlemen perhaps have never laid eyes upon true splendor. Have you not heard of the Shang-lin Park of the Son of Heaven?

"To the east of it lies Ts'ang-wu,
  To the west, the land of Hsi-chi;
On its south runs the Cinnabar River,
  On the north, the Purple Deeps.
Within the park spring the Pa and Ch'an rivers,
  And through it flow the Ching and Wei,
The Feng, the Hao, the Lao, and the Chüeh,
  Twisting and turning their way
Through the reaches of the park;
Eight rivers, coursing onward,
Spreading in different directions, each with its own form.
North, south, east, and west
  They race and tumble,
Pouring through the chasms of Pepper Hill,
Skirting the banks of the river islets,
Winding through the cinnamon forests
  And across the broad meadows.
In wild confusion they swirl
  Along the bases of the tall hills
And through the mouths of the narrow gorges;

Dashed upon boulders, maddened by winding escarpments,
They writhe in anger,
Leaping and curling upward,
Jostling and eddying in great swells
That surge and batter against each other;
Darting and twisting,
Foaming and tossing
In a thundering chaos;
Arching into hills, billowing like clouds,
They dash to left and right,
Plunging and breaking in waves
That chatter over the shallows;
Crashing against the cliffs, pounding the embankments,
The waters pile up and reel back again,
Skipping across the rises, swooping into the hollows,
Rumbling and murmuring onward;
Deep and powerful,
Fierce and clamorous,
They froth and churn
Like the boiling waters of a cauldron,
Casting spray from their crests, until,
After their wild race through the gorges,
Their distant journey from afar,
They subside into silence,
Rolling on in peace to their long destination,
Boundless and without end,
Gliding in soundless and solemn procession,
Shimmering and shining in the sun,
To flow through giant lakes of the east
Or spill into the ponds along their banks.
Here horned dragons and red hornless dragons,
Sturgeon and salamanders,
Carp, bream, gudgeon, and dace,
Cowfish, flounder, and sheatfish
Arch their backs and twitch their tails,
Spread their scales and flap their fins,
Diving among the deep crevices;

The waters are loud with fish and turtles,
A multitude of living things.
Here moon-bright pearls
Gleam on the river slopes,
While quartz, chrysoberyl,
And clear crystal in jumbled heaps
Glitter and sparkle,
Catching and throwing back a hundred colors
Where they lie tumbled on the river bottom.
Wild geese and swans, graylags, bustards,
Cranes and mallards,
Loons and spoonbills,
Teals and gadwalls,
Grebes, night herons, and cormorants
Flock and settle upon the waters,
Drifting lightly over the surface,
Buffeted by the wind,
Bobbing and dipping with the waves,
Sporting among the weedy banks,
Gobbling the reeds and duckweed,
Pecking at water chestnuts and lotuses.
Behind them rise the tall mountains,
Lofty crests lifted to the sky;
Clothed in dense forests of giant trees,
Jagged with peaks and crags;
The steep summits of the Nine Pikes,
The towering heights of the Southern Mountains,
Soar dizzily like a stack of cooking pots,
Precipitous and sheer.
Their sides are furrowed with ravines and valleys,
Narrow-mouthed clefts and open glens,
Through which rivulets dart and wind.
About their base, hills and islands
Raise their tall heads;
Ragged knolls and hillocks
Rise and fall,
Twisting and twining

Like the coiled bodies of reptiles;
While from their folds the mountain streams leap and tumble,
Spilling out upon the level plains.
There they flow a thousand miles along smooth beds,
Their banks lined with dikes
Blanketed with green orchids
And hidden beneath selinea,
Mingled with snakemouth
And magnolias;
Planted with yucca,
Sedge of purple dye,
Bittersweet, gentians, and orchis,
Blue flag and crow-fans,
Ginger and turmeric,
Monkshood, wolfbane,
Nightshade, basil,
Mint, ramie, and blue artemisia,
Spreading across the wide swamps,
Rambling over the broad plains,
A vast and unbroken mass of flowers,
Nodding before the wind;
Breathing their fragrance,
Pungent and sweet,
A hundred perfumes
Wafted abroad
Upon the scented air.
Gazing about the expanse of the park
At the abundance and variety of its creatures,
One's eyes are dizzied and enraptured
By the boundless horizons,
The borderless vistas.
The sun rises from the eastern ponds
And sets among the slopes of the west;
In the southern part of the park,
Where grasses grow in the dead of winter
And the waters leap, unbound by ice,
Live zebras, yaks, tapirs, and black oxen,

Water buffalo, elk, and antelope,
'Red-crowns' and 'round-heads,'
Aurochs, elephants, and rhinoceroses.
In the north, where in the midst of summer
The ground is cracked and blotched with ice
And one may walk the frozen streams or wade the rivulets,
Roam unicorns and boars,
Wild asses and camels,
Onagers and mares,
Swift stallions, donkeys, and mules.
Here the country palaces and imperial retreats
Cover the hills and span the valleys,
Verandahs surrounding their four sides;
With storied chambers and winding porticos,
Painted rafters and jade-studded corbels,
Interlacing paths for the royal palanquin,
And arcaded walks stretching such distances
That their length cannot be traversed in a single day.
Here the peaks have been leveled for mountain halls,
Terraces raised, story upon story,
And chambers built in the deep grottoes.
Peering down into the caves, one cannot spy their end;
Gazing up at the rafters, one seems to see them brush the heavens;
So lofty are the palaces that comets stream through their portals
And rainbows twine about their balustrades.
Green dragons slither from the eastern pavilion;
Elephant-carved carriages prance from the pure hall of the west,
Bringing immortals to dine in the peaceful towers
And bands of fairies to sun themselves beneath the southern eaves.[12]
Here sweet fountains bubble from clear chambers,
Racing in rivulets through the gardens,
Great stones lining their courses;
Plunging through caves and grottoes,
Past steep and ragged pinnacles,
Horned and pitted as though carved by hand,
Where garnets, green jade,

[12] The royal guests at the palaces, pictured by the poet as immortal spirits.

And pearls abound;
Agate and marble,
Dappled and lined;
Rose quartz of variegated hue,
Spotted among the cliffs;
Rock crystal, opals,
And finest jade.
Here grow citrons with their ripe fruit in summer,
Tangerines, bitter oranges and limes,
Loquats, persimmons,
Wild pears, tamarinds,
Jujubes, arbutus,
Peaches and grapes,
Almonds, damsons,
Mountain plums and litchis,
Shading the quarters of the palace ladies,
Ranged in the northern gardens,
Stretching over the slopes and hillocks
And down into the flat plains;
Lifting their leaves of kingfisher hue,
Their purple stems swaying;
Opening their crimson flowers,
Clusters of vermilion blossoms,
A wilderness of trembling flames
Lighting up the broad meadow.
Here crab apple, chestnut and willow,
Birch, maple, sycamore and boxwood,
Pomegranate, date palm,
Betel nut and palmetto,
Sandalwood, magnolia,
Cedar and cypress
Rise a thousand feet,
Their trunks several arm-lengths around,
Stretching forth flowers and branches,
Rich fruit and luxuriant leaves,
Clustered in dense copses,
Their limbs entwined,

Their foliage a thick curtain
Over stiff and bending trunks,
Their branches sweeping to the ground
Amidst a shower of falling petals.
They tremble and sigh
As they sway with the wind;
Creaking and moaning in the breeze
Like the tinkle of chimes
Or the wail of flagolets.
High and low they grow,
Screening the quarters of the palace ladies;
A mass of sylvan darkness,
Blanketing the mountains and edging the valleys,
Ascending the slopes and dipping into the hollows,
Overspreading the horizon,
Outdistancing the eye.
Here black apes and white she-apes,
Drills, baboons, and flying squirrels,
Lemurs and langurs,
Macaques and gibbons,
Dwell among the trees,
Uttering long wails and doleful cries
As they leap nimbly to and fro,
Sporting among the limbs
And clambering haughtily to the treetops.
Off they chase across bridgeless streams
And spring into the depths of a new grove,
Clutching the low-swinging branches,
Hurtling across the open spaces,
Racing and tumbling pell-mell,
Until they scatter from sight in the distance.
Such are the scenes of the imperial park,
A hundred, a thousand settings
To visit in the pursuit of pleasure;
Palaces, inns, villas, and lodges,
Each with its kitchens and pantries,
Its chambers of beautiful women

And staffs of officials.
Here, in late fall and early winter,
The Son of Heaven stakes his palisades and holds his hunts,
Mounted in a carriage of carved ivory
Drawn by six jade-spangled horses, sleek as dragons.
Rainbow pennants stream before him;
Cloud banners trail in the wind.
In the vanguard ride the hide-covered carriages;
Behind, the carriages of his attendants.
A coachman as clever as Sun Shu grasps the reins;
A driver as skillful as the Duke of Wei stands beside him.
His attendants fan out on all sides
As they move into the palisade.
They sound the somber drums
And send the hunters to their posts;
They corner the quarry among the rivers
And spy them from the high hills.
Then the carriages and horsemen thunder forth,
Startling the heavens, shaking the earth;
Vanguard and rear dash in different directions,
Scattering after the prey.
On they race in droves,
Rounding the hills, streaming across the lowlands,
Like enveloping clouds or drenching rain.
Leopards and panthers they take alive;
They strike down jackals and wolves.
With their hands they seize the black and tawny bears,
And with their feet they down the wild sheep.
Wearing pheasant-tailed caps
And breeches of white tiger skin
Under patterned tunics,
They sit astride their wild horses;
They clamber up the steep slopes of the Three Pikes
And descend again to the river shoals,
Galloping over the hillsides and the narrow passes,
Through the valleys and across the rivers.
They fell the 'dragon-sparrows'

And sport with the *chieh-ch'ih;*
Strike the *hsia-ko*[13]
And with short spears stab the little bears,
Snare the fabulous *yao-niao* horses
And shoot down the great boars.
No arrow strikes the prey
Without piercing a neck or shattering a skull;
No bow is discharged in vain,
But to the sound of each twang some beast must fall.
Then the imperial carriage signals to slacken pace
While the emperor wheels this way and that,
Gazing afar at the progress of the hunting bands,
Noting the disposition of their leaders.
At a sign, the Son of Heaven and his men resume their pace,
Swooping off again across the distant plains.
They bear down upon the soaring birds;
Their carriage wheels crush the wily beasts.
Their axles strike the white deer;
Deftly they snatch the fleeting hares;
Swifter than a flash
Of scarlet lightning,
They pursue strange creatures
Beyond the borders of heaven.
To bows like the famous Fan-jo
They fit their white-feathered arrows,
To shoot the fleeing goblin-birds
And strike down the griffins.
For their mark they choose the fattest game
And name their prey before they shoot.
No sooner has an arrow left the string
Than the quarry topples to the ground.
Again the signal is raised and they soar aloft,
Sweeping upward upon the gale,
Rising with the whirlwind,
Borne upon the void,

[13] These appear to be mythical beasts. From this point on the description becomes more and more fantastic.

The companions of gods,
To trample upon the black crane
And scatter the flocks of giant pheasants,
Swoop down upon the peacocks
And the golden roc,
Drive aside the five-colored *i* bird
And down the phoenixes,
Snatch the storks of heaven
And the birds of darkness,
Until, exhausting the paths of the sky,
They wheel their carriages and return.
Roaming as the spirit moves them,
Descending to the earth in a far corner of the north,
Swift and straight is their course
As they hasten home again.
Then the emperor ascends the Stone Gate
And visits the Great Peak Tower,
Stops at the Magpie Turret
And gazes afar from the Dew Cold Observatory;
Descends to the Wild Plum Palace
And takes his ease in the Palace of Righteous Spring;
To the west he hastens to the Hsüan-ch'ü Palace
And poles in a pelican boat over Ox Head Lake.
He climbs the Dragon Terrace
And rests in the Tower of the Lithe Willows,
Weighing the effort and skill his attendants have displayed
And calculating the catch made by his huntsmen.
He examines the beasts struck down by the carriages,
Those trampled beneath the feet of the horsemen
And trod upon by the beaters;
Those which, from sheer exhaustion
Or the pangs of overwhelming terror
Fell dead without a single wound,
Where they lie, heaped in confusion,
Tumbled in the gullies and filling the hollows,
Covering the plains and strewn about the swamps.
Then, wearied of the chase,

He orders wine brought forth on the Terrace of Azure Heaven
And music for the still and spacious halls.
His courtiers, sounding the massive bells
That swing from the giant bell rack,
Raising the pennants of kingfisher feathers
And setting up the drum of sacred lizard skin,
Present for his pleasure the dances of Yao
And the songs of the ancient Emperor Ko;
A thousand voices intone,
Ten thousand join in harmony,
As the mountains and hills rock with echoes
And the valley waters quiver to the sound.
The dances of Pa-yü, of Sung and Ts'ai,
The Yü-che song of Huai-nan,
The airs of Tien and Wen-ch'eng,
One after another in groups they perform,
Sounding in succession the gongs and drums
Whose shrill clash and dull booming
Pierce the heart and startle the ear.
The tunes Ching, Wu, Cheng, and Wei,
The Shao, Huo, Wu, and Hsiang music,
And amorous and carefree ditties
Mingle with the songs of Yen and Ying,
'Onward Ch'u!' and 'The Gripping Wind.'
Then come actors, musicians and trained dwarfs,
And singing girls from the land of Ti-ti,
To delight the ear and eye
And bring mirth to the mind;
On all sides a torrent of gorgeous sounds,
A pageant of enchanting color.
Here are maidens to match
The goddesses Blue Lute and Princess Fu;
Creatures of matchless beauty,
Seductive and fair,
With painted faces and carved hairpins,
Fragile and full of grace,
Lithe and supple,

Of delicate feature and form,
Trailing cloaks of sheerest silk
And long robes that seem as though carved and painted,
Swirling and fluttering about them
Like magic garments;
With them wafts a cloud of scent,
A delicious perfume;
White teeth sparkle
In engaging smiles,
Eyebrows arch delicately,
Eyes cast darting glances,
Until their beauty has seized the soul of the beholder
And his heart in joy hastens to their side."

Unfortunately only a few of the Han *fu* have survived, though among these there are many others which, had I more space, would be worthy of discussion. Some poets, in the manner of Chia I, used the *fu* form to pour out their private thoughts and feelings; others employed it to describe a particular object—a tree, a bird, a musical instrument. But many of the *fu* continued to be on the same grand scale as the works discussed above and to concern themselves with public functions, hunts, sacrifices, or descriptions of the capital. Moreover they frequently followed very closely the wording of the earlier works. In China plagiarism is a compliment, not an offense, and the later *fu* writers paid their predecessors in the art the supreme tribute of stealing not only ideas but whole passages from their works. In the hands of men of lesser talent, the writing of *fu* often became simply a matter of imitation, which is undoubtedly what Yang Hsiung had in mind when he advised a scholar who wanted to study *fu* writing under him, "If you read a thousand *fu,* you will be good at writing them."

In time, however, the *fu* developed new styles, adopted new themes, and was imbued with new life and inspiration. The form holds a place of importance and distinction in later Chinese poetic literature, though to trace its full history would take me far beyond the scope of this volume. I hope the discussion and translations above, however, will give the reader some idea of what it was like in its brilliant, formative years.

SONGS AND BALLADS

Not all early Han poetry is of such grandiose size or pretensions as the *fu.* In addition to these self-consciously literary works, there remains a scattering of shorter songs and ballads, most of them preserved in the histories of the period.

The earliest of these are usually referred to as "Ch'u songs," which seems to indicate that they were sung to a type of music peculiar to that region, perhaps the same style of music used for the "Nine Songs" of the *Ch'u Tz'u.* All the examples preserved are said to have been impromptu compositions, extemporized by various historical persons to express their feelings on a particular occasion. Without an understanding of the circumstances which occasioned them, they are all but meaningless. The following song, for instance, is attributed to Emperor Kao-tsu, the founder of the Han dynasty. The emperor had earlier designated his son by his consort, Empress Lü, as heir apparent, but later decided that he wanted to make the son of his favorite concubine, Lady Ch'i, heir instead. He was vigorously opposed in this move by all the high ministers, and was finally persuaded to abandon the idea when the heir apparent succeeded in attracting to the court four aged recluses whom the emperor had long admired. The song and its narrative setting are taken from Ssu-ma Ch'ien's biography of Chang Liang in *Shih chi* 55. The events described took place in 195 B.C.

The four men proposed a toast to the emperor's health and, when this was finished, rose and departed. The emperor stared after them and then, calling Lady Ch'i to his side, pointed to them and said, "I had hoped to change the heir apparent, but these four men have come to his aid. Like a pair of great wings they have borne him aloft where we cannot reach him. Empress Lü is your real master now!" Lady Ch'i wept.

"If you will do a dance of Ch'u for me," said the emperor, "I will make you a song of Ch'u," and he sang:

> The great swan soars aloft,
> In one swoop a thousand miles.
> He has spread his giant wings
> And spans the four seas.
> He who spans the four seas—
> Ah, what can we do?
> Though we bear stringed arrows to down him,
> Whereto should we aim them?

Another imperial song in the same style, this one by Emperor Wu, is recorded in Ssu-ma Ch'ien's "Treatise on the Yellow River and Canals" (*Shih chi* 29). In 132 B.C. the Yellow River broke through its banks at a place called Hu-tzu and overflowed the region to the south, causing fearful damage and hardship. Several attempts were made to close the gap, but with no success. It was not until 110 B.C., when the emperor traveled through the region on his way to perform the Feng and Shan sacrifices at Mount T'ai, that he realized the true extent of the damage, and the following year he personally supervised while a large force of laborers at last closed the break. The song which he composed on this occasion is in two parts, only the first of which is quoted here.

[The emperor] ordered all the courtiers and ministers who were accompanying him, from the generals on down, to carry bundles of brushwood and help close the break in the embankment. . . . As [he] surveyed the break, he was filled with despair at the difficulty of the task and composed this song:

The river broke through at Hu-tzu;
What could we do?
Beneath its rushing waves,
Villages all became rivers.
The villages have all become rivers
And there is no safety for the land.
Our labors know no rest,
Our mountains crumble.
Our mountains crumble
And the marsh of Chü-yeh overflows.
Even the fish lament
As the winter days press near.
The river raged from its boundaries,
It has left its constant course.
Dragons and water monsters leap forth,
Free to wander afar.
Let it return to the old channel
And we will truly bless the gods.
But for my journey to the Feng and Shan,
How would I have known what it was like?
Ask the Lord of the River for me,
"Why are you so cruel?
Your surging inundations will not cease;
You grieve my people!
The city of Nieh-sang is awash;
The Huai and Ssu brim over.
So long, and yet you will not return—
You break the laws of nature!"

Another famous song, attributed, like those above, to a particular person and dealing with a particular situation, is found in the "Account of the Western Regions" in Pan Ku's *History of the Former Han* (*Han shu* 96B). Around 107 B.C., a princess of the Han imperial family was sent to be the bride of K'un-mo, the aging chieftain of the Wu-sun, a nomadic tribe living north-west of China with whom the Han wished to establish friendly relations. The princess, unable even to communicate with her barbarian husband and desperately homesick, is said to have composed this song to express her grief.

> My family has married me
>   In this far corner of the world,
> Sent me to a strange land,
>   To the king of Wu-sun.
> A yurt is my chamber,
>   Felt my walls,
> Flesh my only food,
>   Kumiss to drink.
> My thoughts are all of home,
>   My heart aches within.
> O to be the yellow crane
>   Winging home again!

Not all the songs preserved in the histories are attributed to particular persons. Occasionally, as their narratives warrant, the historians record songs of the common people or even children's ditties, when these serve to throw light upon the events of the period. Always, however, the songs have to do with some particular occasion. The following, one of the earliest datable examples of five-word verse, is recorded in *Han shu* 90, the biography of Yin Shang.

Sometime around 10 B.C., Yin Shang was made magistrate of Ch'ang-an and, alarmed at the prevalence of crime in the capital, instituted a vigorous clean-up campaign. He had his subordinates round up several hundred thugs, juvenile delinquents, and illegal carriers of knives and other weapons, whom he examined. Those he found guilty he threw into what he called his "tiger dens," holes in the ground walled with stone and fitted with stone lids, where he left them to die. He then had the bodies carted off and buried temporarily east of his office gatepost, setting up a board

with their names listed on it. After a hundred days, he ordered
the families of the dead men to come and take away their corpses.
According to the historian,

The parents and relatives of the dead wept and wailed, and the streets
were filled with sobbing. In Ch'ang-an they sang a song:

> Where will you look for your dead one?
> East of the post in the place of young men.
> When he was alive he was rash indeed.
> Now how will you bury his dry bones?

Finally a word should be said about the *Yüeh fu* or *Music
Bureau* ballads. Around 120 B.C., Emperor Wu set up a bureau
of music in order to provide songs and musical accompaniments
for the various new sacrifices which he instituted. It was abolished
in 6 B.C., but its functions were carried on by officials of other
bureaus. Because of their connection, or supposed connection,
with the work of the bureau, many early poems are referred to
as *Yüeh fu* poems.

There are three types of poems or songs which go by this desig-
nation. First are the hymns composed by officials of the bureau to
meet imperial needs, many of them recorded in the *Han shu*
"Treatise on Rites and Music" (*Han shu* 22). They are stately,
dull pieces, written in archaic language and employing a four-
word meter. Obviously patterned after the hymns in the *Book
of Odes*, they are of even less general interest than their prototypes. Presumably they satisfied the Han demand for liturgical
music, but, being consciously archaic in nature, they contributed
little to the advancement of poetry.

Second are the anonymous *Yüeh fu* ballads. The officials of the
bureau were said to have gathered folk songs from various parts
of the empire, in order to provide inspiration for their own compositions and also, as was supposed to have been the case with

the *Book of Odes*, to ascertain the temper of the common people. The *Han shu* "Treatise on Literature" lists a number of collections of songs from various regions, which are presumably the anthologies compiled by the officials. Unfortunately it is impossible to say with certainty whether any of these folk songs survive. We do have a handful of anonymous ballads recorded in later works that are said to date from Han times. But we have no way to verify this assertion, nor can we more than guess to what period of the 400-year span of the dynasty's rule they belong. The allegedly older ones are often in irregular meters, while those of later date employ the five-word line that won such popularity from late Han times on. Because of the uncertainty of their provenance and the rather battered state in which many have been handed down, it seems best not to attempt to treat them in detail here. I shall quote two examples, however, the first a brief and lusty oath of friendship, the second a dirge said to have been sung at the funerals of the Han nobles. Both employ irregular meters.

> By Heaven!
>   I will be your comrade
>   And may our friendship never fail.
>   When mountains have no peaks
>   And rivers run dry,
>   When thunder rolls in winter
>   And summer snow falls—
>   Only then will I desert you!

> Dew on the leek,
>   How quickly it dries!
> Dew that dries
>   Will fall again tomorrow morning;
> But a man gone away in death,
>   When will he return?

Works of real beauty and feeling are to be found among the *Yüeh fu* ballads: love songs, complaints of poverty and hardship, attacks on rapacious officials, marked by all the simple passion and sincerity that characterize the *Odes* folk songs at their best. Many of them, however, are of little more than antiquarian interest. Lest, in spite of this assurance, the reader should feel that he is being cheated of untold delights, the following example of the latter type, which loses nothing at all in translation, may reassure him.

> Father, do not ford the river!
> Father went and forded the river.
> Into the river he sank and drowned.
> What's to be done about father?

The third group of works included under the title *Yüeh fu* consists of literary pieces composed by later poets, in most cases known by name, in imitation of these early ballads. They bear the same titles as the original folk songs, though they were not intended to be sung and it is not certain how faithfully they follow the wording and spirit of their prototypes. Most of them are in the five-word meter.

Much discussion among scholars, which need not concern us here, has centered about the origin of five-word poetry. It is sufficient to note that the form was in existence among the common people at least by the end of the Former Han (as attested by the brief song on the executed criminals quoted above), and in Latter Han times was taken up as a vehicle for serious literary expression. It soon won wide popularity, and almost all the important poetry of the following two or three centuries is in this meter. The few works in the meter attributed to the Han, such as the famous "Nineteen Old Poems," therefore, belong properly to a new phase of development in Chinese poetry, to describe which would take me far beyond the scope of this volume. I shall accordingly take leave of Chinese poetry at the point it had reached around 100 A.D., when *fu* writing, though past the peak of its earlier brilliance and originality, was still developing vigorously, a ballad literature of considerable merit (only fragments of which have been preserved) flourished among the people, and Chinese poetry was about to flower forth in the new five-word meter.

SUGGESTED READINGS

TRANSLATIONS

Book of Odes

Arthur Waley. *The Book of Songs.* 2d ed., 1954.
Bernhard Karlgren. *The Book of Odes.* 1950.
Ezra Pound. *The Classic Anthology Defined by Confucius.* 1954.

The *Ch'u Tz'u*

Arthur Waley. *The Nine Songs: A Study of Shamanism in Ancient China.* 1956.
Arthur Waley. "The Great Summons," in *More Translations from the Chinese.* 1919.
David Hawkes. *Ch'u Tz'u: The Songs of the South.* 1959.

Early *fu*

Arthur Waley. *170 Chinese Poems.* 1919.
Arthur Waley. *The Temple and Other Poems.* 1923.
Burton Watson. *Records of the Grand Historian of China: Translated from the* Shih chi *of Ssu-ma Ch'ien.* 2 vols. 1961. (See the Biographies of Ch'ü Yüan and Master Chia; The Biography of Ssu-ma Hsiang-ju.)

Ernest Richard Hughes. *Two Chinese Poets: Vignettes of Han Life and Thought.* 1960. (Contains partial translations of two *fu* on the Han capitals.)

Ch'u songs and *Yüeh fu* ballads

Robert Payne. *The White Pony.* 1947.
Arthur Waley. *170 Chinese Poems.* 1919.
Burton Watson. *Records of the Grand Historian of China* 2 vols. 1961.

CHRONOLOGY

	Important Events	History	Philosophy	Poetry
B.C.				
1122	Traditional date of founding of Chou dynasty			
	Western Chou			
770	Chou capital moved to Loyang	Earlier portions of Book of Documents	Book of Changes	
	Eastern Chou			
700				
600	Spring and Autumn period, 722–481	Spring and Autumn Annals		Book of Odes compiled[?]
500	Confucius, 551–479		Analects	

CHRONOLOGY (continued)

	Important Events	History	Philosophy	Poetry
400		*Tso chuan* *Kuo yü*	*Mo Tzu*	
300	Warring States period, 403–222	Later portions of *Book of Documents*[?]	*Lao Tzu*[?] *Chuang Tzu* *Mencius* *Book of Lord Shang* *Kuan Tzu* compiled [?] *Yen Tzu ch'un-ch'iu*[?] *Hsün Tzu* *Han Fei Tzu* *Lü shih ch'un-ch'iu* *Lieh Tzu*[?] Appendices to *Changes*[?]	Ch'ü Yüan, *fl. about* 300 Sung Yü, *fl. about* 275
221	Unification of China by First Emperor of Ch'in dynasty	*Chan-kuo ts'e*	*Classic of Filial Piety*[?]	
206	Founding of Han dynasty			

200			Chia I, 201-169 Mei Sheng, d. 140 Ssu-ma Hsiang-ju, 179-117
100 Western or Former Han	*Shih chi*	*Huai-nan Tzu* *Ch'un-ch'iu fan-lu*	Yüeh-fu ballads
		Book of Rites and *Ta-Tai li-chi* compiled *Yen t'ieh lun*	
A.D. 1 Reign of Wang Mang, 9-23	*Han shu*	*Fa yen* and *T'ai-hsüan-ching*	Yang Hsiung 53 B.C.–A.D. 18
		Lun heng	
100 Eastern or Latter Han	*Han chi*		Development of five-word poetry
			Present text of *Ch'u Tz'u* compiled
200			
220 Fall of Han dynasty			

Index

"Abundant Dew of the *Spring and Autumn*," see *Ch'un-ch'iu fan-lu*
"Account of the Western Regions" (Pan Ku), 287–88
Ai, duke of Lu, 144–45, 188
Analects, see *Lun yü*
Anthology of Literature, see *Wen hsüan*

Ballads, 285–92 *passim*
Bamboo Annals, see *Chu-shu chi-nien*
"Behavior of a Confucian," see *Ju hsing*
Berlin, Isaiah, 100
"Biographies of Assassin-retainers" (Ssu-ma Ch'ien), 101–3
Book of Changes, see *I ching*
Book of Documents, see *Shu ching*
Book of Lord Shang, see *Shang-chün shu*
Book of Odes, see *Shih ching*
Book of Poetry, see *Shih ching*
Book of Songs, see *Shih ching*
Book of Rites, see *Li chi*
Book of Rites of the Elder Tai, see *Ta-Tai li-chi*

"Canon of Yao," 34
Chan-kuo ts'e or *Intrigues of the Warring States*, 24, 74–91, 96, 101, 109, 113, 114, 132, 175
Chang Hsüeh-ch'eng, 152–53
Chang I, 77
Chang Liang, 286
Ch'ang-an, lord of, 87–90
Ch'ang-sha, king of, 255
Ch'ang-yang Palace, The (Yang Hsiung), 267
Chao, duke of Lu, 48

Chao, queen dowager of, 87–90
Chao hun or *Summons to the Soul*, 253–54
Chao K'uo, 64
Chao Tung, 64
Chaucer, Geoffrey, 241
Ch'en Tsun, 266
Cheng Hsiu (consort of King Huai), 85–86
Cheng Hsüan, 212
Ch'eng, emperor of the Former Han, 266
Ch'eng, king of Chou, 26, 34, 36
Ch'eng I, 128
Ch'eng T'ang, king of Shang or Yin (founder of the dynasty), 29, 106–7
Chi, King, 35
Chi Shih, duke of Shao, 216
Ch'i, Emperor, 32
Ch'i, Lady, 285–86
Ch'i, queen of, 83–84
Ch'i, lord of, *see* Hsiang, duke of Ch'i
Ch'i Tzu, 58–60 *passim*
Chia I, 115n, 255–58
Chieh, Emperor, 29
Chien, crown prince of Ch'i, 83–84
Chien Shu, 58–62 *passim*
Chien Ti, 246
Chih Po, 101–3 *passim*
Chin t'eng or "Metal-bound Casket," 34–36
Ch'in Shih-huang-ti (First Emperor of the Ch'in dynasty), 21, 37, 74, 96, 174, 175, 178, 186
Ching, duke of Ch'i, 183–86
Ching, duke of Chin, 64–65
Ching Ch'a, 260

Ch'ing-hsiang, king of Ch'u, 232, 237, 251

Chiu pien or "Nine Arguments," 251–53

Cho-tzu, 70

Chou, emperor of Shang or Yin, 28, 29

Chou, duke of, 20, 26–31 *passim*, 35–36

Chou kuan, see Chou li

Chou Kung, *see* Chou, duke of

Chou li or *Rites of Chou*, 139

Chu Hsi, 131, 133, 134, 138, 140, 213

Chu-shu chi-nien or *Bamboo Annals*, 37

Chu-shuo or "Collected Stories" (Han Fei Tzu), 247

Ch'u, king of, 175, 185

Ch'u Che, 88–90

Ch'u Han Ch'un-ch'iu or *Spring and Autumn of Ch'u and Han* (Lu Chia), 96

Ch'u Shao-sun, 103–4

"Ch'u songs," 285

Ch'u Tz'u or *Elegies of Ch'u*, 231–54

Ch'ü Yüan, 231–54 *passim*

Chuang, duke of Ch'i, 183

Chuang, duke of Chu, 65–66

Chuang Chou (Chuang Tzu), 160–69

Chuang Tzu (Chuang Chou), 123, 156, 160–69, 169–70, 190

Ch'un ch'iu or *Spring and Autumn Annals*, 37–40, 41–44 *passim*, 97–98, 109, 111, 124, 135, 148n

Ch'un-ch'iu fan-lu or "Abundant Dew of the *Spring and Autumn*" (Tung Chung-shu), 135–36

Chung Li, 188

Chung yung or *Doctrine of the Mean*, 128, 140; see also *Ssu shu*

Ch'ung-erh (Duke Wen of Chin), 67, 68

Classic of Filial Piety, see Hsiao ching

Classic of History, see Shu ching

Classic of the Great Mystery, see T'ai-hsüan-ching

"Collected Stories," see *Chu-shuo*

Confucius, 13, 21, 26, 32–33, 38–40 *passim*, 63, 97, 117, 119, 124–30, 134, 137, 141, 142, 144–46, 148–50, 165–66, 172, 188, 194, 202, 211–12, 229

Conversations from the States, see Kuo yü

Critical Essays, see Lun heng

Crump, James I., 77 and n

"Deathbed Commands," see *Ku ming*

Debates on Salt and Iron, see *Yen t'ieh lun*

Divination, 251

Doctrine of the Mean, see *Chung yung*

Documents of Antiquity, see *Shu ching*

"Duties of a Student, The," 180–81

Elegies of Ch'u, see *Ch'u Tz'u*

Embracing the Sands, see *Huai sha*

Encountering Sorrow, see *Li sao*

Erh ya, 148n, 194

Fa yen or *Model Words* (Yang Hsiung), 13, 136–37

Fan Ning, 64

First Emperor of the Ch'in dynasty, *see* Ch'in Shih-huang-ti

Fisherman, The, 251

Five Classics, 148n

Fu (rhyme-prose), 254–85

Fu-ch'a, king of Wu, 67, 256, 257n

Fu Hsi, 32

Fu on the Owl (Chia I), 255–58

Fu on the Shang-lin Park (Ssu-ma Hsiang-ju), 270–84

Fu Yüeh, 257 and n

Generalities on History, see *Shih t'ung*

Goddess, The, 259–60, 263

Graham, A. C., 170n

Graves, Robert, 167n

Great King, 35

Great Learning, see *Ta hsüeh*

Great Summons, see *Ta chao*

Han chi or *Records of the Former Han* (Hsün Yüeh), 108–9

Han Fei Tzu, 159n, 175–77

Han Fei Tzu, 80n, 175–78, 247

Han Shu or *History of the Former Han Dynasty* (Pan Ku), 5, 94, 103–8, 109, 116, 266, 287–89, 290

Han Yü, 13
Hawkes, David, 232–33, 241, 242 and n, 245n, 236, 254
Heavenly Questions, see *T'ien wen*
Henryson, Robert, 19
Hightower, James Robert, 9, 138
History of the Latter Han Dynasty, see *Hou Han shu*
Hou Chi, 224, 225, 246
Hou Han shu or *History of the Latter Han Dynasty*, 104
Hsi Ch'i, 59–62 *passim*
Hsi-ch'i (son of Lady Li), 70, 72
Hsi tz'u or *Appended Words*, 152–53
Hsiang, king of Ch'i, 83
Hsiang, king of Ch'u, 260–64 *passim*
Hsiang, duke of Ch'i, 54–55
Hsiang, duke of Sung, 214
Hsiang-tzu, 101–3
Hsiang Yü, 96
Hsiao, king of Liang, 269
Hsiao, duke of Ch'in, 173
Hsiao-ch'eng, king of Chao, 87–88
Hsiao ching or *Classic of Filial Piety*, 125, 148–51
Hsien, duke of Chin, 67, 69–73 *passim*
Hsien Chen, 60–62
Hsien Kao, 59–60
Hsü, lord of Ch'eng-pei, 86
Hsü Shen, 194
Hsüan, emperor of the Han, 116
Hsüan, queen dowager of Ch'in, 84–85
Hsün Ch'ing (Hsün Tzu), 45, 49, 133–35, 140, 144–45, 147, 176
Hsün Hsi, 70
Hsün Tzu (Hsün Ch'ing), 45, 49, 133–35, 144–45
Hsün Yüeh, 108–9
Huai, king of Ch'u, 85–86, 232
Huai-nan Tzu, 189–91
Huai sha or *Embracing the Sands*, 248–51
Huan (physician), 64–65
Huan, duke of Ch'i, 76, 179–80
Huan, duke of Lu, 54
Huan K'uan, 192, 193–94
Huang-fu Mi, 150n
Hui, king of Ch'in, 84–85
Hui, king of Wei, 82
Hui Shih, 82

Hui-wen, king of Chao, 87
Hung fan or "Great Plan," 26

I (minister), 32
I Chi, see *Kao Yao mo*
I ching or *Book of Changes*, 124, 148n, 151–53
I K'uan, 184
I li or *Ceremonial*, 139
I-wu, Prince, 68
I Yeh-ku, Lord, 66
Institutes of Chou, see *Chou li*
Intellectual Adventure of Ancient Man, The (Frankfort *et al.*), 168
Intrigues of the Warring States, see *Chan-kuo ts'e*
Itō Jinsai, 128

Jan Ming, 63
Ju hsing or "Behavior of a Confucian," 140

Kao-shih chuan (Huang-fu Mi), 150n
Kao-tsu, emperor of the Han (Liu Pang), 96, 285–86
Kao-yang, Emperor, 233
Kao Yao mo or "Pronouncement of Kao Yao," 27, 31
Karlgren, Bernhard, 25, 32n, 35, 41, 50
Kou-chien, king of Yüeh, 67, 257 and n
Ku liang Commentary, 39–40
Ku ming or "Deathbed Commands," 34–35
K'u, 246
Kuan Chung (Kuan I-wu), 63, 179
Kuan Tzu (Kuan Chung), 48, 63, 131, 167, 179–83
K'uei (music master), 188
Kun (minister), 235
K'un-mo, 287
Kung, king of Ch'u, 56–57
Kung-sun Lung tzu, 156
Kung-sun Wu-chih, 54–55
Kung-sun Yang, *see* Wei Yang
Kung yang Commentary, 39–40, 97, 135
Kuo yü or *Conversations from the States*, 20, 63, 66–73, 75, 83, 95, 98, 109, 167, 202–3

Lai Chü, 61
Lament for Ch'ü Yüan (Chia I), 255
Lao Tan (Lao Tzu), 79, 123, 157–60, 191
Lao Tzu or Tao te ching (Lao Tan), 79, 123, 157–60, 170, 190–91
Li, king of Chou, 63
Li, Lady, 69–73
Li, Lady, 163 and n
Li cheng, 29
Li chi or Book of Rites, 7, 125, 128, 134, 139–47, 148n, 149, 177
Li K'o, 70–72
Li sao or Encountering Sorrow (Ch'ü Yüan), 232–41
Li Ssu, 257 and n
Liang Ch'iu-chü, 184
Liang Hung, 61
Lieh Tzu (Lieh Yü-k'ou), 169–72
Lieh Yü-k'ou, 169
Ling, king of Ch'u, 46
Ling, duke of Ch'i, 183
Liu An, king of Huai-nan, 189, 232
Liu-ch'en-chu Wen hsüan (Lü Hsiang), 264
Liu Chih-chi, 53
Liu Hsiang, 105, 106, 231
Liu Hsin, 41, 105, 106
Liu Pang, see Kao-tsu, emperor of the Han
Liu Te, king of Ho-chien, 207
Lu Chia, 96
Lü, empress of the Han, 285–86
Lü Hsiang, 264
Lü hsing or "Code of the Marquis of Lü," 26–27
Lü Pu-wei, 186
Lü shih ch'un-ch'iu or Spring and Autumn of Mr. Lü, 186–89
Luan Chih, 61
Lucan, 167n
Lun heng or Critical Essays (Wang Ch'ung), 194–97
Lun yü or Analects (Confucius), 7, 32–33, 38–39, 117, 119, 123, 125–30, 137, 148n 202; see also Ssu shu

Man, Prince, 59
Manyōshū, 230

Mao (editor of Shih ching), 203, 207–26 passim
Mei Sheng, 268, 269
Mencius, 31, 33, 49, 134, 153
Mencius, see also Ssu shu
Meng, Lady (wife of Li K'o), 71
Meng Tzu or Mencius (Mencius), 31, 33, 38, 123, 128, 130–32, 148n
Meng Yang, 54–55
"Metal-bound Casket," see Chin t'eng
Millet, Lord, see Hou Chi
Mo Ti (Mo Tzu), 150, 153–56, 167–68, 175–76
Mo Tzu (Mo Ti), 131, 153–56, 167, 175–76
Mount Kao-t'ang, 259
Mu, duke of Ch'in, 167
Music Bureau ballads, see Yüeh fu

"Nine Arguments," see Chiu pien
"Nine Declarations," 248–51
"Nine Songs, The," 241–45
"Nineteen Old Songs," 291–92
Nü Hsü, 235

Pan Chao, 105
Pan Ku, 39n, 103–8, 152, 239, 263, 287–89, 290
Pan Piao, 104, 115n
Pao-ssu, 226
P'eng Hsien, 237
P'eng Sheng, 54
P'eng Sun, 60
Pharsalia (Lucan), 167n
Pi (attendant of Duke Hsiang of Ch'i), 54–55
P'i Cheng, 70
Plutarch, 99
Po I, 59–62 passim
Po-li Meng-ming, 59–62 passim
Po-yung, 233
Polybius, 111–12
"Praise for the Orange Tree," 248
Preface to commentary on the Fa yen (Ssu-ma Kuang), 137
Preface to the Ku liang Commentary (Fan Ning), 64
Preface to the Li sao (Pan Ku), 239

Records of the Historian, see *Shih chi*
Remonstrance on Wine (Yang Hsiung), 266–67
Rhyme-prose, see *Fu*
Rites of Chou, see *Chou li*

Seven Incitements (Mei Sheng), 268, 269
Shang, Lord, *see* Wei Yang (Kung-sun Yang)
Shang-chün shu or *Book of Lord Shang*, 173–74
Shang shu, see *Shu ching*
Shao, duke of, 35, 216
Shao, Lord, *see* Shao, duke of
Shao kao or "Announcement to the Duke of Shao," 30
Shao Kung, 63
Shen Nung, 32
Shen-sheng, crown prince of Chin, 67, 68, 69–73
Shih (actor), 71–72
Shih chi or *Records of the Historian* (Ssu-ma Ch'ien), 37, 77–78, 92–103, 105, 106–7, 109, 112–14 *passim*, 132, 174, 178, 185, 202, 213, 222, 232, 248, 255–58, 270, 273–84, 285–87
Shih-chih Fen-ju, 54–55
Shih ching or *Book of Odes*, 6, 7, 13, 20, 124, 148n, 201, 202–230, 252, 263
Shih t'ung or *Generalities on History* (Liu Chih-chi), 53
Shou, emperor of Shang or Yin, *see* Chou, emperor of Shang or Yin
Shu-ch'i, 88–89
Shu ching or *Book of Documents*, 20, 21–36, 48, 95, 98, 109, 124, 148n, 223
Shun, Emperor, 31–33 *passim*, 188, 236
Shun tien, see *Yao tien*
Shuo-wen chieh-tzu (Hsü Shen), 194
Songs, 285–92 *passim*
Sorceror of Mulberry Field, 64–65
Sources of Chinese Tradition (de Bary, et al.), 115n
Spender, Stephen, 6
Spring and Autumn Annals, see *Ch'un ch'iu*

Spring and Autumn of Master Yen, see *Yen Tzu ch'un-ch'iu*
Spring and Autumn of Mr. Lü, see *Lü shih ch'un-ch'iu*
Ssu-ma Ch'ien, 77–78, 91–103, 105, 106–7, 108, 112–14 *passim*, 115–16, 132, 152, 202, 222, 232, 248, 255, 263, 265, 270, 285–87
Ssu-ma Ch'ien: Grand Historian of China (Watson), 116n
Ssu-ma Hsiang-ju, 265, 269–84
Ssu-ma Kuang, 137
Ssu-ma T'an, 92
Ssu shu or *Four Books* (Chu Hsi), 128, 131, 140
Su (historian), 69–70
Su Ch'in, 77
Summons to the Soul, see *Chao hun*
Sun Hui-tsung, 116 .
Sung Yü, 251, 259–64 *passim*, 269

Ta chao or *Great Summons*, 253–54
Ta hsüeh or *Great Learning*, 128, 140; see also *Ssu-shu*
Ta-Tai li-chi or *Book of Rites of the Elder Tai* (Tai Te), 146–47
Tai Te, 146–47
T'ai-hsüan-ching or *Classic of the Great Mystery* (Yang Hsiung), 138
T'ai-kung Wang, 35
"Taking over the Rule of the State," 181–83
Tan, *see* Chou, duke of
T'ang the Completer, King, *see* Ch'eng T'ang, king of Shang or Yin
Tao te ching, see *Lao Tzu*
T'ao Yüan-ming, 229
Testament of Cresseid (Henryson), 19–20
Three Ways of Thought in Ancient China (Waley), 154
Thirteen Classics, 148n
Thucydides, 23, 81
T'ien Chiu, 175–76
T'ien Tzu-fang, 119
T'ien wen or *Heavenly Questions*, 245–48
Ting, duke of Lu, 46–47
Topics in Chinese Literature (Hightower), 9, 138

Toynbee, Arnold, 23
"Treatise on Literature" (Pan Ku), 5, 39n, 290
"Treatise on Rites and Music" (Pan Ku), 289
"Treatise on the Yellow River and Canals" (Ssu-ma Ch'ien), 286–87
Trilling, Lionel, 7
Tseng Tzu, 148
Tso chuan or *Tso Commentary* (Tso Ch'iu-ming), 13, 24, 40–66, 75, 81, 83, 95, 98, 109, 127, 179, 211
Tsou Chi, 86–87
Tso Ch'iu-ming (Tso-ch'iu Ming), 40, 66
Tu Fu, 230
Tu Yüan-k'uan, 73
Tuan Kan-mu, 119
Tung Chung-shu, 119, 135–36
T'ung-chien kang-mu (Chu Hsi *et al.*), 138–39
Tzu-ch'an, 51, 63
Tzu-fa, 190–91
Tzu-hsia, 189
Tzu-kung, 46–47, 145, 146, 165–66, 172

Waley, Arthur, 11, 154, 156, 169, 210n, 227, 272–73
Wang Ch'ung, 194–95
Wang I, 231, 241, 248
Wang Mang, 41, 104, 138
Warner, Rex, 81
Way and Its Power, The (Waley), 11, 156, 169
Wei, king of Ch'i, 86–87
Wei, king of, 85
Wei Ch'ou-fu, 84–85
Wei Hung, 208
Wei Yang (Kung-sun Yang), Lord Shang, 173–74
Wen, emperor of the Han, 255
Wen, duke of Chin, 58–61 *passim*, 76; *see also* Ch'ung-erh
Wen, king of Chou, 29, 146, 151, 224
Wen, marquis of Wei, 119
Wen hsüan or *Anthology of Literature*, 260, 267, 268

Wen-shih t'ung-i (Chang Hsüeh-ch'eng), 152–53
Wen-ying, 61
Wind, The, 260–65
Wright, Arthur, 29
Wu, emperor of the Han, 92–93, 191, 265, 269–70, 286–87, 289
Wu, king of Chou, 26, 27, 35, 146
Wu, king of, 13
Wu i, 31
Wu-ling, king of Chao, 80–81
Wu Ting, king of Shang or Yin, 257 and n

Yang Chu, 169, 187 and n
Yang Ch'u-fu, 62
Yang Hsiung, 136–39, 195, 263, 266–67, 269n, 284
Yang Sun, 60
Yang Yün, 116–19
Yao, Emperor, 22, 31–34 *passim*
Yao tien or "Canon of Yao," 27, 31–33
Yellow Emperor, 32
Yen (diviner), 58
Yen, queen of, 89–90
Yen Hui, 172
Yen t'ieh lun or *Debates on Salt and Iron*, 191–94
Yen Tzu ch'un-ch'iu or *Spring and Autumn of Master Yen*, 63, 131, 183–86
Yen Ying (Yen Tzu), 63, 183–86
Yin, viscount of Ch'u, 46–47
Yin Shang, 288–89
Yoshikawa Kōjirō, 55
Yu, king of Chou, 226
Yü, Emperor, 30, 32
Yü Jang, 101–3
Yü kung or "Tribute of Yü," 26, 34
Yüan Jang, 145–46
Yüan tao (Han Yü), 13
Yüeh fu or Music Bureau ballads, 289–91
Yung Jui, 85

Zücher, E., 170n